Total Body Training

Robert S. Gajda, MS RKT has a BS degree in Physiology, an MS in Exercise Physiology (both from George Williams College) and a Ph.D. in Biomechanics (dissertation pending) from the University of Illinois. Bob is a registered Kinesiotherapist. He has been the Director of Professional and Public Education for the American Cancer Society, Assistant Director, Drug Education for the Robert Crown Center for Health and Education, faculty member and research assistant, Department of Health and Safety Education at the University of Illinois, Executive Director of Health Plus Network in Bannockburn, IL, Co-Chairman for the Chicagoland Council on Physical Fitness, Sports and Health and VP Moving Force Systems the innovative fitness equipment company. He has personally trained a "Who's Who" list of top professional athletes, including greats like: Bill Buckner, Scott Sanderson, Rocky Blier, Gary Fencic, Richard Dent, Jim McMahon, Mike Singltary, Bret Hall, Dennis Savard, Al Secord, Andrea Yeager, Tracy Austin, John McEnroe, Jimmy Conners, Yannick Noah, as well as working with many college, Olympic and professional teams like the 1984 and 1988 U.S. Men's and Women's Olympic Volleyball Teams, Chicago Sting soccer team, Chicago Black Hawks, Harvard Tennis Team... Bob is also a former Triple Crown winner: Mr. America, Mr. USA and Mr. Univierse, a highly regarded public speaker, consultant, author and a great guy.

Also by **Robert S. Gajda, MS RKT**
Power Tennis

RICHARD H. DOMINGUEZ, M.D. is a board certified orthopedic surgeon and Co-Medical Director of the SportsMed Center for Fitness in Carol Stream, Illinois. He is Chief of Staff at GlenOaks Medical Center, Glendale Heights, Illinois and past Chief of Staff at Central DuPage Hospital, Winfield, Illinois. He is a clinical instructor of orthopedic surgery at Loyola University Medical Center, a member of numerous professional organizations including the American College of Sports Medicine, the American Academy of Sports Physicians, the American Orthopaedic Society for Sports Medicine and both the North American and International Arthroscopy Associations. He is the author of *The Complete Book of Sports Medicine* and *The Gift of Healing*. He is President of the U.S. Swim Team's Sports Medicine Society and has served on the Illinois State Medical Society Sports Medicine Committee.

Also by Richard M. Dominguez, M.D.

THE COMPLETE BOOK OF SPORTS MEDICINE

Total Body Training

RICHARD H. DOMINGUEZ, M.D.,
AND ROBERT S. GAJDA

MOVING FORCE SYSTEMS • EAST DUNDEE, ILLINOIS

The treatments and activities suggested in this book have been developed by the authors from their experience in the practice of sports medicine, rehabilitation, and fitness training. However, the training and rehabilitation programs described in this book may not be appropriate for everyone. Persons recovering from an injury of any sort should consult their physician regarding the advisability of undertaking any of the training programs outlined in this book. Injury can result from any training program, especially if it is not followed properly. Neither the authors nor the publisher shall be responsible for any harm or injury resulting from the training or rehabilitation programs or use of the exercise devices described herein.

Illustrations by Jon M. Nelson

Library of Congress Cataloging in Publication Data

Dominguez, Richard H.
Total body training.

Includes index.
1. Physical education and training. 2. Sports—Accidents and injuries. I. Gajda, Robert S. II. Title.
GV711.5.D65 613.7'1 81-21269
ISBN O-684-17320-4 AACR2

Printed in the United States of America.

3rd Printing, 1994

To Sam Dominguez . . . he was always "Mr. Sam" to me. He is "Uncle Sam" to a multitude of nieces and nephews and "Grandpop" to his twenty grandchildren. We all love you, Dad!

R.H.D.

To Steve Gajda, my dear father and earliest mentor, who each payday brought home what he called "useful books" about the human body. Thank you, more than any, for planting the seeds of love and inspiration that continue to flow within today.

B.G.

We must thank our friends

Joanne Hampe
Paul Mouw
Dr. Karen Gajda

for all of their expert help
in the preparation of this manuscript.

R.H.D. & B.G.

Contents

PART TWO/ THE TOTAL BODY TRAINING PROGRAM

PART ONE

TOTAL BODY TRAINING THEORY

1

A Great Opportunity

This book brings help for the healthy, hope for the injured, and aid to those wanting maximum performance. No matter whether you are a professional athlete, an active amateur, or a weekend warrior, and no matter what your sex or age, we have good news for you that will help you live up to your physical potential and even improve your performance.

The news we bring you is in the form of a comprehensive training system—the one that helped Bill Buckner recover from an injured ankle to win the National League batting title and that helped Eric Soderholm come back to bat close to .300 for the Yankees after injuring his knee so badly that almost everyone had given up on him. It's the system that helped the Chicago Bears' Gary Fencik recover from an injured knee to be an All-Pro safety and Tom Hicks fill the famed middle linebacker spot previously occupied by Dick Butkus, despite shoulder and knee injuries.

Arno Steffenhaggen, the all-star midfielder of the Chicago Sting Soccer Club, uses this system, and it was a key part in the training of the Sports Performance and Rehabilitation Institute Cosmics volleyball team, which won the Women's National AAU volleyball championship. Dr. Karen Gajda, the wife of one of the authors, followed this system when she won her world championship in power lifting.

What is this system? What does it involve, and what are its advantages?

First, it is a unique way of thinking. It is holistic in that we attempt to help you improve all parts of your body, not just certain locomotor power muscles or those that are normally associated with a particular activity. We'll prove to you that this holistic approach is not only best, it is necessary if you are to live up to your full potential.

Second, it is low cost. You don't need expensive machines, which tend to be incomplete anyway. We will discuss the machines, but only to help you survive exercising on them. Most of the expensive exercise machines exercise muscles only on one plane and cannot provide the overall effects you'll get with our simple devices. And these devices are so inexpensive that even if you go "deluxe," they will still cost you less than $100. If you go "junk-city special," you may be able to put these devices together for no cost at all.

Third, the effects on your body will be beneficial whether you are rehabilitating or healthy. Healthy individuals will probably increase their performance and, even more important, avoid certain injuries. Think of this system as insurance that pays immediate dividends. Injured individuals will find that the system provides both a means of rehabilitation and a way to evaluate progress. In many cases they may end up being even better than they were before they received the injury.

A fourth point is that our system does not always follow conventional thinking. In fact, we believe that some of the conventional training methods seen in popular magazines and books may actually be extremely harmful. We will give you explanations of simple body mechanics that may make you want to change your warm-up and stretching routines—and you'll never do some of them again! If you get static from your coach or your friends, explain that you read a book written by a unique combination of individuals: One developer of this system is an orthopedic surgeon who specializes in sports medicine and is in the forefront of this exploding field; the other is a kinesiologist (an expert in body motion) and a champion weight lifter who has proven credentials in both increasing athletic performance and rehabilitating injured elite athletes.

Finally, while this system provides a great opportunity, it is not magic. You must put time and effort into the training. The key to success is to not take shortcuts, but to read carefully and do the routines exactly as we outline them. As the products of a technological age, we often look for "magic" medicines or machines. Let us realize that our bodies are the magic machines, and our minds provide the magic medicines.

Ecclesiastes 1:9 states "There is no new thing under the sun." We agree. The system, idea, and principles outlined in this book are old, but, unfortunately, have almost been forgotten. How unfortunate that the principles and methods outlined here are so old that they seem new!

It is our contention that the popular methods currently used in rehabilitation and training come either from an American philosophy that "machines can do it better" or from a recent upsurge of interest in Eastern religions. Machines *can't* do training better, and the yoga-induced mania for stretching is simply dangerous!

So, back to the "old-new" or the "new-old," whichever you prefer to call our complete training system. It has worked for others and it can work for you.

A WORD ABOUT GENDER

All of the techniques described in this book are applicable to both sexes. The training of women should not be different from the training of men. Some women are afraid to do strength training because they fear they will develop bulging muscles. This fear should not be a deterrent for two reasons. First, women can have a 50 percent increase in strength without any increase in the size of the muscle, because the female sex hormone permits this kind of strength improvement without increasing muscle bulk. Second, North Americans' attitudes toward beauty and attractiveness are changing. Women with athletic bodies and builds are creating a new standard of feminine beauty. Women are at the vanguard of the fitness revolution. Even so, the training slogan all too often still holds: "Women fear they will look like Arnold Schwarzenegger; men fear that they won't."

Both men and women need appropriate strength training. The body build that you achieve from such a program will depend more on your genes than on how much you weight lift. As Arthur H. Steinhaus, a world-renowned physiologist, once said, "You can't make a chihuahua into a St. Bernard."

If your parents have large well-defined muscles and broad shoulders, chances are that you will develop that kind of build as well. Even so, don't avoid exercise and training out of fear that you will grow "too big." It's better to be firm, with well-defined muscles, than to be flabby. You'll look better and feel better about yourself. The key here, as in all life, is to make the best out of yourself and what you've been given.

As for those of you who wish to develop large, bulging muscles and who have thin, angular parents: You will probably be able to achieve enormous increases in strength, but chances are you will never have the body of a Mr. America.

Traditionally females have not had the athletic background and opportunities that males have had. And so we believe they may derive more benefits from this book than males will, especially in being able to decrease injury rates. In fact, this lack of background in resistance training and exercise routines may be of added advantage in that the bad training and exercise habits passed from male to male will not have been burned into the minds of females. Women may find it easier to learn the proper training techniques and the safe, stable manner in which to exercise.

But whether you are male or female, you must understand and act on the concepts described in the next three chapters: The core, stabilization, and dynamic range of motion. These three concepts are the prerequisites of performance. No matter where you are on the physical scale, whether you are an elite pro athlete or a weekend warrior, you need these three. In fact, our system is designed to help you develop these to the level you desire and to the level that fits your needs.

If you understand the following chapters, you will have the framework for increasing performance, rehabilitating your severe or frequent injuries, and, perhaps most important of all, preventing injuries. That's a lot to promise, but based on our success rate, it's one that we can keep.

2

The Core

The first essential concept in total body training is that of the "core," which is our term for the muscles of the center of the body. These muscles stabilize the body while we are in an erect, antigravity position or are using our arms and legs to throw or kick. They maintain our structure while we do vigorous exercises, such as running, jumping, shoveling snow, and lifting weights overhead. These are the muscles that control the head, neck, ribs, spine, and pelvis.

When guarding an opponent or trying to tackle another player, you don't watch his head, arms, or feet—you watch his hips. This is because as his bellybutton goes, so goes his body. The good defenseman also watches his opponent's body to see which way it is turning. The golf instructor always says, "Move your hips and body through the shot."

The pitching coach will observe approvingly that a pitcher "throws with his whole body," or, derogatorily, that he tried to "arm it." When a tennis pro teaches you the proper backhand or forehand, he teaches you how to hit with your body, moving it through the shot. In all athletic endeavors, the good coaches and the

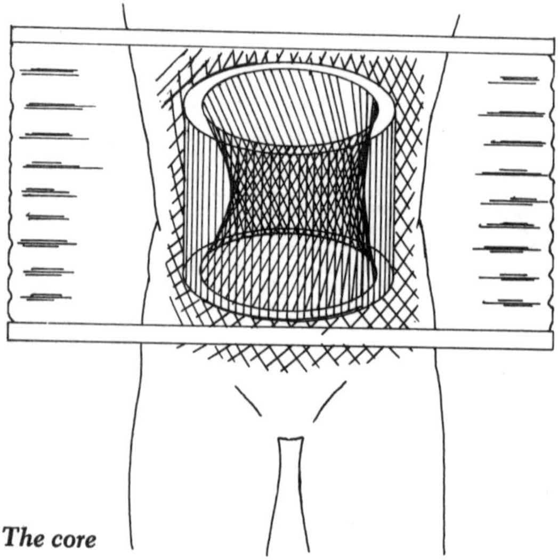

The core

good trainers stress the need for using your "body," not just your limbs, in the key maneuvers.

We call this important main part of the body the core. The experts know the importance of the core to achieving maximum performance. Unfortunately, very few people emphasize any training of this core. Nucleus, middle, dead center, focal point—the core of the human body is those muscles that keep the trunk and neck in a tubelike form. In a sense, we are basically a semirigid tube with a flexible spine up the back.

This semirigid, firm cylinder is mechanically a very strong design. However, when it loses its rigidity, it is very, very weak. This is similar to the trick of taking an unwrinkled piece of paper and rolling it into a tube. You can lay a book on the rolled-up piece of paper and it will support the weight. But if you wrinkle the paper, the tube will not support that same book.

Your body works in a similar fashion. If it is firm and rigid, it can do the activities it is intended to do. If the rigidity is enhanced, then you can maximize your athletic performance. If, however, your cylinder is not rigid, it will never obtain maximal performance and there will be inordinate strain on your lower back.

We can't repeat enough that core training is essential for performing at maximum in sports and is a key factor in preventing injury to the spine (back), head, and neck. It is insurance against the plague of low back pain that affects 70 percent of the population.

The core muscles are those that stabilize (or anchor) and move the central pillar of the body, including the head–neck, spine–ribs, and spine–pelvis. Most of the activity of the core muscles is tonic (stabilizing) rather than phasic (moving), which means that the muscles are acting continually throughout the day when you are moving, standing or sitting.

Since normal sitting or standing activities occur in what we call a gravity-neutral (G0) plane (the body is balanced through the body center line), a full range of development is never encouraged. That is why we designed training exercises to utilize the pull of gravity in what is called positive gravity (G+). These exercises are done across or horizontal to the straight downward line of gravity.

Try this experiment to understand the principle that the erect position of the body is maintained by equal contraction of the

Essential core muscles *Note how the muscles above the hip blend into the muscles around the abdomen and chest, which continue up to the shoulder girdle.*

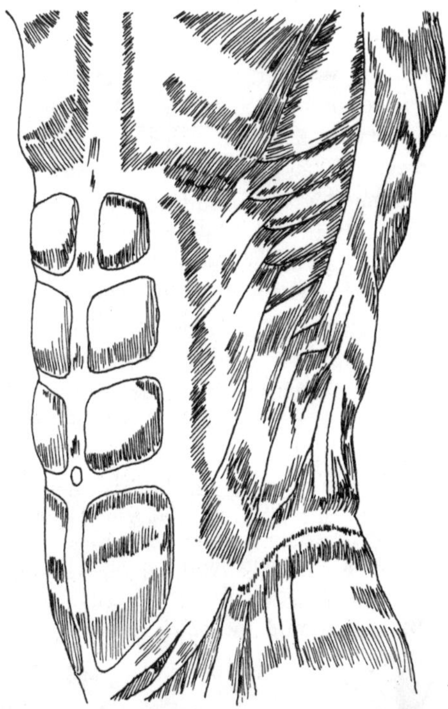

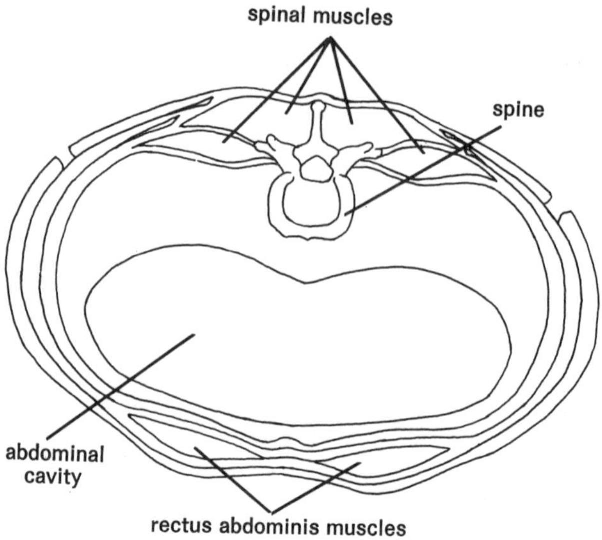

Cross section of the core *This cross section of the body at about the level of the waistline shows that the body is a semirigid cylinder with a flexible spine up the back, stabilized by core muscles all the way around.*

muscles located on the front and the back of the body. While standing erect (gravity-neutral posture) place your right hand on your lower back and your left hand on your abdomen. Note the amount of tone present in both sections. Bend backward and you will experience an increase in tone of the abdominal area, especially if the ribs are pressed down; that is, if the rib muscles are contracted. (By the way, the proper way to bend backward is by contracting the muscles.) Now, bend forward and note the increase in muscle tone in the back area that you can perceive with your right hand.

This muscle action is called the antigravity mechanism. It is a check system that prevents dislocation and distortion of the core skeleton. In these movements, only part of the total potential range of motion is worked, so strength is not developed through the entire range of motions, and a person exercising in only this one plane could not resist the strain that sports activities produce.

In contrast, lie face-up (supine) on the floor, place your hands as sensors on your abdomen and do the following set of exercises:

1. Press your lower back toward the floor.
2. Depress or pull down your ribs (as in exhaling) and sternum, pressing downward toward the pelvis.

3. Rotate your pelvis upward.
4. Draw your chin in and down, lengthening the back of your neck.
5. Bend your neck forward.
6. Lift your vertebrae slowly off the floor; do it in segments, starting with the upper end (cervical vertebrae) first and the lower (lumbar vertebrae) last. It is very important while doing this maneuver to become aware of each part of your spine as it moves off the floor in a controlled fashion. You should not jerk up. The idea is to move upward in a slow, controlled fashion, maintaining the position of the sacrum flat on the floor, and exhaling with a hiss sound to aid movement.

Your abdominal muscle tone will reach maximum as the last lumbar vertebra leaves the floor at about a one-quarter sit-up position. At the same time, the muscles of the back will be lengthened to the maximum, thereby becoming reciprocally relaxed. This is called reciprocal inhibition. It involves an automatic turn-off or relaxation of opposing muscles so that you aren't pulling against yourself, and it is the proper way to restore muscle balance and range of motion. (We'll discuss the concept of range of motion in Chapter 4.) Note that this is not passive stretching; rather, it is an active contracting and strengthening over a full range of motion.

IMPORTANT: The exercise just described is the only case where forward bending should be practiced. It is our recommended substitute for the dangerous exercises listed below, which **must** be stopped (see also high-risk exercises in Chapter 6).

- All vertical standing toe-touching exercises.
- The commonly practiced sit-up exercises.
- All sit-and-reach stretching exercises.

The exercise above is just one of a set we have designed to build up the core. We treat these exercises separately in Chapter 14, but this one is included here because we can't emphasize enough the importance of developing this core.

In fact, the only advice we will ever give you that is more important involves the neck. Nothing is more important than developing a strong neck, because injuries to this area are among the most devastating of all. The emphasis here should be on prevention.

Rehabilitation is very difficult and sometimes not possible at all—nor would it be necessary if more athletes spent at least as much time developing the neck as they spend on the biceps!

In sports such as boxing, wrestling, rugby, and football, neck training is a must for survival. Even a nonathlete can benefit greatly from proper neck training. Whiplash injury as a result of automobile accidents is all too common today, but its severity could be reduced significantly if more people practiced proper neck training.

The neck muscles support and balance a fifteen-pound head. Picture an oblong bowling ball sitting on top of a short pole. The ball is filled with fluid, which makes up 70 percent of its total weight, and contains a three-and-a-half-pound fish (the brain) that has already been caught and is being pulled through a two-inch hole by a nerve line (the spinal cord).

Almost all body balance is controlled from within this fishbowl. The cerebellum controls coordination and balance. The three semicircular canals of the ears control the vestibular system, which is also important for balance. The eyes are part of the righting eye reflex. Thus, the more control between head and body, the more stable and protected is this command control center. Imagine the precise control supplied by the gyroscope within an intercontinental missile when blasting off, and then compare the instantaneous corrections, both fine and large, required by the running, jumping, or diving human body. The movement of the neck, head, and face is a marvel in nature and represents a wonder not yet duplicated in science.

How many dads can recall the time when pregame football introductions included the player's name, position, body weight, and neck size? Twenty-one-inch necks were not uncommon back then. Somehow a false sense of security has developed. It's much like the polio vaccination problem in public health. When extensive vaccination programs had successfully lowered the incidence of polio, the public became negligent and didn't continue to receive the necessary vaccinations. Now the incidence of severe neck injuries in football has been drastically lowered. But some coaches and trainers have become overly secure, and would do well to practice an ounce of prevention to avoid the one hundred pounds of cure.

Along with the rest of the core exercises, we've included sets of exercises in Chapter 14 to help you build up the vital neck area.

Stabilization

A famous poem reads:

For want of a nail the shoe is lost,
For want of a shoe the horse is lost,
For want of a horse the rider is lost,
For want of a rider the battle is lost,
For want of the battle, the kingdom is lost.
—George Herbert

We rephrase that poem:

For want of a stable foot the knee is lost,
For want of a stable knee the hip is lost,
For want of a stable hip the back is lost,
For want of a stable back the shoulder is lost,
For want of a stable shoulder girdle the arm is lost,
For want of a stable head and neck all is lost!

Or, to put it in a form understood by all who sit in a football stadium on a September Saturday, watching the gladiators below:

For want of a stable foot, the ankle was sprained,
Because of the sprained ankle, the tackle was missed,
Because of the missed tackle, the touchdown was scored,
Because of the touchdown, the game was lost:
For want of the game, the season was lost,
All for want of a stable foot!

These poems illustrate a principle called serial distortion. This means that if a part is not in a structurally stable position, it will put abnormal pressure and distorting forces on the structures above and below it, causing them to become distorted in turn.

For example, at every All Star baseball game, someone mentions Dizzy Dean. One of the sport's great pitchers, Dizzy was struck on the foot by a line drive during an All-Star game. He compensated, and the end result was that he damaged his arm. His arm was never the same again, and he was forced to retire much earlier than his original skills would have dictated.

Another example is the knock-kneed person. He or she has abnormal forces and stress on both the ankles and the muscles near the ankles and in the feet. These stresses are transmitted in turn to the pelvis and spine. In addition, abnormal stress is put upon the knee joint itself, which, in a knock-kneed person, is not properly aligned. We also know that joints that are not perfectly aligned don't wear normally, wearing out faster and becoming arthritic.

To avoid serial distortion, and the chain of damage that one unaligned part begins, we emphasize structurally stable positions. Fostering these mechanically stable positions is what we call maintaining the structural integrity of the body. We wish to avoid the distorting forces that bring on serial distortion (of which poor posture is an example). To encourage your structural integrity, we must get you into **stabilization training,** which is a new, systemically progressive method of developing the body's interrelated segments to act as a stable system during both static and dynamic activities.

STATIC STABILITY

The major difference in theory between this book and others available in the same field is the emphasis we place on the value of *specific* stabilization strength. This specific strength can be thought of as the glue that joins together all the body segments. It is the glue that fuses the body parts into one solid foundation. This strength has value throughout the entire spectrum of sports performance, as evidenced by the experts' comments on "a solid foundation." And, obviously, this specific stabilization strength is a goal of rehabilitation as well.

Many systems of training exist, such as power training, endurance training, cardiovascular training, and rehabilitation strength training. But none is more important, nor more ignored, than specific stabilization training. It is primary to all others.

You'll see that specific stabilization training requires more than lifting heavier and heavier weights or jumping higher than before. It requires knowledge of proper body alignment, what we call structural integrity. Drawing on the principles of architecture, engineering, and biomechanics, we can knowledgeably train an athlete or a performer (such as a dancer) to be more efficient in their movements.

To the engineer or architect, stabilization is the very foundation of their science. Making a bridge or a building withstand pressures is more important than beauty. It's only when both stabilization and beauty exist that we can have a true work of art.

This concept of stable bridges and buildings needs to be applied to human bodies as well. The science of bioengineering or biomechanics tells us that human architecture and design must withstand the same forces that stress bridges and buildings; they all require inherent strength, called *static stabilization.* The rules governing any such system cannot be violated, or else structural decay sets in and the total system fails or collapses.

Self Test

How structurally stable are you? Here are some easy tests to see how you measure up for static stability. If you've been injured, these tests are a good guide for judging to see what you need to improve and how ready you are to train for high-performance athletics.

It's best to do these tests in athletic shorts, with only socks or tights on, or perhaps barefooted. Ideally, they should be done in front of a full length mirror.

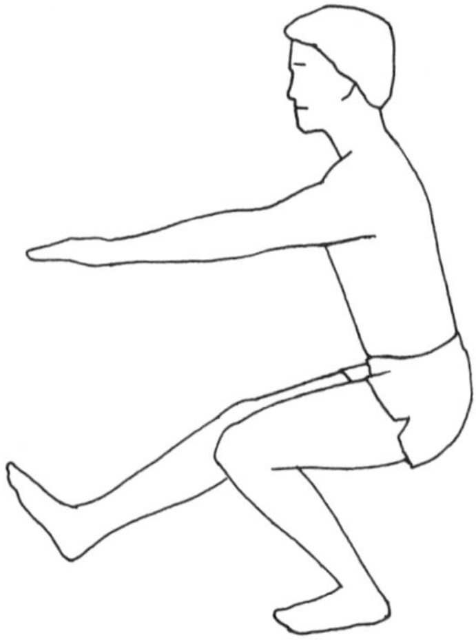

Stability test—the full squat *You are not structurally stable or fit to run until you can hold this position for 30 seconds.*

For the first test, lift one leg in front of you. Can you still stand still? Are you stable? Are you rocking back and forth on your foot? Now try this test with your other leg. If you've had a leg injury and cannot stand on that leg, you are unfit for any athletic endeavor, and it would be harmful and wrong for you to do any running with your injury.

If you passed the first test, do a quarter squat. Then do a half squat. If you cannot, you are not fit to run or play any sport at all until you have properly rehabilitated yourself.

The reasons behind this should be obvious. In running or any sporting endeavor (including dance), you spend much of your time on only one leg or the other. If one of your legs cannot support you in your own room while standing, then there is no conceivable way that it is strong or stable enough to do so in an athletic setting, or even to withstand the stresses of running. The forces involved in running and in various sports are four to ten times greater than the forces involved in simply standing or trying a simple squat.

This test illustrates the importance of one of our basic concepts: You must be stable before you can perform. Without stability, you risk injury and you cannot perform at your maximum. We've seen many athletes who tried to get back into extremely demanding sports when they did not have this stability. Then they wondered what was wrong with their bodies as other injuries hit them while they tried to compensate for the instability. They were unfortunate examples of the results of serial distortion.

We call the next test the mirror test, for which you need a mirror, preferably a full-length one. Stand sideways and look at yourself. Do you have what is commonly called a swayback, which gives you a potbellied appearance? Are you round-shouldered? Does your neck stick out like a road-runner's?

Now begin the test. Can you pull your head back and tuck in your chin? Can you pull your shoulders back, much like a West Pointer? Can you "suck in your gut" as if you were going to be punched by Sugar Ray Leonard? Can you rotate your pelvis? (You should be

Structurally stable position *Note that the feet are stable, with the kneecaps lining up approximately with the second toe. The position of the spine and shoulders is ideal. The neck is straight and tall and the head stable.*

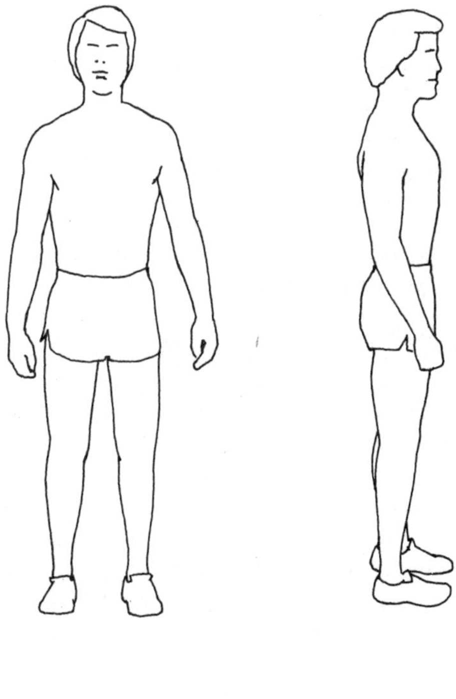

able to rotate your pelvis approximately thirty degrees.) If you can't do all of these maneuvers—that is, do them securely and hold them—then your important trunk muscles do not have a strong, stable core. You must have core stability before you can perform or return to performing any athletic endeavor with any kind of safety.

Flexibility Is Not the Key

Unfortunately, the ability to be a contortionist and assume abnormal yoga positions is becoming the standard by which many athletes judge their ability to perform. If maximum flexibility were the test for athletic prowess, then victims of polio would be our best athletes. Legs that are partially or completely paralyzed by polio have almost complete flexibility. But these partially or completely paralyzed legs are extremely unstable, and incapable of supporting weight of any sort. What we really need for athletic performance is stability throughout a full range of motion of the joint.

There is absolutely no scientific evidence that stretching a joint beyond its normal range of motion is beneficial. In fact, traditional orthopedic teaching has been that the ability to assume these postures and positions is abnormal. The three most common medical conditions that are characterized by hyperflexibility are polio, Ehlers-Danlos syndrome (the "India-rubber man"), and hypotonia (loss of tonicity of the muscles).

If you compare the structure and abilities of a gorilla and a man, you will understand what we say about stability. The man is much more mobile. The gorilla is much stronger, but it can stand erect for only short periods and spends most of its time crouched in an all-fours position. It uses its shoulder girdle, collarbone, and scapula much like a pelvis. The huge pectoral, serratus, and latissimus dorsi muscles act like a suspension bridge for the entire torso.

While we are not recommending that our readers walk around on all fours, we are suggesting that you can learn about stability from a friendly gorilla.

The linebacker who is taking on a big running back and the power lifter who is breaking a world record in the squat could both use the stability approach of the gorilla. But the finesse and the elegant movement of the virtuoso pianist or violinist are matched in the soft touch of a quarterback's pass or the finger action of a basketball jump shot.

We hope we've convinced you of the importance of static stabilization. Our system is unique in that it will completely train you—or rehabilitate you for return to maximum athletic endeavors—by allowing you to exercise and perform in a stable fashion that never violates sound mechanical principles.

DYNAMIC STABILITY

The human machine must also withstand dynamic forces as it moves. The body must be continuously stabilized, and stabilization during motion is called dynamic stability. Dynamic stability involves rotation, holding together, and braking. When the human athlete is dynamically stable, his performance is efficient, and he uses his energy economically and safely. His performance is smooth, rhythmical and beautiful; he looks skilled.

Part of dynamic stability is a concept called essential synergy. Whenever you swing your arm or move your leg, it goes where you want it to go. The movement is aligned and kept on track by the synergistic (cooperative) balancing efforts of almost all of the muscles in your arms and legs.

One of the hardest parts of anatomy to learn is which actions the various muscles perform. It should be obvious that the biceps bends your elbow and the quadriceps straightens your knee. However, if you check an anatomy book for each action, there are always at least two muscles that are involved in it, and sometimes four or more. It gets even more confusing if you actually study which muscles work (and when) as you are walking or running. *All* of the muscles in your hips and legs work, and they are constantly turning off and on. The reason they are all involved is that they frequently act as midcourse correctors, much like the side rockets on a spaceship. To go where you want to go, you must use all of these muscles. And it should be obvious that to train for maximum performance, you must train and strengthen all of these muscles. You must increase your options so you can move with control throughout all of your possibilities. Our training program is designed to keep you stable even while you are moving and jumping, and to give your body the ability to alter and change course, and, even more important, to keep in alignment and on course.

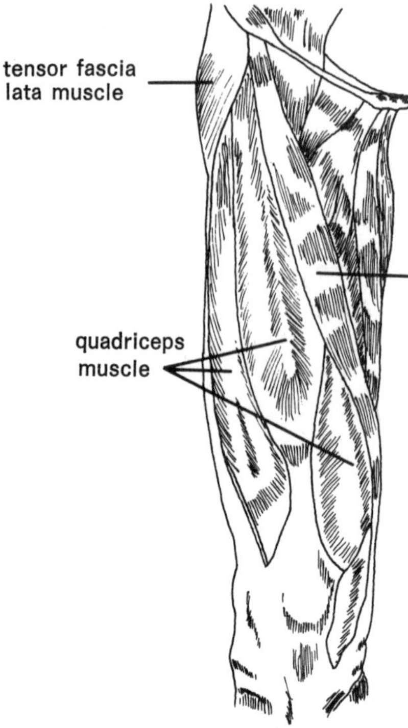

Thigh muscles, front view Some muscles curve around both sides of the knee, and four muscles come together and join in the front to become the well-known quadriceps muscle.

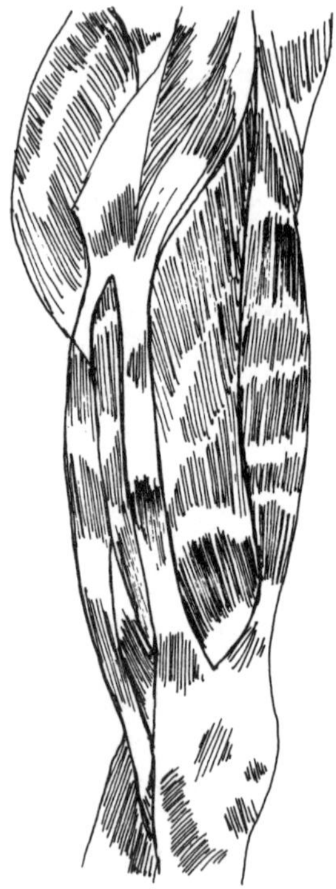

Buttocks and thighs, side view *Muscles cross not only in front of the hip and knee joints, but along the sides as well. You must train all these muscles because they are significant in maintaining your stability.*

If you don't train the synergistic muscles, then you won't be able to reach your maximum potential. That is why we believe in training you for balance and teaching stability. If you don't train all the necessary bodily systems you will never reach your full potential and you will risk injury. You have to train your balancing system and muscles as well as your stabilizer muscles if you want all of them to perform.

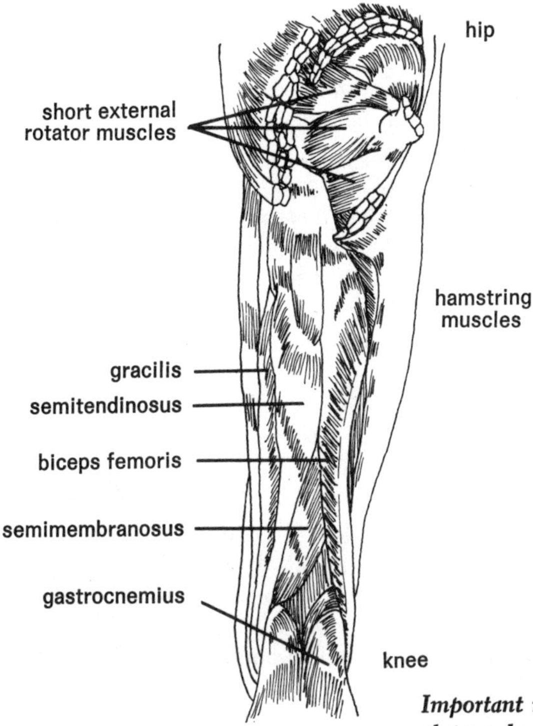

Important rotational muscles *The large gluteus buttock muscles have been removed to show the important rotational muscles. Note the hamstring muscles, which curve around both sides of the knee. Also note the short external rotators at the hip. These rotators must be trained because they can easily fatigue from overuse.*

One part of dynamic stability involves rotation. It is obvious in watching any sporting event that no performance is conducted in a straight line. When you look at an event like the 100-yard dash in slow motion, you can see obvious rotational changes in the thighs, legs, and feet throughout each stride. Unfortunately, the use of machines in traditional training methods has emphasized moving the arms and legs in a straight direction only, because of constraints imposed by the machines. These machines are useful, but the training they give is clearly incomplete. It should be obvious that if you twist, spin, and rotate while performing, you must train yourself to perform these maneuvers and to do so in a stable fashion, so that you can maintain the structural integrity of your body. You must train not only the movers of your body, but also the spinners, the twisters, and the rotators.

A second part of dynamic stability involves holding together. When you run, jump, throw, or lift heavy weights, you use one system of muscles to propel you. But you also use another system of muscles and nerve interactions to hold the parts together. Your body is constantly working both to help you move and to keep you together.

A basic principle of physics also applies here. It is an engineering fact that the best lever action for a third-class lever, which is what our arms and legs are, requires a solid fulcrum. It's like hauling in a shark out of the Gulf of Mexico. The shark is pulling at one end of the fishing pole. You're hanging on to the middle of the pole, and the bottom end is braced against your body or in a holder. If it weren't braced, and braced well, you would have a tough time getting any lever action on the fish end of the pole.

The same principle applies to the stabilization of a particular part of your body, such as a leg. For you to be able to kick or run or move well, your femur must have a good axis point in your pelvis. If the axis point is stable, you will get more force from the action of your muscles. Certain parts of the body must be fixed and stable for other parts to move.

Conversely, as you increase the force that you can apply to a part of your body, you must also be able to provide greater braking action or counterreaction. Unless your body compensates for a strong movement, it will be torn apart or twisted out of control. And the stronger the acceleration, the stronger the countermovement must be.

Kinesiologists call the actions of the accelerators and brakes spurt and shunt functions.

The system we are outlining specifically provides for that explosive starting action so essential to most sporting maneuvers and activities. Part of our goal is to train you so that you can move quickly and safely in a stable fashion. But even more important is the training of the brakes or the "shunts."

This is especially true in throwing, where most exercises are aimed at the powerful throwing muscles. But usually left untrained are the muscles at the back of the shoulder blade that attach the shoulder and shoulder blade to the chest and are responsible for the braking and, literally, the holding of the arm to the core. Every pitching coach in the country will say that to throw safely and efficiently, you must use your whole body. In effect, they are telling you that you must train all the muscles associated with your shoulder —and especially the brakes or shunts.

STABILIZATION TRAINING

It is vital that the stabilizer system be built up sufficiently to accommodate increases in speed, strength, power, and magnitude. As you increase your abilities to propel your body or appendages, you will be in trouble if you don't also build up your body's stabilizers. In effect, what goes up must come down, softly.

In Chapters 13 through 21 we will show you how to build up these stabilizer systems. You will need some equipment not usually seen in training areas, but it is equipment that you can purchase at low cost or make. We'll show you how to use the unstable "O" balance beam, kinesthetic primer board, mini-trampoline, power bands, and the soft down jump box.

These simple tools will help you develop both **primary stabilization** and **secondary stabilization.** Primary stabilization is that which occurs within the core. We call it primary because of its extreme importance and because the core is the axis point for all arm and leg movements. It is primary stabilization that provides for good posture and for an erect spine, neck, and head.

Arm and leg movements are outside the core, but they also need stabilization. This type of stabilization differs from core stabilization because arm and leg movements are comprised of segmented actions. Thus, stabilization that occurs in the arms and legs is called secondary stabilization. But don't be misled by the term. While we call it *secondary* stabilization, ask any pitcher with arm trouble, or any one of the thousands with knee trouble, if it is secondary to performance.

The good news is that stabilization training can be preventive and rehabilitative. In Chapter 7 we will discuss injuries and how to prevent them, and in Chapter 22 we will give you specific stabilization training for both increased performance and rehabilitation of knee injuries.

We believe that stabilization training is a prerequisite for rehabilitation. While stability of joints is recognized as an important factor in rehabilitation work, very few therapists in the United States include stability as a goal of training in itself. This may seem incredible, but an inspection of programs shows great gaps in application. Several factors contribute to this mistake and they are mostly related to a heavy dependence upon machines.

In most prescriptions for knee rehabilitation exercise, we find instructions like the following: "Work quad extension"; or "Work Nautilus thigh curl." Other prescriptions seem totally reliant on the Cybex exercise machine, which works concentric extension and concentric flexion at the same time. The major problems with prescriptions for machine work are the following:

- Machines only exercise in one plane, but all normal body movement is in more than one plane. Because the machines are stable, it is possible to train and strain in an unstable fashion. This increases your chance of injury while training (see Chapter 8). Because the machines stabilize the weights, you can't train your stabilizers and midcourse correctors. Thus, machines provide incomplete training.
- None of the commonly available exercise machines trains rotation or twisting movements—and all of sport and dance is a study in twisting and turning.
- Machines provide too much resistance too soon. Most machines use ten-pound increments. One-pound or even half-pound increments are more appropriate.

While it is obvious that major stabilizing muscle work is performed by those muscles that are actively engaged in stabilizing the pivot point on which the movement takes place, most skillful movements involve action that is not confined to only one or two joints but is actually diffused over the whole body. For example, when you throw a ball, the shoulder blade (scapula) must be stabilized for efficient action, but it must also be maintained within the proper track, which moves through three planes of action—forward, backward, and sideward. Furthermore, the shoulder blade is part of the shoulder-girdle assembly, which also includes the clavicle (collarbone). The shoulder girdle in turn moves in relation to the body as a whole, so you can see that while the position of the scapula is a crucial factor in throwing, stabilization control is also needed for the shoulder-girdle complex and the entire body.

INSTABILITY

We've discussed the importance of stability. Perhaps we can give further motivation for stabilization training by showing you what happens when certain stabilities are lost.

Canoe Feet

When a performer wobbles or is unable to maintain balance when standing upon one foot, we say he has "canoe feet." If you don't understand this, try to stand up in a canoe sometime. The performer's wobbly foot indicates that the muscles in his leg are weak and unable to maintain the foot in a stable position while standing. If, for example, when landing from a skip or a jump you wobble and are not stable, your canoe foot is due to muscles that are unable to maintain a stable position while lengthening. This is called eccentric supination of the foot: The arch is unable to maintain appropriate alignment and stability, and as a result the ankle cannot be controlled within its normal bony limits.

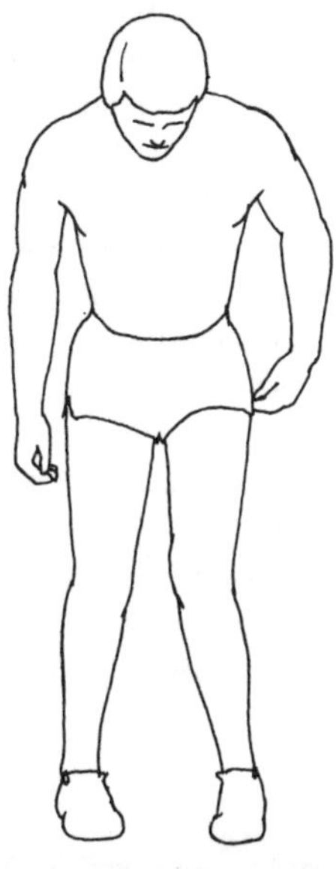

Unstable foot position *The right foot is supinated and the left foot is slightly pronated. Also note the poor position of the classic X-knees. This is an extremely unstable position. Also, the head, neck, and spine are in an unstable position.*

The most severe type of unstable foot is where the arch collapses and the foot rolls outward, rolling the ankle inward. This is called a pronated foot. If your muscles are incapable of supporting your arch, or if your foot rolls out because of loss of the arch, you may need orthotics, which are custom-made arch supports that will help maintain your foot in the proper position and avoid serial distortion. Any athlete, especially a high-performance athlete with this problem, will benefit significantly from orthotics.

X-Knees

We prefer the term "X-knees" to the more commonly used "knock-knees." The proper medical term is "valgus knees." Whatever you call it, it is a structurally unstable position. It is much more common in women than in men because women have a wider pelvis than men, which causes their thigh bones to come in at more of an angle. X-knees is also common in children as a normal phase of development. One of the possible causes of X-knees is bony alignment that cannot be changed. However, there are several causes that can be corrected and those are the ones that we want to stress.

The first is canoe feet, or the valgus (or pronated) foot. As the foot rolls out, stress is transferred onto the knee, forcing it into an X-kneed position. An athlete with this problem frequently needs orthotics to maintain structural alignment.

In children, and especially adolescents (who often have problems with ligamentous laxity), X-knees are usually the result of loose ligaments and weak hip muscles, usually the muscles that rotate the hips out (the external rotators). In children with this condition, stability training and strengthening are essential to prevent this posture from becoming a permanent unstable condition.

A third type of treatable X-knees occurs often in athletes, most commonly female performers with weak hip muscles: As their hips rotate in, their posture becomes X-kneed. Strengthening the hip muscles will help this weak and unstable alignment.

Whatever the cause, X-knees is an unstable position and proper training can benefit anyone who has this problem. Obviously those performers with bony deformities cannot be corrected with training and exercises; but with proper instruction they can be taught to perform in a more stable fashion by turning their legs out, thus increasing their ability to perform and decreasing their risk of injury.

A

B

Stable and unstable positions *The ideal foot and knee position for stability and structural integrity is shown in figure A. Figure B demonstrates the X-kneed position. Note how unstable the athlete appears, as if he is about to collapse. In fact, that is what will happen!*

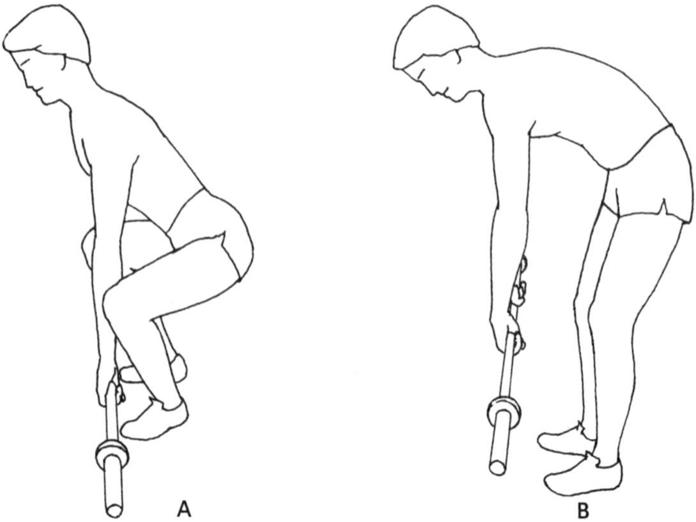

Banana back vs. correct back *Figure B shows the banana back position, which puts enormous strain on the ligaments and discs in the back. It is one of the prime causes of back pain; in fact, anyone who lifts in this position is risking a slipped disc, especially if a twisting maneuver is added to it. Figure A demonstrates the proper position for lifting weights off the ground. Note the full-squat knee position, the facet-locked stable spine, and the neck and head position.*

Banana Back

When lifting or training (except if performing the torso-curl exercise), you must avoid the banana-back position. In other words, your back should never be curved forward like a banana. This is because there are two little joints in each spinal segment of your back. In the stable position shown in the illustration on page 30, these joints (called facet joints) are locked. In this stable position, called facet lock, strain is maximally distributed across all the segments of the spine and discs, thereby minimizing the chance of injuring any of these structures.

If you bend forward in the banana-back position, you unlock the facet joints. Once this happens, some of the stress is taken off the bony supports (called pedicles) in the back and abnormal stresses

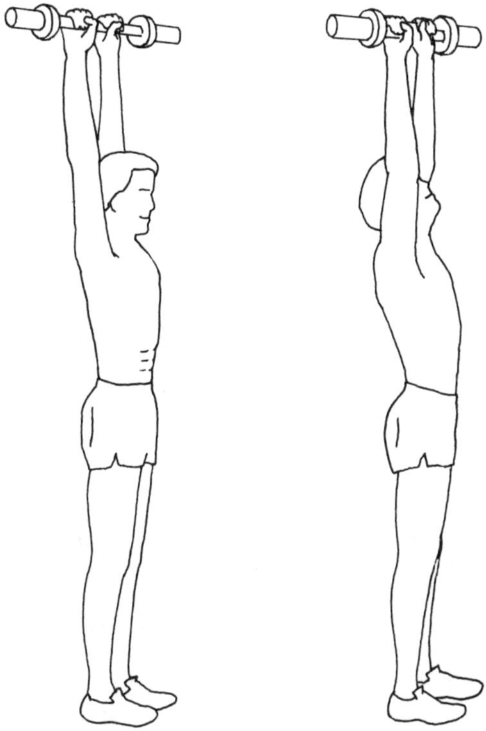

A B

Overhead positions *Figure B shows an improper stance; he is looking at the bar, his spine is out of its stable facet-locked position and is in fact hyperextended. The proper position is shown in figure A. Not only is this posture stable, it also allows breathing.*

are placed upon the discs and ligaments in the back. This also makes the muscles in the back work much harder, so in this structurally unstable position you are much more likely either to injure a disc ("slipped disc"), cause ligament strain ("low back strain"), or injure the muscles (so-called muscular back pain). Furthermore, when the facet joints are unlocked, the spine is more vulnerable to twisting motion. In the locked position the facets can't twist. Twisting motions of the spine cause shear forces. Shear forces put enormous stress on the discs in the back and it is these shear forces that are the primary cause of ruptured discs and disc problems in

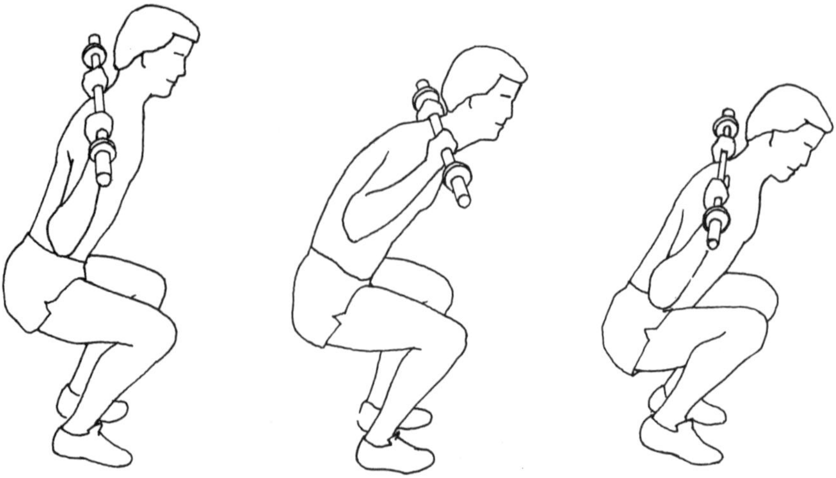

A B C

Good and bad weight-lifting positions *Figure A illustrates the stable, full-squat position. Note the proper head and neck position. The spine is in the facet-locked stable position, and the knees and feet are also stable. Figure B demonstrates the terrible banana-back position. Note also the roadrunner head and neck position plus the poor foot position. This is a classic example of serial distortion. When one segment is unstable, the rest of the body follows. Figure C shows a deep knee bend. This is beyond the normal full-squat position and it is quite easy to tear the lateral meniscus or cartilage in your knees by going into this deep, injury-producing position.*

Proper structurally stable position *Note the position of head, neck, spine, knees, and feet.*

the lower back. So to prevent disc injuries, it is essential that you maintain the facet-locked stable position.

The back-bend position is normally prevented by the bony processes (projections) that protrude backward from the spine (spinous processes). However, it is possible to perform sporting maneuvers that force back bends, such as the three-point stance of a defensive football lineman, the back-walkover in gymnastics, and the butterfly stroke in swimming. These place abnormal stress on the pedicles, and can and often do lead to a stress fracture. That is why it is absolutely essential that you maintain the structurally stable position of your lower back and entire spine if you want to avoid injury and maximize your performance.

Because in the facet-unlocked, banana-back position you are putting abnormal stresses and shear forces across the discs, we strongly advise against toe-touching exercises. Alternate toe-touching, because of the shear forces, and stiff-legged dead-lifting exercises are even more hazardous. All of these put your low back in its worst, most unstable position and put maximum dangerous stresses across your discs.

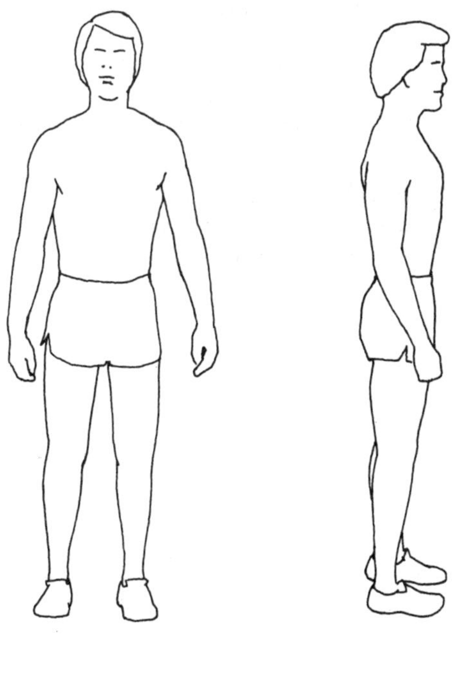

Ideal head and neck position *You need to think tall and keep your chin in. Holding your chin in without thinking tall will give you the unstable "West Point position."*

Bowling-Ball Head

Roadrunner neck usually connects to bowling-ball head. You really shouldn't stick your head out there like a bowling ball. Head position is a critical factor in performance. There are reflexes (such as the righting reflex) which at times can force abnormal motions upon the head. One of the maneuvers in calf roping is simply to twist the calf's head, and a reflex automatically flips the rest of the body around. It is not the strength of the cowboy that twists the entire calf's body, but the strength of the reflex that moves all the calf's feet out to the side and lets it fall to the ground.

Humans do not have that degree of righting reflex, fortunately. However, the same connections are there. So there is no question that abnormal head position and constant head motion can throw us off ever so slightly, and in many activities—such as catching a ball, shooting a jump shot, or hitting a ball—if you don't hold your head still, your performance will suffer.

In other situations, if you stick your bowling-ball head out on your roadrunner neck, not only are you inviting failure but you are courting disaster and complete paralysis: Unfortunately, broken necks still do occur in sporting activities. This is why we spend hours at the Sports Performance and Rehabilitation Institute teaching our performers to maintain control. It improves performance and enhances survival. The important thing to learn here is to use your eyes more while stabilizing your head, rather than whipping your head all over the place.

4

Dynamic Range of Motion

After core and stability, the third concept of maximum performance is that of dynamic range of motion. According to this concept, you must be able to actively control your joints through their full individual potential range of motion ("potential" means "not beyond anatomical possibilities"). We call this D'ROM (pronounced D-prime-R-O-M) for short.

First, note that D'ROM calls for full muscle control throughout the range of motion. If you don't have this control, your body will risk injury when force is applied to a joint during a phase of less control.

Second, note that D'ROM calls for the *fullest* potential range of motion that is not beyond anatomical possibilities. In some cases, an individual's actual range of motion (AROM) may be greater than his or her dynamic range. This will happen if the person has been a practitioner of yoga or other ill-advised stretching maneuvers that have stretched ligaments and tendons beyond what is normal. In this case the joints are usually less stable than they should be. Various kinds of injury could also cause AROM to be greater than D'ROM.

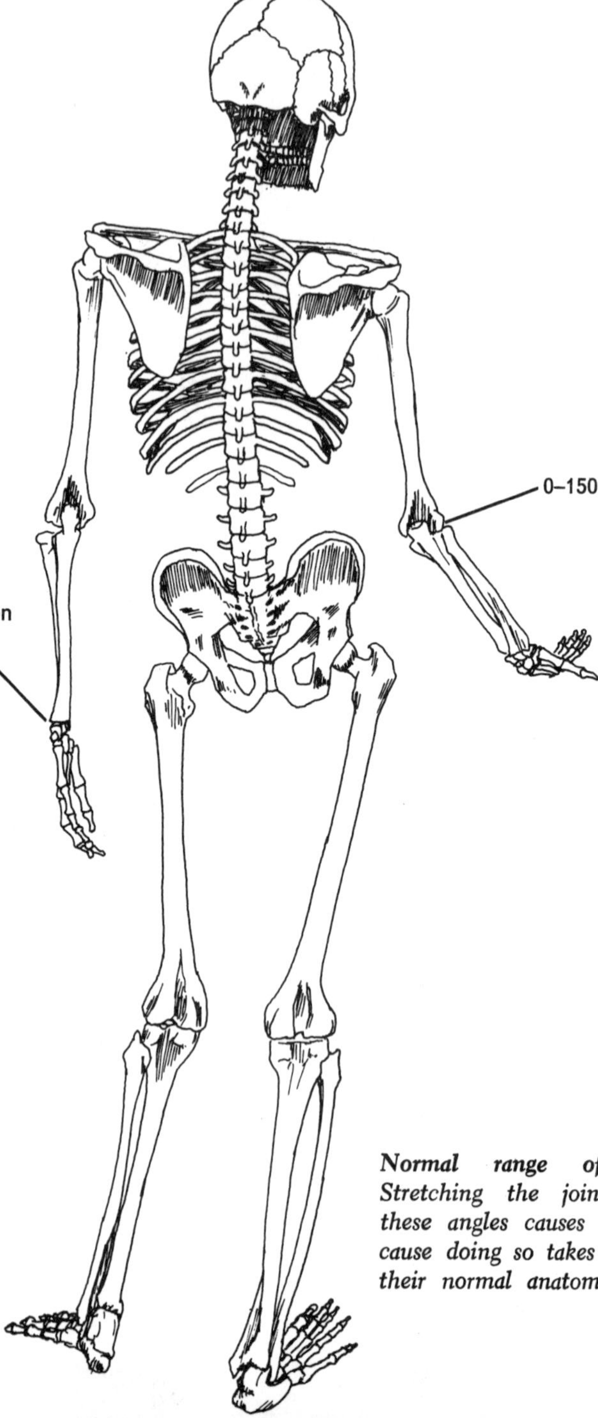

Normal range of motion
Stretching the joints beyond these angles causes injury, because doing so takes them past their normal anatomical limits.

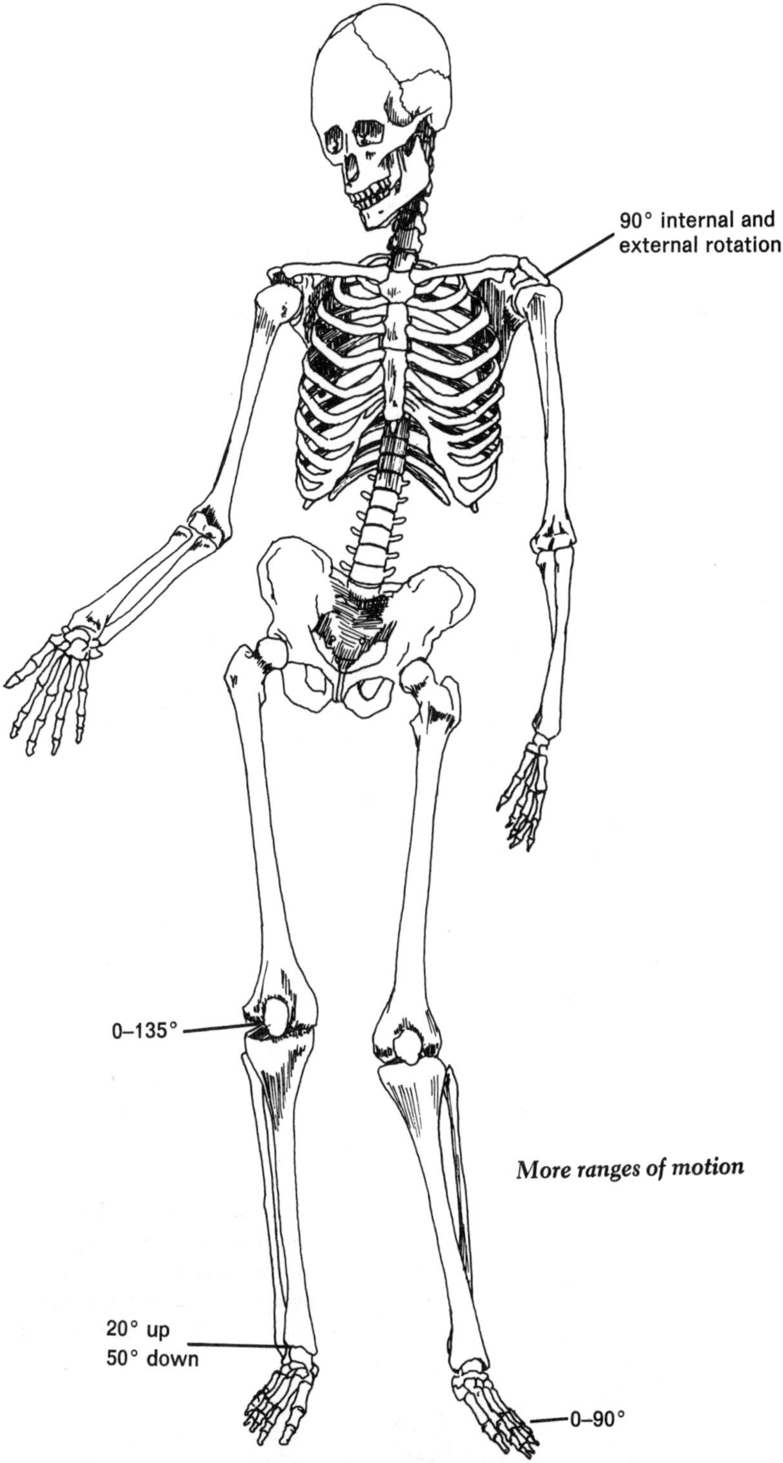

More ranges of motion

Thirdly, note that D'ROM calls for the comprehensive range of motion in which all possible options are open to the athlete. The limits of the range of motion depend upon the actual anatomical construction of the joint, the ligaments around the sides of the joint, the tendons that connect the muscles to the bones that move the joint, and the muscles themselves that move the body part. Thus any injury could cause your actual range to be somewhat less or significantly less. Recovery following an injury or even a lack of development can cause a loss of range of motion. It is possible, by active exercise, to increase range of motion (ROM) significantly, up to the anatomical limits of the joint. Part of our program is designed to improve your performance by increasing your actual range of motion to D'ROM.

Dynamic range of motion (D'ROM) is different from desirable range of motion (DROM). For each sport or activity you would have a desirable range of motion that is necessary for performance in that particular sport. This desirable range obviously varies with each sport. For example, certain gymnastic maneuvers require more range in some joints than, say, a sport like basketball does. It is important to identify your desirable-range-of-motion needs and compare them with your actual range of motion. If your AROM is less than the DROM you need for a sport, then you must work on increasing that range in order to be able to function even minimally.

These may seem like simple concepts, but they are extremely important for increasing your performance. Your best performance and your insurance against injury come from developing the D'ROM for your body. Developing your D'ROM will give you the racer's edge in any sport; it will permit you to maximize your athletic potential.

In rehabilitation, D'ROM training is the first step. Obviously, until you can move your injured joint through its full motion, you have only begun your rehabilitation process. It is now an accepted fact that active muscular control enhances healing. Furthermore, active motion will cause the gentle, natural reordering and loosening of scar tissue, promoting the healing process.

It is possible under deep anesthesia, with biofeedback, or through yoga training to reduce muscle tone to almost zero. The opposite of this is muscle spasm, where there is such a dramatic increase in tone that the muscle becomes spastic and usually quite painful;

you can't control it. Of course, there are varying degrees between the two extremes.

At either extreme, injury and/or pain is quite possible. At the extreme of spasm, you would have a great deal of pain. At the other extreme, minimal or no tone, you would have virtually no muscular control over the joint in question. You literally hang by your ligaments, stretching on your ligaments with no muscle tone to guard them. The yogi is able to achieve his contortionist positions by minimizing his muscle tone and stretching his muscles beyond their normal limits. There are no proven athletic performance benefits from such maneuvers, and discussion of the effects of this relaxed state upon the athlete's psyche is beyond the scope of this book.

Our goal is to help you successfully rehabilitate and train for maximal athletic performance. To do this, you must have active control of your joints throughout their full range of motion. It is for this reason that we recommend beginning your workout with a D'ROM set that uses gravity and the weight of your arms and legs. Don't waste fifteen to thirty minutes of warm-up doing stretching that is not beneficial and may potentially be harmful (see Chapter 13). Once you have completed your D'ROM workout, then progress to bands, beams, and boards, and eventually boxes. Your performance will increase and it will speed up your rehabilitation.

Some of the alleged benefits of stretching routines are in fact the results of performing a modified D'ROM-type routine. Unfortunately, most people don't realize that it is the active, controlled muscular activity that is the beneficial part, and not the stretching.

5

Are You Training to Run Slower?

In the "dark ages" before everyone realized the benefit of resistance exercise (weight lifting), there was the image of the musclebound power lifter who couldn't run fast or do other athletic maneuvers. Once the period of enlightenment came, the concept "musclebound" became outmoded. Experts said that weight lifting would not bind you up but instead would improve your speed.

As with many old concepts that have been forgotten, we must resurrect the idea that lifting weights can make you musclebound. Lifting weights can bind you up and make you run slower. Rockey Blier of the Pittsburgh Steelers is a prime example of this. He was highly motivated, and in trying to rehabilitate his war-injured leg, he was doing the "big four": power squats, power cleans, bench presses, and curls. He noted that as he worked harder on just these four exercises, he began to tie up and run slower. He sought out Bob Gajda and began to use the training systems we present in this book. He then began to improve dramatically. His problem was that he had been strengthening only one group of his thigh muscles, and so the increased strength and muscle tone he developed "bound him up." He needed to balance his strength and put his energy into properly training all his muscles.

We are seeing more and more of this type of problem now that many high-school football teams require a certain amount of strength in the "big four" to make the team. Weight lifting is a valuable exercise, but if you train only in those routines, you may become musclebound; you could even succeed in training yourself to run slow!

If your goal is to achieve your maximum athletic potential, you are going to have to train smart. This book has a complete system to help you achieve your goal. But training smart doesn't come with any short cuts. It is the quality of your training that is important, and it takes time and determination to TRAIN SMART!

Before the explosion of interest in aerobics and aerobic training in North America, the conditioning and training of athletes tended to be a bit haphazard. That, coupled with the success of Russia and the Eastern European countries in the Olympics (apparently because of the scientific approach that they took), led to interest in a more effective way to train athletes. This new scientific approach studied professional athletes and teams, and resulted in the observation that many of the professionals were in woeful aerobic condition.

We agree that aerobics are important to good health and good conditioning, but, unfortunately, aerobic conditioning is basically endurance training, and most of the popular sports in the United States are not aerobic-type activities; they are anaerobic. Being successful in baseball, football, or the 100-yard dash does not require great aerobic capacity or fitness, and aerobic training alone will not necessarily lead to marked improvement in performance of these anaerobic types of activities. While aerobic conditioning can contribute to a decrease in injury rates by eliminating fatigue as an injury factor, it isn't the answer to improving performance in anaerobic sports, nor will it necessarily help in the rehabilitation of injuries.

To understand what we are trying to accomplish, you have to understand the basics of exercise physiology, and what the different types of training activities will achieve.

THE DIFFERENCE BETWEEN PERFORMANCE AND PHYSICAL FITNESS

Physical fitness is cardio-respiratory biased. If you think of this in terms of work, increased fitness means the ability to do more work. It is a concept best applied to events such as cross-country skiing, marathon running, and long-distance swimming; it doesn't apply very much to sports like racquetball, football, tennis, and baseball.

Performance, on the other hand, emphasizes efficiency, and success in it is based upon skill development and structural integrity. Performance is looking to conserve energy. Performance tends to concentrate more on quality, less on quantity. Because efficiency of action requires all systems to be in the best possible operating condition, it follows that training for performance must maintain that optimal operating condition, and that any activity or repetition pattern that destroys or lessens operating conditions should be changed.

Traditional training philosophy was based on physical fitness, and demanded catharsis, caloric expenditure, heavy breathing, and perspiration. Its goals were based on quantity.

Training for performance, we believe, must weigh the costs against the benefits. No exercise should exceed the limitations of bone and ligaments. You don't want premature muscle strain, or wear and tear on joints. You want to minimize the risk of injury while maximizing performance.

That is why we believe that in all training the recommended exercises must be noninjurious, specific to the activities of the sport, and at a level appropriate for both the performer and the sport.

For example, many racquetball players jog for cardiovascular value in the hope of improving their play. Unfortunately, as rated by performance ratio, jogging is low in efficiency. It costs a person more than it returns in benefits. According to *Runner's World* magazine, six out of ten joggers suffer from joint injury. Not only is the technique of heel-strike and flat-footed running inappropriate to the sprint requirement of racquetball, but the pressure jogging exerts on the foot, knee, and spine is tremendous.

Unfortunately, many players falsely believe that jogging is the only way to attain cardiovascular fitness. Not only is this belief false, it is counterproductive as well. There are many other alternatives, and jogging in a straight line is nonspecific and not at all like the running done in racquetball.

Simply stated, as a sport racquetball entails more than enough running. Any additional running is just a waste of time.

This illustrates why we believe that exercise should be more than just exercise. It should be systematic and purposeful. If you want to develop your performance, do not concentrate on the ends—how much, how often, how far. Rather, concentrate on the means: quality, style, form, and technique.

AEROBICS

Aerobic capacity is the ability of the lungs to take in large amounts of air and the heart to pump oxygen to all the muscles of the body for energy. All the energy that a muscle uses comes from the burning of oxygen within that muscle. Aerobic means "with air," so aerobic training trains the heart, lungs, and muscles to use oxygen directly for energy formation. The larger your aerobic capacity, the more oxygen you can use and burn, and the more efficient your heart, lungs, and circulatory system will be in getting the oxygen to the muscles.

In practical terms, your aerobic energy system is not important and does not begin to function in athletic events and maneuvers until two minutes has elapsed. Therefore, any sporting activity that requires less than two minutes of continuous activity—and *continuous* is the key word here—is not an aerobic event. Any sport or activity that does require more than two minutes of continuous activity is an aerobic event. In practical terms, this means that aerobic training requires more than two minutes of continuous, vigorous, athletic activity. If you stop in less than two minutes, then you are not really using or training your aerobic system. (The aerobic system actually begins to function after fifteen to thirty seconds of athletic activity, but it is not until after two minutes that it functions enough to have any training benefit.)

ANAEROBICS

In the first two minutes of any physical activity, or until the aerobic system kicks in, you are utilizing anaerobic energy. Anaerobic means "without oxygen," and this type of energy is already stored in the muscles. Baseball is a classic example of an anaerobic sport. In it there is no play or activity that lasts two minutes, so baseball makes very little aerobic demand on the body. That is why walking eighteen holes of golf may provide more aerobic activity than does playing a baseball game (depending on your position). It also explains why baseball players can often get away with being "out of shape"; the longest they ever have to run is 120 yards—and that would be for an inside-the-park home run, which is an extremely rare play. Normally they have to run only thirty yards every thirty or forty minutes.

To improve your speed and performance you must train anaerobically. You must increase your strength if you want to be faster, and it must be increased throughout the full range of motion required by the activity if your performance is to be improved. This is the desirable range of motion, or DROM. A passive flexibility does not count. You must have strength and control throughout the entire range of motion.

Furthermore, you not only need strength, but you must improve your stamina so you can do a maneuver more than once. The system outlined in Chapter 14 will show you how to increase both strength and stamina, and also power (which is the strength and ability to do something quickly). Increasing power is the key to increasing speed. Chapter 14 describes a complete system of resistance training for all three: strength, stamina, and power.

Our bodies have two types of anaerobic energy systems. The first one is the instantaneous, which gets us moving on a split-second basis; the second involves the slightly slower type of anaerobic energy which is stored in the form of glycogen in our muscles. We are able to burn glycogen (a carbohydrate) to keep us going until our aerobic energy system kicks in and starts to take over, after about two minutes.

However, you will remember that we said that all muscle energy comes from the burning of oxygen. We just described an energy system that functions without supplying oxygen to the muscles. That is why when you run anaerobically you develop an "oxygen debt."

Eventually, oxygen will be necessary to replace the energy that was burned anaerobically. The aerobic system will have to kick in to repay the oxygen debt for the energy burned anaerobically. Oxygen must be provided to recharge the anaerobic energy system in the muscles for the next time they have to function anaerobically.

MUSCLE TYPES

To understand the types of training necessary, it is helpful to know about muscle types and their function (muscle physiology). Basically our muscles are made up of two types of fibers, called slow-twitch and fast-twitch fibers.

The slow-twitch fibers are the endurance type of muscle fiber. They are thought to function aerobically; that is, they need oxygen to function. Muscles that have a high number of slow-twitch fibers are good endurance muscles. Endurance athletes such as long-distance runners and marathoners usually have a high percentage of slow-twitch muscle fibers.

Fast-twitch fibers are the fibers that function anaerobically. There really are two types of fast-twitch fibers: super-fast or instantaneous, which are the ones that get us from a standstill to a quick motion; and the basic fast-twitch fibers. Muscles with a high percentage of fast-twitch fibers are usually quick and are most commonly found in sprint-type athletes—those who run the 100-meter dash, do high jumping, pole vaulting; baseball players, and so forth. For anaerobic training these athletes must train both types of anaerobic fast-twitch muscle fibers.

Some experts believe that with specific training it is possible to change the proportion of fast-twitch and slow-twitch fibers in your muscles, selectively improving either your endurance capacity or your speed. Others, however, believe that the individual's ratio of fast-twitch to slow-twitch fibers is fixed and can never be changed. But all the experts agree that both aerobic and anaerobic functions can be improved with proper training. Since none of use ever reach our full potential, that is the fact that is important to remember.

As we stated, endurance events require slow-twitch fibers; short-duration events require fast-twitch fibers. For sports that require both sprinting and endurance, such as soccer and basketball, it is best to have approximately a 50-50 mix.

ANAEROBIC TRAINING

What makes anaerobics so important in rehabilitating injuries and training athletes?

First and most obviously, anaerobic training causes an increase in strength in the muscles, which brings with it an increase in strength in the tendon and, if the training is done properly, strengthening where the tendons attach to bone. By strengthening all three parts of the muscle–tendon unit, you decrease the chance of injury to muscles and tendons and, in addition, gain an increase in function.

Second, anaerobic training and increasing strength naturally create an increase in flexibility. We believe that this is the best way to gain useful and safe flexibility. By "safe" we mean readily immune to injury; if you gain flexibility without appropriate gains in strength, you increase your chances of injuring a muscle, a tendon, or both. But if you have the proper strength to go with the increased flexibility, the chances of injury are much less.

Third, you increase circulation. The heart pumps blood that has high oxygen content to the muscles through the arteries. The blood returns by flowing through the veins back to the heart and then the lungs for more oxygen. While the heart is the main pumper of blood to the muscles, it does not pump it through the veins. The blood is returned through the veins by muscle work, muscle use, muscle action.

One of the things that can happen if you are out of shape and rest for a long time is that muscle tone is lost and an arm or a leg will begin to swell somewhat. This occurs because your arm or leg muscles aren't pumping enough fluid back to the heart. The only way to decrease this swelling is through muscle activity. It is also muscle activity that improves circulation and decreases the swelling that occurs after an injury. Until such activity occurs, circulation will not improve, and swelling will not go away.

Fourth, when you increase muscle strength you increase protection against injuries to the joints by improving their stability and strength. The stronger your muscles are, the more stable they make the joints and the more protection you get.

Fifth, anaerobic training increases muscles, anaerobic function, and your ability to do anaerobic activities. Initially it increases the muscles and your tolerance to lactic acid buildup. As muscles burn energy, lactic acid is formed as a kind of "exhaust" from these little motors. The lactic acid can cause muscle ache and pain, making it increasingly difficult for you to perform the activity. Some runners call this "rig," which is short for rigor mortis. Lactic acid buildup is what is going on when you hear about a runner "tying up."

Anaerobic training enables muscles to tolerate lactic acid buildup in several ways. It increases the ability of your muscles and blood to take care of the lactic acid by buffering it, the same way that an antacid decreases the acidity in your stomach. Increased buffering in your muscles and blood decreases the acid effect of increased lactic acid. You increase the circulation in the muscles with anaerobic training, so this helps wash the lactic acid out of the muscle faster. The training will increase your tolerance to this particular type of painful or noxious stimulus within the muscles and permit you to function longer. Anaerobic training will also increase blood-vessel tone, by increasing not only venous circulation but arterial circulation as well.

A sixth benefit believed by some experts to be conveyed by specific anaerobic training is an increase in the percentage of fast-twitch fibers in your muscles and a corresponding increase in your ability to do anaerobic activities. Seventh, if you anaerobically exercise different groups of muscles without long rests in between the exercises, you will achieve an aerobic training effect as well. In a sense you can kill two birds with one stone if you consistently work at an anaerobic exercise group for a longer period of time than the usual less than two minutes. And eighth, with the increase in the size of muscle fibers comes the ability to store more glycogen for energy, which makes the muscle stronger and able to work longer and possibly faster.

STRENGTH, STAMINA, AND POWER

To understand the difference between strength, stamina, and power, picture a fifty-pound weight.

The ability to move that fifty pound weight at all would show a certain amount of strength.

The ability to move that fifty-pound weight continuously for ten minutes would show a certain amount of stamina.

The ability to thrust that fifty-pound weight one foot in one-hundredth of a second would show a certain amount of power.

Strength is the ability to do work; the larger a resisting object you can move, the stronger you are. Stamina is the ability to work continuously over a period of time; the longer you can move a resisting object, the more stamina you have. And power is the ability to work rapidly; the faster you can move a resisting object, the more power you have.

COMMON TYPES OF RESISTANCE TRAINING

We have discussed aerobics and anaerobics and the different muscle types. Now we need to discuss the common resistance-training exercises, what they accomplish and what their limitations are.

Isometric ("Same Measure") Exercises

In isometric exercises there is no movement. Examples of isometric exercises are pulling on a bar that does not move; with your leg straight out, tightening the muscles as tight as you can and holding the position; and pulling one arm against the other with no movement. Isometric exercises are a very effective and usually quite safe form of strengthening. They can be used for body building and increasing strength and for rehabilitation. Isometric exercises are the least expensive form of resistance-training exercise, since no special equipment is required.

To effectively strengthen joints throughout their full range of motion, however, you must do the isometric exercises with your joints in different positions. Otherwise, you will only be strong in one position. For example, if you do an isometric exercise with your knee straight, the knee will be very strong in that position, but in all other positions it could still be quite weak.

The benefit you receive from isometric exercises is directly related to the work you do. Since there are no gauges to go by, it is sometimes quite difficult to see progress in isometric exercising. But all in all, it is a very inexpensive and effective method of strengthening and training. Everyone can do isometrics, and they can be done anywhere: in your bedroom, in your front yard, or in a hotel room. All it takes is a little knowledge, imagination, and work. One potential problem is "breath holding" and straining. This is an improper way to do isometrics and can be harmful. Breathe, don't hold your breath if you are doing isometrics.

Isotonic ("Same Tone") Exercises

When most people think of weight training and strengthening exercises, they think of isotonic routines. "Pumping iron" is the classic form of isotonic exercise. It involves taking a weight, such as a 20-pound barbell, and moving it. Isotonic training, too, is relatively inexpensive. If you are handy, you can construct various weights from concrete in cans and pipes, or you can even use books, and have a good set of isotonic-exercise weights for little money.

The main problem with isotonic exercises is that people frequently perform them incorrectly, and do not get full benefit from doing them. In addition, the benefits differ for different positions of the joints, much as they do in isometric exercises. If you have ever lifted a barbell, you know that it is difficult with your arms straight, it gets easier in the midpositions of bending the elbow, and then becomes quite difficult the last little bit. The same is true with the return motion. This is due to the position of the joints and muscles. Unfortunately, when you fatigue the muscles you may begin to cheat, cutting out those extremes or end points of motion that sometimes need the most protection. So it is very important to do properly the exercises we outline in order to get maximum training benefit.

The Universal Gym system of weights with pulleys and levers eliminates the need for a spotter (a partner who can lift the weights off of you if you lift too much and get pinned), but is much more expensive than free weights and is somewhat limited in the exercises that can be done with it. However, it is an isotonic type of training that can be done safely alone, and it has many of the advantages of free weights.

The Paramount is similar in many respects to the Universal Gym. It is glistening, shiny, and quite expensive, and is basically another type of isotonic-exercise apparatus that eliminates the need for a spotter. Its main selling point: Because you exercise arms or legs individually, you can't "cheat" by relying more on your stronger arm or leg to lift weights. While the Universal requires both arms and both legs at every station and at every exercise routine, the Paramount eliminates this disadvantage of the Universal setup.

Isokinetic ("Same Motion") Exercises

We are in the isokinetic age of strengthening at the present time. It is not clear whether we are at the end of it or in the midst of it, however. Theoretically, isokinetic strengthening is a good way to strengthen joint function throughout the full motion of a joint. Isokinetic strengthening machines are more expensive (at times much more expensive) than the other types of training apparatus we have discussed.

Isokinetic strengthening maintains a constant resistance throughout the full motion of a joint so you get strengthening throughout a full range of motion. Unfortunately, some isokinetic machines are designed to exercise in only one direction. This wastes a lot of time: Once you have completed your movement you must go back to your starting point with no resistance and change either your position or the machine to exercise in the opposite fashion. The typical bending action or shortening of the muscle is usually referred to as a concentric contraction, and the lengthening as an eccentric contraction. There is value in doing both, one after the other, as part of your training routine. This can't be done easily on some of the isokinetic machines.

TRAINING THEORIES

While it may seem that there are hundreds of different theories as to how to train for specific athletic events, we think there are really three basic theories, and all the rest are only variations of these.

First is what we would call "nonspecific" training. That is, you only train in your activity; you do not do exercises designed specifically for increasing your strength for your activity. If you are a swimmer, you only swim; if you are a runner, you only run; if you are a baseball pitcher, you only throw the baseball, etc. You may have heard coaches who advocate this system make statements such as, "You compete in the water, you're only going to train in the water." Except for the purely endurance events, this can be considered a bit oldfashioned.

However, there are some people who adhere to this theory of nonspecific training, but who advocate general strengthening of muscles by either isometric, isotonic, or isokinetic methods. The reason they do not want to do strength training in their specific events is that they fear that they will learn improper technique; they don't want to learn how to throw a 20-pound shot when the shot in competition is only 12 pounds, since they may use different motor patterns and different form in throwing a 20-pound shot than they would in throwing a 12-pound shot. There is merit to this type of system since it does recognize the fact that for anaerobic events, general anaerobic training will be beneficial. These coaches and trainers do recognize the need to increase strength to improve performance.

The second type of training is aerobic training. Most people recognize that we are in an aerobic era, and aerobic training is in vogue. There are many benefits to health and performance that will come from aerobic training. But if you are an athlete in a primarily anaerobic event, aerobic training alone will result in only a relatively small benefit on performance. This improvement in anaerobic performance will occur if there is enough aerobic training to complement anaerobic training, by creating more efficient circulation. A good example of this is what happened in swimming several years ago. The training of most swimmers used to be primarily of the aerobic type, that is, long, slow, distance swimming. Although approximately 80 to 90 percent of all swimming events are anaerobic events, training was primarily aerobic, yet we still saw tremendous improvements in time. But now that training also stresses anaerobics, we are seeing even more rapid improvements.

The third category is the type we would label "specific." That is, there are weight-training and strength-training techniques for each specific activity the athlete is trying to perform. One example of this would be a shot-putter throwing a 20-pound, a 30-pound, or even a heavier shot-put than he would throw in competition, in order to increase strength. Another example is a baseball player's swinging a leaded bat, a bat that is much heavier than the one he would use in competition. This is done to increase strength in the specific activity. A variation of the same principle would be to then throw a lighter shot or swing a lighter than normal bat in order to increase performance speed by training at a faster than normal speed. Training is thus specific to increase speed and increase strength. Yet another example of this is marathon runners doing what are called intervals or wind sprints—short bursts of high-speed running, faster than they might normally do in a race—to increase their overall speed.

These specific training methods are, of course, usually correlated with generalized strengthening exercises as well. Another variation of this type of training utilizes isokinetic equipment to simulate the activity, such as an isokinetic swim bench for swimming, or a tennis-racquet handle attached to a Mini-Gym for performing various tennis strokes against isokinetic resistance.

Another application of the same principle involves performing the activity—whether it is a shot-put, tennis stroke, throw, run, or jump—in slow motion. Instructors in various sports have discovered that a very effective way to learn a technique, even a fast maneuver, is to first do it very, very slowly and break it down into its components. If it can be done correctly in slow motion, it has been learned properly. This is an effective way to eliminate faults in technique, and it is also an extremely effective way to gain strength and control throughout an entire maneuver. Strength and control prevent injuries not only because they increase stability, but also because they eliminate the faults that can cause injury. Isokinetics performed in slow motion can also be very effective, just as they are at normal or high speed.

Nonspecific, aerobic, and specific training seem to be the three main theories that are being used at the present time. We think you will find that the type almost any coach you encounter uses will fit into one of these three broad categories, and that by understanding the reasons behind each you can increase the benefits you receive from the training programs.

We believe you must be eclectic in your approach to training and take the best from every system. We want to help you to rehabilitate and strengthen and prepare yourself for athletic participation, with maximum performance as the ultimate goal. In Part Two of this book we describe training devices and routines designed to help eliminate flaws in performance that are not corrected by usual training programs. These training techniques are probably different from those you are used to, but they are based on experience and sound scientific principles. The methods are proven—don't ignore them because they seem simple.

6

Warning: These Exercises Can Be Dangerous to Your Health!

STRETCHING EXERCISES

Everybody stretches, from the youngest baby to the hundred-year-old grandparent. When we awaken in the morning or start moving after being in a rested position, stretching is the normal and natural thing to do.

Unfortunately, the cult of flexibility is sweeping this country, and part of its luggage is an unnatural stretching. People are no longer limiting themselves to that gentle, beneficial, natural stretching; now they are trying to become contortionists.

Whether this flexibility craze is an effect of the upsurge of interest in yoga or just of the impact of the flexibility addicts on the runners of the nation, everybody is being told to "really stretch." And they are being assured that it "prevents injuries." Yet there is no real evidence that it does. In fact, every week we see more injuries from stretching than injuries that are a result of stiffness.

Everyone wants to be flexible, and there is no question that a certain amount of motion is good and useful. Certainly, stiffness isn't good and useful. The problem is that too much flexibility can be devastating. We mentioned earlier Ehlers-Danlos syndrome, or the "India-rubber man." Unfortunately, people who suffer from this marked type of flexibility have unstable joints. Their shoulders, kneecaps, elbows, and even hips may pop out of place.

Flexibility should not be a goal in itself, but the result of muscle strengthening and training. Yet one cannot go to a road race or a gym without seeing people trying to be contortionists.

Remember that too much stretching can be harmful to your health!

The problem is that flexibility without the strength to control it will lead to injury, and the flexibility faddists have lost track of that obvious fact. If you can bend a joint beyond your ability to control it with muscle strength, you risk either tearing the muscles, tendons, or ligaments that support the joint, or damaging the joint surface itself through abnormal pressure upon it.

A strengthening of the muscles around the joint naturally increases flexibility, so improvement in flexibility is a natural outcome of proper training and strengthening—it should not be a goal in itself.

People vary in their flexibility, probably due to differences in the natural elastin content of their tissues. There are inherent differences in degrees of stretchability of tissues, just as there are differences in skin color, height, and body build. Some stretchability can be enhanced with proper strengthening exercises, but most people will never be able to be contortionists, and many of us will never be able to be good at some of the yoga positions because we just have less elastic tissue. It is better to have appropriate strength and adequate flexibility than marked flexibility and inappropriate weakness!

Another reason that people stretch is for the treatment of tendinitis. The theory underlying this is that because tendinitis is an inflammation of the sheath or the tube covering of a tendon, the inflamed sheath will tend to scar down to the tendon and stop the tendon from moving, and gentle motion breaks up the adhesions that are developing and decreases the severity of tendinitis. But this has led to the unfortunate dogma that stretching is the solution to tendinitis when, in fact, the main cause of tendinitis is that there was too much stress upon the tendon in the first place. As we discussed above, proper strengthening naturally increases flexibility and moves the tendon. This is why we believe that proper strengthening and *gentle* moving of tendons is a much better and more appropriate way to decrease tendinitis and prevent it in the future.

THE EXERCISE HIT LIST

The new stretching exercises aren't the only ones on our hit list; there are also some old standards, such as toe touching and sit-ups. We've divided the list into two categories: Free Exercises and Weight Lifting. We may seem extreme in our judgments about these exercises, but if you had seen the injuries we've seen, you would take an extreme position, too.

The lists are arranged in order of decreasing relative danger.

Free Exercises

1. Yoga plow
2. Hurdler's stretch
3. Duck walk (and deep knee bend)
4. Toe touching
5. Ballet stretches
6. Stiff leg raise
7. Knee stretch
8. Sit-ups

Weight Lifting

1. Stiff-legged dead lift
2. Stiff arm pullover
3. Bent-forward rowing
4. Jefferson lift
5. Supine horizontal flexion (supine flys)
6. Overhead press

No matter who advocates these exercises and no matter what magazine covers you see them pictured on, we contend that they are high-risk activities that in and of themselves can and often do cause injury. It is our firm belief that they should never even be attempted. Any slight benefit they may convey is more than offset by the high risk of injury that you entail doing them.

Here are some details.

1. Yoga plow. One of the few exercises known to modern man where you can injure your neck and back while sustaining a stroke, all in one maneuver, is the yoga plow. The plow puts inordinate

Yoga plow *Although this maneuver is recommended by many running books and magazines, it is exceptionally dangerous. It can cause a stroke by pinching off one of the essential arteries in your neck. It is also devastating to the lower back; you can sustain serious back injuries by performing this useless, harmful maneuver. It has no proven benefits, but it can certainly cause great harm.*

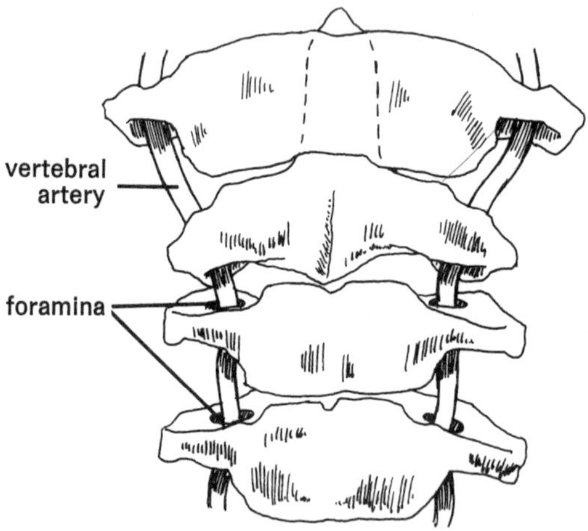

The yoga plow's effect on the spine *The vertebral artery curves through openings in the bony segments of the spine, called foramina. Stretching the spine beyond the normal limit, as can happen if you do a dangerous movement like the yoga plow, easily kinks this artery and can cause a stroke.*

stretch and stress on the blood vessels to the brain and the upper spinal cord, and as a result, strokes have occurred because the circulation to the brain or spinal cord was cut off. This position is even more dangerous if you are wearing a football helmet and pads. The arteries travel through holes in the cervical vertebrae, and the plow can cause the arteries to kink, resulting in cut off circulation and possible stroke.

The plow is very dangerous for the back. It places a great load on the cervical vertebrae, which are really too weak and too fragile to support the body's weight. In fact, this exercise places an inordinate amount of pressure on discs and ligaments throughout the entire spinal column. In this position you take away the natural protection of each interlocking vertebra, so the pressures on bone and connective tissue are tremendous. At the end point of the movement, when your feet are at the opposite end from where they belong, you are literally tearing at the ligaments of your back muscles. Doctors call the injury that can result low-back myofascial strain.

To make matters even worse, the movement approaches the limits of actual nerve-fiber length, thus creating the possibility of fiber destruction in the cauda equina and sciatic nerves and their connections. It's as though you are trying to pull out your nerves. In addition, further nerve damage can occur through repeated stretching of the spinal structures and nerves.

As a famous physiologist wrote, "Save the plow for your visit to the farm."

2. Hurdler's stretch. Ah, doesn't the hurdler's stretch look like something right off the covers of running magazines? Unfortunately, it is high up on the list of most dangerous exercises. Because of the explosion of running and stretching, this is probably the most frequently performed of the exercises on our hit list. But it stretches the muscles and ligaments in the groin region farther than they

Hurdler's stretch *This maneuver can cause gradual, harmful stretching of the ligament on the inside of the knee (the medial collateral ligament) and of the tissue in the groin, resulting in fascial groin pulls.*

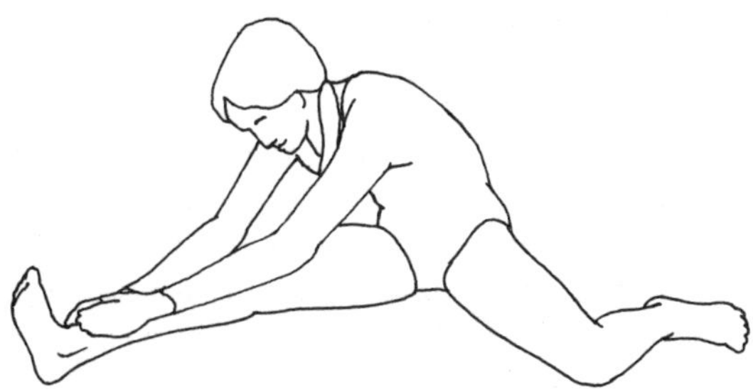

were normally intended to go. This can lead to a chronic groin pull, or at least make you more vulnerable to a groin pull.

In addition, the hurdler's stretch unduly stretches the medial collateral ligament, which is the important stabilizing ligament on the inner side of the knee. Over a long period of time, it may stretch this ligament enough to lead to instability in the knee. Ligaments tend to resist jerks or snaps, but succumb to prolonged pressure. The resultant destruction is insidious, because it can occur gradually over two or three years of repeating the movement. The position also puts enormous stress on the meniscus cartilage in the knee and can lead to injury of the cartilage. As a surgeon who has looked at hundreds of knees, I can tell you it is not worth the risk (unless, maybe, you're posing for a cover and getting paid for it).

In older athletes, hurdler's stretch frequently causes back pain by stretching the sciatic nerve. Many of the people who relate their back pain to jogging and running should instead blame the stretching exercises they do prior to running. This particular exercise is one of two prime offenders for causing back pain in runners. (Toe touching is the other.)

Sometimes we despair of being believed, though. Professor Robert Shelton of the University of Illinois Kinesiotherapy Clinic campaigned for thirty years against this exercise, and his opponents resisted the campaign with almost religious fervor!

3. Duck walk (and deep knee bend). The first exercise ever to be condemned by orthopedic surgeons and finally the President's Council on Physical Fitness was the duck waddle or duck walk (walking like a duck in a deep knee position). This exercise technique is the cause of many knee injuries incurred by football players who are simply doing calisthenics. The deep knee bend position puts enormous pressure on the outer or lateral meniscus (lateral cartilage) in the knee, and can cause a tear of this cartilage which results in permanent disability and requires surgery.

4. Toe touching. Before the explosion of interest in running and stretching, toe touching was the most commonly performed risky exercise in the United States. The toe-touching maneuver puts enormous strain on all the structures in the lower back and stresses the ligaments beyond their normal limits. The muscles of the back cannot give any support when you are toe touching; you are actually stretching and hanging by your ligaments.

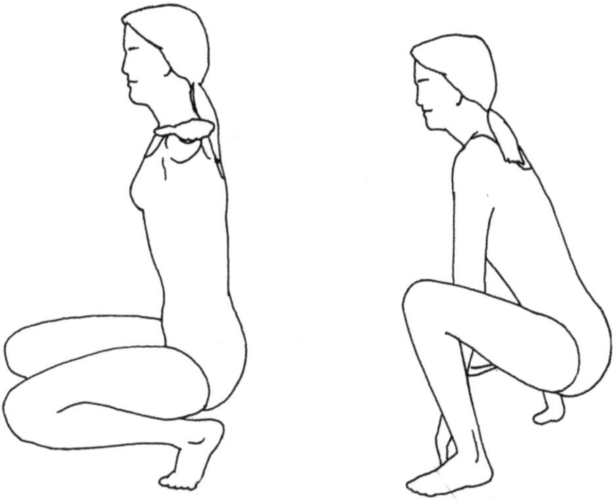

Duck walk and deep knee bend *The deep knee bend position that is assumed in order to perform the duck walk is very harmful for the knee cartilage, especially the lateral meniscus. It is possible, simply by performing this maneuver, to tear the lateral meniscus.*

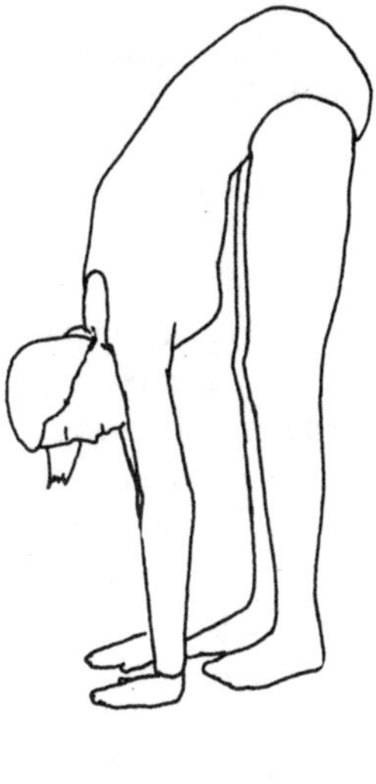

Toe touching *This stretching exercise is one of the most common causes of back pain in runners, because it puts undue stress on one of the main supporting ligaments in the spine, the posterior longitudinal ligament. It is also possible to injure a disc by putting your spine in this dangerous position.*

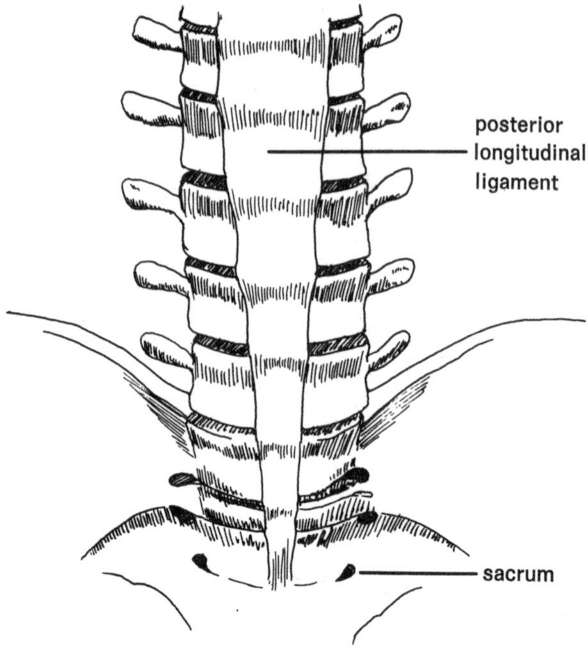

Posterior longitudinal ligament *One of the main stabilizing ligaments of the spine, the posterior longitudinal ligament helps hold the discs in place. Note how it tapers down at the lowest lumbar segments of the lower back; one of the reasons ruptured discs are so common in these lowest segments is that they do not have the full protection of this ligament. Because the toe-touching position puts undue stress on this ligament it is one of the more common causes of back pain in athletes.*

Toe touching also puts a great deal of stress on the discs, and can cause ruptured discs in an adult who has an underlying disc problem. In addition, what we said earlier about stretching the sciatic nerve and pulling it out of its connections also applies here. Stretching this nerve is a common cause of back pain.

Toe touching has been thought of as a good exercise to "relax" or "stretch" a tight back, but it does just the opposite. It will make your back muscles even tighter because of the strain. This exercise and the hurdler's stretch are the prime causes of back pain in runners. You will get no benefit from this exercise, only pain—and you also risk serious injury in the process.

5. Ballet stretches. Ballet has one of the highest injury rates of any of the common sport or dance activities. Ballet itself places

Ballet stretch *The sciatic nerve comes out of the spine around the back of the hip joint and through the pelvis, and down the back of the leg into the foot. Performing the ballet stretch with any back trouble at all can cause pain to radiate down the sciatic nerve, simply because you are stretching the sciatic nerve beyond its normal length.*

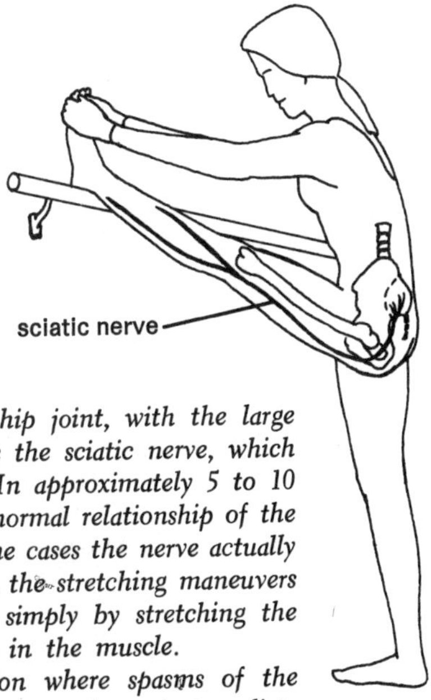

Hip joint *This is a back view of the hip joint, with the large gluteal muscles removed for clarity. Note the sciatic nerve, which comes out under the pyriformis muscle. In approximately 5 to 10 percent of the population, there is an abnormal relationship of the sciatic nerve to the pyriformis, and in some cases the nerve actually goes through the muscle. In these people, the stretching maneuvers that we warn against can cause sciatica simply by stretching the nerve through its abnormal configuration in the muscle.*

The pyriformis syndrome is a situation where spasms of the pyriformis irritate and pinch the sciatic nerve, causing pain to radiate down the back of the leg to the foot. This painful sciatica is common in athletes, in high-performance volleyball players, and in runners who do too much stretching or who have not trained their rotational muscles. A lack of proper jump training can cause spasms of the pyriformis and sciatica.

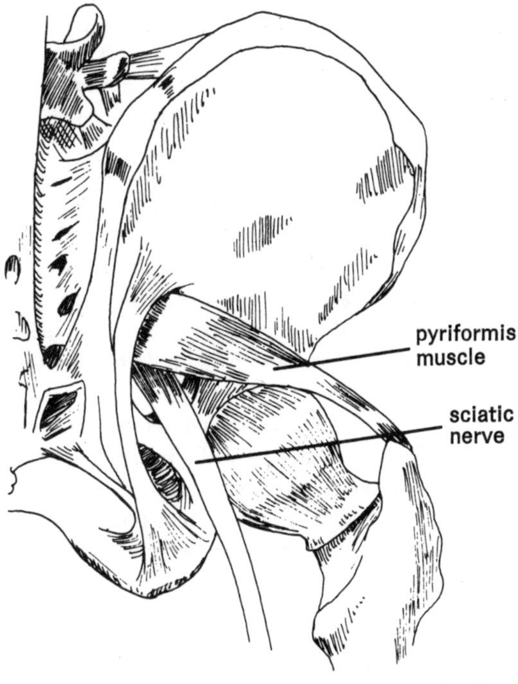

inordinate, abnormal demands on the hips, knees, ankles, and feet. Ballet stretches help the ballet dancer stretch his or her body so these abnormal, injury-producing postures can be assumed. If you are seriously involved with ballet, then this is a risk you take—or the price you pay. But the fact still remains that ballet exercises excessively stretch the back of the knee, low-back ligaments, muscles, joints, discs, and especially the sciatic nerve. They are a common cause of back and leg pain.

6. **Stiff leg raise.** The stiff leg raise (and its cousin, the stiff leg raise with weights) is a feat of strength. To do it properly you must keep your spine in a flat position—on the ground—and few people are capable of that. Lifting the spine off the ground puts great strain on the low back. We do not recommend that you take this significant risk of ligament, muscle, or even disc injury in the lower back. Instead, we recommend spine-strengthening exercises and the reverse torso curl. (See Chapter 14.)

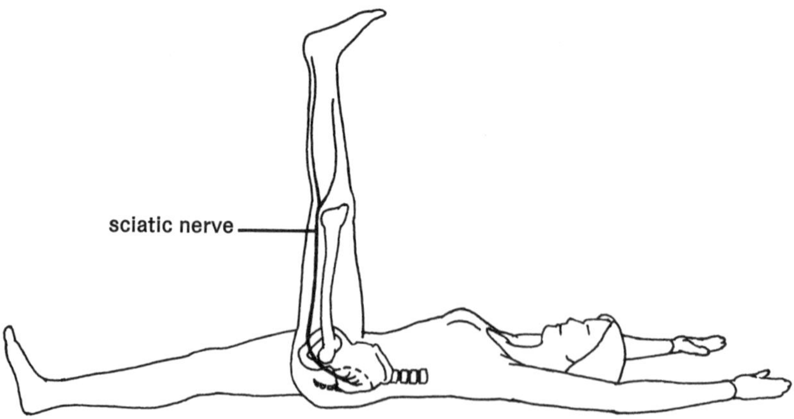

Stiff leg raise *Performing the stiff leg raise can cause sciatica and back pain by overly stretching the sciatic nerve. Bending the knee takes the tension off of this important nerve.*

7. **Knee stretch.** Another popular "dislocation activity" is the knee stretch. If you look at the angle of the lower leg, in the illustration you see that it clearly exceeds the actual skeletal range of motion of the knee. This distortion can produce a stretching of the patellar ligament of the knee and also strain the collateral ligament due to

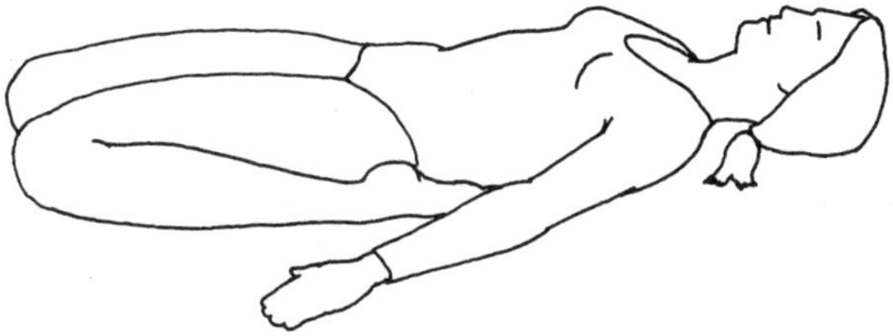

Knee stretch *This popular stretching posture puts abnormal pressure on the cartilages inside the knee (the menisci), and can cause tearing of them. In addition, it stretches the ligaments on the inner border of the knee (the medial collateral ligament) beyond their normal length and can cause unstable or stretched and loose knee ligaments.*

the obvious twisting. There is no value in stretching a joint beyond its normal range of motion; only harm can result.

8. **Sit-ups.** The sit-up exercise and its numerous variations are the subject of much controversy at this time. Many experts believe that they are one of the major causes of low-back problems in later life. To sit up with momentum and pass the upright or gravity-neutral

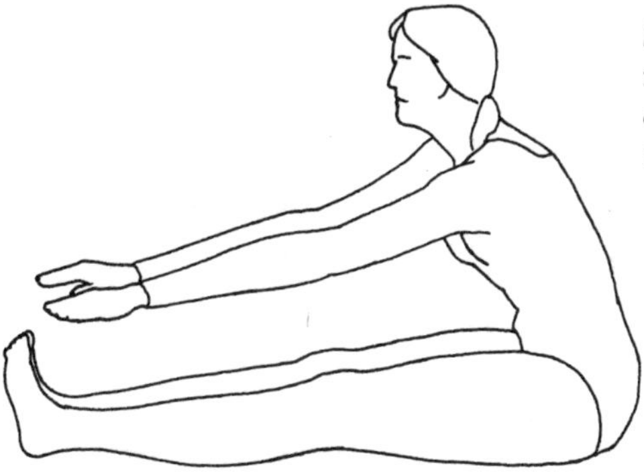

Sit-up *This exercise can result in back strain and abnormal elongation of nerves.*

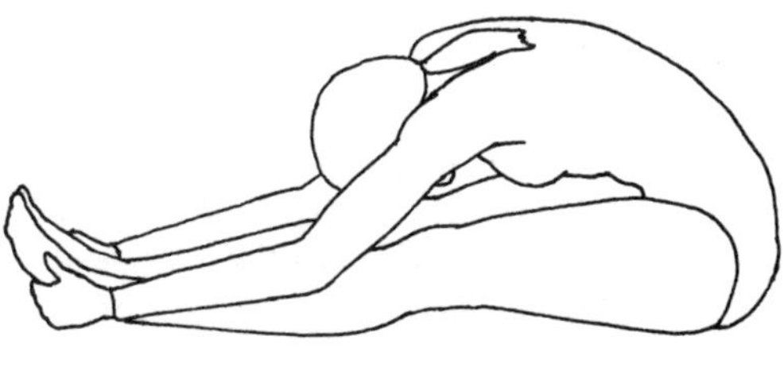

Sit and reach *This posture stretches the posterior longitudinal ligament beyond its normal anatomical bounds, and puts a great deal of stress on the sciatic nerve. Stretching either or both of these structures is a common cause of back pain and sciatica.*

position results in back strain and nerve elongation. Yet the sit-up family of exercises is practiced throughout the world.

People love to do sit-ups, and the following questionable beliefs concerning sit-ups are frequently encountered.

"Sit-ups will help me lose weight," or more specifically, *"Sit-ups will help me to lose weight around the middle."* Remember that adipose or fat tissue is part of a general metabolic system. This means that you cannot work "spot reduction"; instead, you must look at the total amount of fat in the body because fat enters the general metabolic system regardless of the region of storage. Fat is caused by the intake of more calories than you burn. Since it is possible to take in many calories more quickly than you can burn them, effective weight control is really a balance between eating and aerobic exercises. Long distance runners are among the leanest athletes in town, despite the fact that many are junk-food addicts, looking for calories on every plate and in every glass.

"Hundreds of repetitions of sit-ups will do me good." This is part of the principle that if ten repetitions are good, then a hundred repetitions are better. We tend to look at our goals in extremes, such as "How many," "What is the highest number," "How far," "How fast . . ." But in exercising, quality is usually more important than quantity. When you are doing an exercise that could tend to be harmful, the application of "the more the better" principle could be the final straw that breaks *your* back.

"Sit-ups should be fast paced, because the faster you do them, the more conditioning you'll get." It is not true that the two-minute-how-many-can-you-do sit-up test is a gauge of your condition. Fast-paced sit-ups are momentum based, and the throwing forward past the upright position creates many of the same pulling problems we saw in other exercises. Besides, if you are talking about overall fitness, judging only by the abdominals is not a true test of conditioning.

"Abdominals require a lot of work." This reflects a mistaken belief about the predominance of abdominals over other muscles. As with other muscles, abdominals require concentrated, controlled effort to develop strength and full range of motion.

"Sit-ups will help me thin my waistline." The action of the rectus abdominus is to shorten the distance between the pubes and the breast bone. Like any other muscle group, these muscles get larger when worked. Core work will thicken the waist, not reduce it. Re-

member, reduction of fat is based on calorie control, not repeating one exercise.

One common belief regarding sit-ups does have merit however. The most common variation of sit-up recommended for people with back pain is the bent-knee sit-up. The bent-knee position does relax the sciatic nerve and is less likely to stretch it than the regular sit-up is. Stretching the sciatic nerve is the most common cause of back pain from doing sit-ups. If you are going to do sit-ups and have back trouble, at least bend your knees. Some authorities recommend the bent-knee sit-up for the wrong reason. They state that it relaxes the iliopsoas muscle (this muscle runs along the spine, through the pelvis, across the hip joint, and attaches to the femur). But to truly relax the iliopsoas muscle, you must bend your hips 90 degrees.

However, if you have back trouble, we advise that you not attempt sit-ups that won't accomplish what you want and may aggravate your back. Instead, we strongly recommend you do the torso-curl exercise (see Chapter 14). If you don't have back trouble, then do all of the core exercises instead of sit-ups.

We have given you the eight worst offenders, but do not assume that these are the only ones. Instead, try to apply the principles behind the discussion. See if you can explain the reasons for not doing the following exercises.

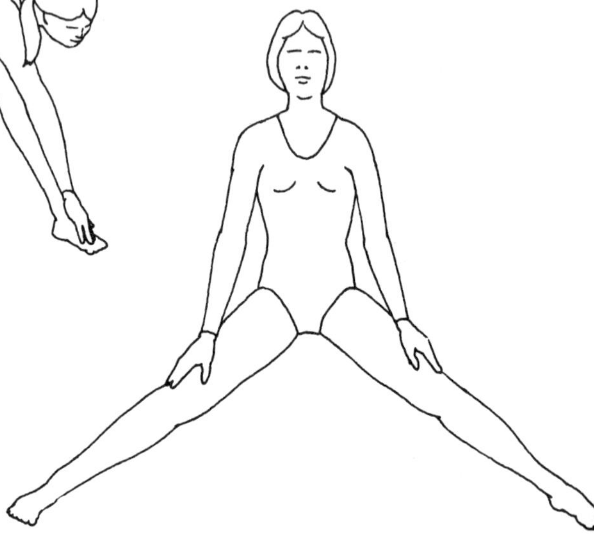

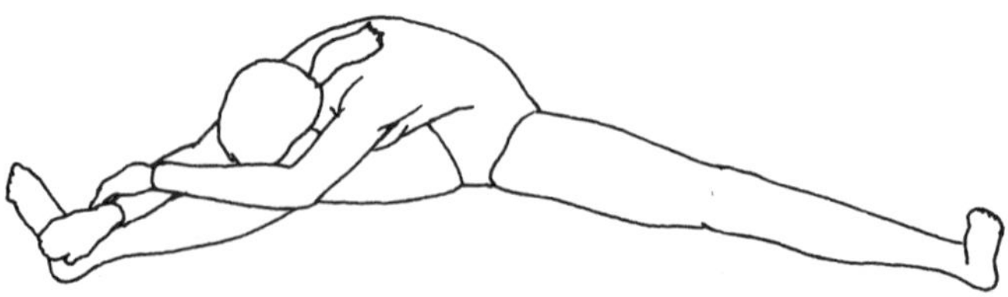

The previous exercises were the so-called free exercises—they did not involve the use of weights, barbells, or weight machines. The next six are our top forbidden weight-lifting exercises. Because of the use of weights, the relative possibilities of danger to your body are much more significant.

1. Stiff-legged dead lift. While lifting weights off the floor with your legs stiff is bad enough, it is even worse to stand on a bench and reach below it with the weight. Reaching off the bench, this maneuver stretches one of the major ligaments in the back (the posterior longitudinal ligament) beyond its normal limits. Because of this, the obvious danger is serious back injury and disc herniation. In addition, because the exercise stretches the ligaments and muscles beyond where they were normally intended to go, there is a high risk of muscle pull and of strain on the small joints in the back (the facet joints). Not only is this an extremely dangerous exercise,

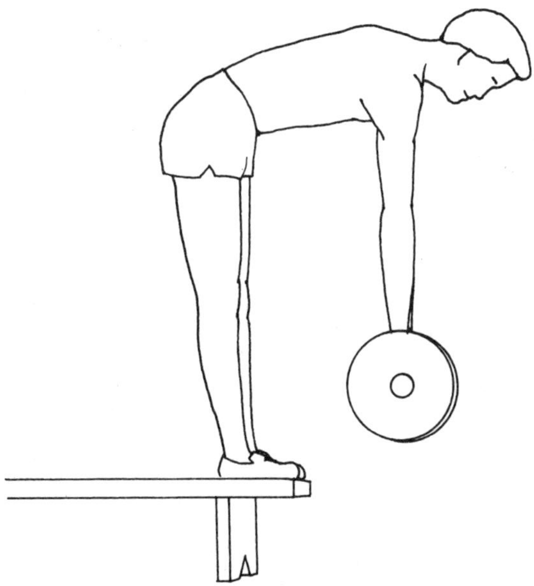

Stiff-legged dead lift *This is the most destructive weight-lifting technique that we know. It stretches the posterior longitudinal ligament beyond its normal limits and is one of the most common causes of ruptured discs in weight lifters. We recommend that you never do this exercise. Stiff-legged lifting of weights off the floor is bad enough; never do it on a bench, as illustrated here!*

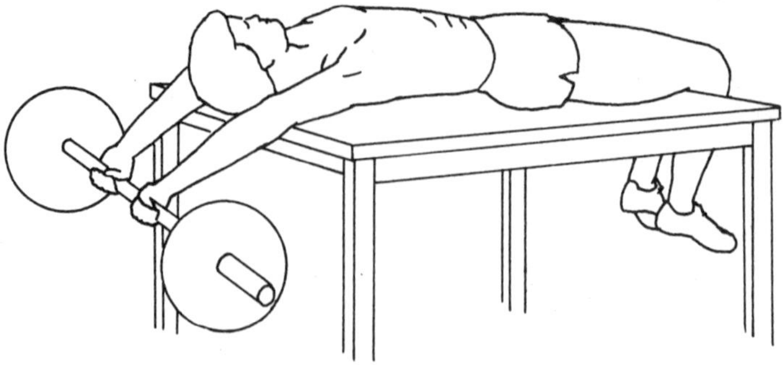

Stiff-arm pullover *This is a high-risk exercise that can cause severe muscle strains and dislocated shoulders, and is probably the most common cause of stretch marks in weight lifters.*

but there is nothing advantageous to be gained from doing it. It should never be done.

2. Stiff-arm pullover. The stiff-arm pullover is done in a supine position with barbells or dumbbells. This exercise is a feat of strength and puts maximal strain on the shoulder joints. If you unfortunately attempt it with more weight than you can safely hold and don't let go, you run the risk of dislocating your shoulder joint. In addition, you also run a high risk of straining the muscles around the shoulder or tearing them. This exercise is probably one of the prime causes of stretch marks around the shoulders of weight lifters.

Jefferson lift *Do not ever perform this exercise! It is an extremely unstable, dangerous position. Note the twist in the spine, which puts shear force—the most damaging force of all—on the discs, causing ruptured discs in the lower back.*

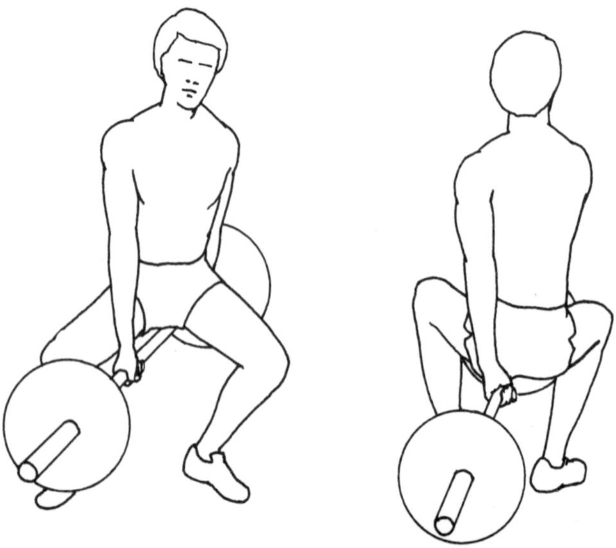

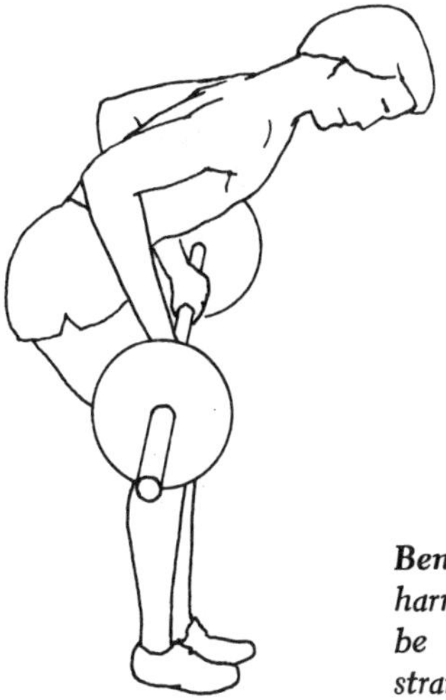

Bent-forward rowing *This is a very harmful posture. This exercise should not be performed because it puts undue strain upon the lower back.*

3. Jefferson lift. The Jefferson lift is a maneuver in which barbells are picked up from the floor from a position between the legs. It puts a great deal of torque on the spine, which causes a shearing force on the discs in the back. Shear is the most damaging force you can put on the lower back. There are much better ways to strengthen the back than with this exercise, and we recommend that you never do it.

4. Bent-forward rowing. The bent-forward rowing exercise puts the lower back in an exceedingly vulnerable position. It is extremely

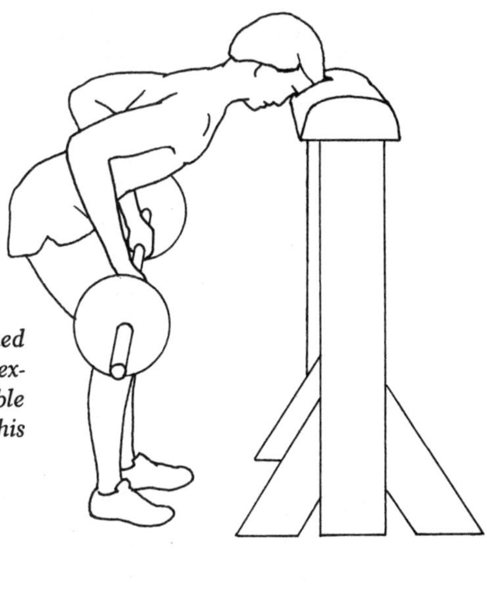

Stable position *If you are determined to do bent-forward rowing, use an external support for your head. This stable position will permit you to perform this exercise with much less risk.*

difficult to hold the position properly, and it causes enormous spinal strain. If it is improperly done or you are fatigued, you run a high risk of injury both to the lower back muscles and to the discs. We recommend that this exercise not be done without some other support, such as resting your head on a shelf or bar.

5. **Supine horizontal flexion (supine fly).** Supine flys are done by lying flat on a bench with your arms straight out on each side, lowering the weights to the floor, then bringing them from the floor to the horizontal position and from there to straight up over the body. This exercise should never be done with heavy loads, because at the beginning of the maneuver there is tremendous strain involved in lifting the weights from the floor to the horizontal position. This stress can lead to small tears in the pectoral muscles. Also, your body may reflexively act with what is called a stretch reflex, which tightens up and increases the strain within the muscle without any gain in strength. This can result in an imbalance in the muscles that move the shoulder girdle, with eventual harm to the stabilizers of your shoulders.

If this exercise is performed, we recommend very light loads so that there is no straining when you begin to lift.

Supine fly *The supine fly is an extremely difficult exercise to perform, and we recommend that you don't do it. If you must, start out with very light weights. The supine fly is the most common cause of tears of the pectoral muscles.*

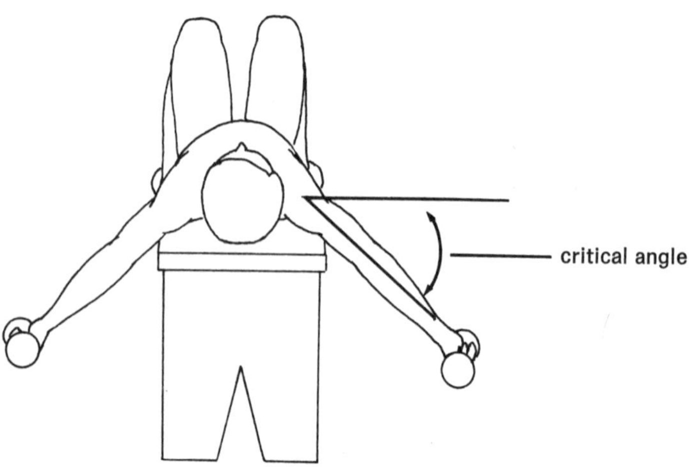

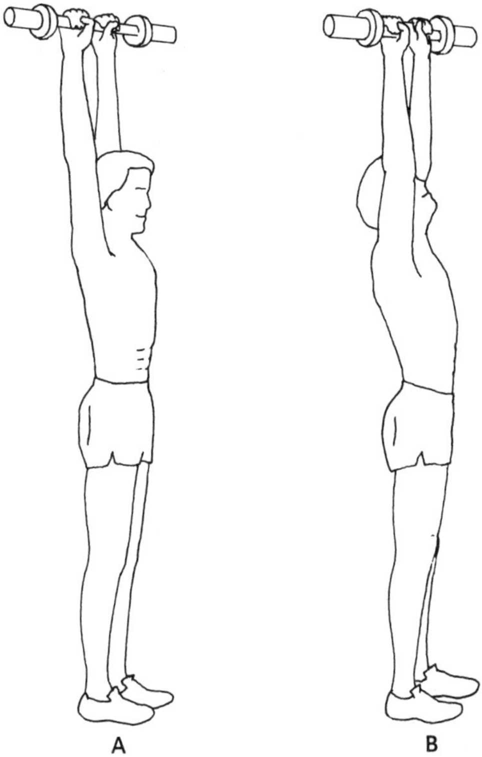

Overhead press The unstable position, figure B, is improper because you should not look up at the bar, hold your breath, or lean back while performing this exercise. The proper position is shown in figure A.

6. **Overhead press.** We have seen more injuries from the overhead press in young boys than from any other, because they often lose control of the weights and drop them. This exercise requires proper form and great stabilizer fixation strength in the abdominal muscles in order to protect the lower back.

Unfortunately, if your abdominals have not been sufficiently strengthened or your technique is not excellent, it will put a tremendous strain on your back. If you hold your breath, you will run a risk of blacking out. To perform this exercise safely, never look up at the bar, don't lift your ribs upward while lifting the weights overhead, and don't hold your breath. And don't get under falling weights!

While we don't prohibit this exercise, we strongly advise carefulness and good form.

To summarize our discussion of weights: We have talked a lot in this book about stability and the core. The same principles that apply to training for stability and training the core apply to weight training and free exercises, and you must apply them to all of your training and rehabilitation. We strongly recommend that you re-evaluate all your training and set up a program that will safely enable you to perform at your maximum capability.

7

Injury Prevention

Most coaches, trainers, and physicians now agree that getting proper training is the best way of preventing injuries. But, very few have a clear idea of the specific benefits of proper training. So we are going to list the injuries that can be prevented or minimized through proper training, and explain how they can be prevented and the basic treatment for when they do occur.

To explain fully the more common injuries, we will first discuss the different types of injuries—those afflicting skin, tendons, muscles, bones, and so on—then we will specifically discuss the most common injuries.

TYPES OF INJURIES

Bruises

Probably the most common of all athletic injuries occuring in any sport, are bruises. Frequently they are trivial and require no specific treatment, but they can be so extensive and serious that they even require hospitalization. They most commonly result from a blow or a direct injury to a part of the body.

Bruises are areas of bleeding beneath the skin. The bleeding can occur in joints, in muscles, and around tendons and ligaments. Bruises that are beneath the skin but not in the muscles can frequently be quite colorful—blue, black, green, or yellow—in various stages of healing. This can be disconcerting, but bruises that are not within the muscle usually cause no disability at all.

However, a bruise within a muscle indicates that there has been bleeding in it and that some of the muscle fibers have been torn. Stretching a muscle that has bled recently can increase the bleeding, delay recovery, and decrease the overall strength of the muscle. It can be quite harmful to stretch what are called "deep muscle bruises," even though it is now in vogue to do so.

The best treatment for bruises in any location is the application of ice, ideally four or five times a day for fifteen minutes at a time. This will decrease the bleeding, promote healing, decrease swelling, and decrease pain, all desired effects. The application of heat to a deep bruise within the first seventy-two hours runs a significant risk of increasing the bleeding and markedly prolonging the recovery time, so heat should never be applied to a bruise in the first three days after the injury.

The one problem with using ice for treating bruises is that cold increases stiffness. So if ice is applied immediately before a vigorous event, it may lead to a poor performance because the muscle may be sluggish and stiff. For this reason experienced trainers sometimes alternate heat and ice during the healing phase of bruises.

You may begin strengthening exercises of bruised arm or leg muscles and the muscles of the opposite arm or leg when there is 75 percent range of motion of the joint that the muscle moves (see Chapter 13). Until you have that 75 percent range of motion, only you yourself should exercise the joint; no stretching by a trainer or therapist should be done during the healing phase of a deep muscle bruise.

Three to five days after all bleeding has stopped, alternating heat and ice treatments can be performed, with heat applied right before the exercises are started and ice immediately after they are completed. After any deep bruise, the athlete is permitted to return to normal play when he has normal strength and motion. Stiffness and loss of motion are signs that healing is not complete, and that the athlete is vulnerable to reinjury or a more severe injury.

Tendinitis

Tendinitis is the inflammation of a tendon, which is a strong, specialized "leader" that connects a muscle to a bone. Tendinitis is the reaction of a tendon to injury. The two most common causes of tendinitis are a direct blow to the tendon and excessive stress of the tendon, either from a single vigorous pull or as a result of fatigue from repetitive stress applied over a long period of time.

Tendons glide through tubes called tendon sheaths. These sheaths are lubricated with fluid very similar to joint fluid. When a tendon or its sheath has been injured, there is a possibility that the tendon may stick to the sheath. This causes pain and marked loss in movement of the tendon. Attempting to overcome this problem may be the reason that the "flexibility school" has gained such popularity.

There is no question that gentle motion at an early stage of healing can prevent adhesions from developing between a tendon and its sheath. This gentle motion promotes healing and also prevents the formation of adhesions and decreases stiffness in the tendon. But if stretching is overly vigorous and the treatment is not coupled with proper rest, permanent damage and chronic, almost incurable tendinitis can result. Even worse, it is possible to rupture the tendon if the injury is not properly rested or if it is overly stretched.

For the first seventy-two hours after an injury or the onset of tendinitis, ice alone is the best treatment because it decreases inflammation, decreases swelling, decreases pain, and promotes healing. While ice theoretically should cause stiffness in a tendon because of decreased elasticity, this is not a practical problem because the beneficial effects of the decreased swelling and decreased inflammation outweigh any stiffness that might occur. Icing an area of tendinitis does in fact increase motion.

If the tendinitis is more than three to five days old, you may find that alternating heat and ice will be quite helpful. For some athletes, heat alone promotes healing and increases motion, but it should never be applied within the first three to five days after an injury. Heat may be applied through hot packs, by soaking the injured part in a hot shower, or by treatment in a warm whirlpool. Trainers and therapists also can deliver heat to deep structures through various therapy machines, such as ultrasound, medcosound, Dyna-Wave and other wave applicators.

But better than any treatment for tendinitis is prevention, especially after recovery has taken place. This is best done by proper strengthening of the muscles that move the tendon and the muscles on the other side of the joint that pull against the tendon (so-called antagonists). One of the causes of tendinitis is the overpowering of the muscle–tendon unit by muscles on the other side of a joint that have been markedly strengthened with training. Such overdevelopment of one set of muscles can cause a chronic stress or even a rupture or tear in the tendon by pulling it too strongly the other way. By increasing the strength and endurance of the muscles on both sides of the joint, you really decrease the strain and stress on the tendons and help prevent tendinitis. In addition, proper strengthening of the muscles will lead to strengthening of the tendons themselves, which is another preventive measure. The exercises and training systems outlined in Chapters 13 through 19 will show you how to properly balance and strengthen the muscles and tendons so that you will minimize the development of tendinitis. In addition, the training techniques learned on the beam, the boards, and the boxes will help prevent that sudden one-time stretch that can also cause tendinitis. The most common causes of tendinitis in the shoulder and arm are improper throwing mechanics and improper training so that you "arm" it and do not get your body core into it. The reason we have discussed and stressed the core's stability is that with a properly strengthened core and a stable base from which to throw, you significantly decrease your chance of developing a severe tendinitis in the arm or shoulder. If you perform in a stable fashion and have full strength through a full range of motion, you will minimize your chance of developing tendinitis. Our entire system is aimed at accomplishing these goals. If you train smart, you will avoid the plague of tendinitis.

Ligament Injuries

Ligament injuries are the most feared, the most misunderstood, and frequently the most mistreated athletic injuries that occur. Ligaments hold joints together. In most joints the strong ligaments are on the sides, but some joints have strong ligaments in the front and back and even inside the joint.

If you have a mild ligament injury, there has been only a slight stretching of the ligament. The ligaments are still strong because they have only a small area of injury and will heal with rest from stress. Mild ligament injuries, if they are truly minor, may heal in a few days, but most take seven to ten days to heal. Moderate and severe ligament injuries can take from three to eight weeks to heal. Unfortunately, there are a few ligaments that never heal without surgery. The two best examples of these types of ligaments are the cruciate (crossing) ligaments inside the knee joint and the ligaments in the front of the shoulder joints. When these ligaments are torn, they never heal without surgery. Severe ligament injuries around the knee theoretically take one year to return to full strength, function, and flexibility. Even though function is restored in less than a year with proper rehabilitation, full, complete microscopic healing still does not occur for up to one year.

The treatment of ligament injuries depends upon two main factors: the severity of the injury, and which ligament is injured. Some joints are much more stable than others, and because of this, injuries to their ligaments frequently heal even if the injury is major. The ankle, the elbow, and the hip are such stable joints, while the knee, the shoulder, and the joints of the thumb are unstable. Unstable joints require strong ligaments to hold them together; without strong, tight ligaments these joints tend to become loose and arthritic. Inherently stable joints frequently can function normally after ligament injury, even if the ligaments have not healed up well and are not tight. Another variable is the sport to which the athlete wishes to return. Each sport makes different demands on different joints.

Certified athletic trainers usually are quite good at separating minor ligament injuries from ones that need to be evaluated by an orthopedic surgeon or sports-medicine physician. Only an experienced orthopedic surgeon or sports-medicine physician can separate moderate ligament injuries from severe ones.

There are differences in expertise in evaluating the athlete, the injury, and the demands made by their sport. For the mild or moderate injury, the key is to begin exercises that don't put stress on the ligament. A mild or moderate injury can become a moderate or severe injury if the ligament is stressed, because this will stretch out the ligament, leading to permanent weakness and even instability. An unstable joint will not function normally and will usually become arthritic early. So the price of improper rehabilitation or rushing an injury is too high a risk to take. However, exercises can be safely done if properly supervised. We recommend a registered physical therapist or certified athletic trainer in most of these instances. In some cases braces can protect the injury and permit exercises to begin earlier than otherwise.

The problem in rehabilitating ligament injuries is that the athlete is usually a poor judge of the timing and degree of rehabilitation. An experienced trainer or therapist is a much better judge. The athlete usually wants to get back to running and jumping as part of the rehabilitation rather than as a goal of rehabilitation. The risk of running and jumping too soon is great. If you are not stable and fully recovered, running and especially landing after jumping create a significant risk of further injuring your ligaments or injuring something else.

Use your brain—train, don't strain!

Fractures

A broken bone is a fractured bone is a broken bone. A chip fracture is a broken bone. Many people think that a fracture is worse than a break, and some think the opposite. In fact, these are all merely different terms for the same type of injury. The rehabilitation of the athlete who has sustained a broken bone begins as soon as the bone has been set, casted, or treated. Usually it is possible to exercise all the uninjured parts of the body and try to maintain conditioning. In fact, gently exercising the broken arm or leg *with proper supervision* will decrease the time it takes for the fracture to heal.

Caution: Before exercising a broken limb, check with your physician and see Chapter 8.

The most serious types of fractures an athlete can sustain are those that involve a joint surface. If these fractures are not lined up perfectly and do not heal perfectly, permanent disability will result despite the best possible rehabilitation procedures. Usually these injuries require surgery. Fractures of the ankle joint, knee joint, or hip joint surface do not heal perfectly, and sustaining one of these injuries usually will eliminate the possibility of playing certain sports.

For example, long distance running is not a realistic goal for a person who has had such an injury, and some other types of activities, such as swimming, bicycling, or rowing, must be substituted.

Bone can be very slow in healing. Full recovery after a broken bone can take up to a year, and sometimes even longer. Although moving the muscles and joints around the fracture as soon as possible can sometimes speed up the healing process, too-early motion can sometimes slow down healing and even lead to the fracture's never healing without additional surgery. So it is very important to follow the recommendations of your orthopedic surgeon as to the timing of exercise. There is no "cookbook" approach to this.

The complications attending fractures (in addition to the imperfect healing of joint-surface fractures) are that a fracture can sometimes trap muscles and tendons in it, causing them to stick to the area around the broken bone. Early motion and exercise can sometimes prevent this. Usually these adhesions are not severe, and with proper exercise, ice and heat treatments, and sometimes gentle assisted motion, these adhesions can gradually be loosened up so that function is restored. Motion will gradually loosen these adhesions so that the microscopic structure will eventually change into more normal tissue.

Nerve Injuries

Nerve injuries are more common in athletes than many people realize. Usually they are quite minor and are no more severe than most of us have had when we have bumped the "funny bone" on the inside of our elbow. The "funny bone" is our ulnar nerve, and the stinging or electric sensation we get is what it feels like to bruise a nerve. The other kind of very minor nerve injury that most of us have had is from sitting on a hard bench or a toilet seat too long and having a leg "go to sleep." This is a pressure injury to the sciatic nerve. The important thing to note about this is that it is a good example of how nerve injuries heal. The leg went to sleep and the nerve was injured without any degree of pain or discomfort; it was actually quite insidious. Until you stood up, you did not even realize that you had done something to your leg. However, once the pressure was off, there was that obnoxious phase of healing with the "pins and needles" sensation we are all familiar with. This is the healing phase of a nerve injury. The important thing to note here is that the healing phase of nerve injuries frequently can be more obnoxious than the injury itself. In severe nerve injuries, this phase can be quite painful and can last from one to two years before there is complete recovery, nerve tissue being the slowest-healing tissue in the body.

If there is weakness or paralysis from a nerve injury, the aim in rehabilitation is to maintain motion and prevent stiffness. This is one instance where some gentle stretching is essential: You do not want to have stiff joints once the muscles get their nerve function and stimulation back. This stretching is best done by a trained physical therapist. Since there are no exercises that speed up nerve healing, our goal in their rehabilitation is to prevent complications and reinjury.

Unfortunately, the pain in the healing phase of severe nerve injuries can be quite intense. Even the strongest pain medication that you can take by mouth does not usually affect the pain significantly. It is usually not worthwhile taking any pain medicine at all, since the pain is probably intermittent rather than constant, coming in electriclike shocks and disappearing in a flash, before you have even had time to find a pill to take, much less let it take effect.

If you have had a significant nerve injury and do not have weakness, you should see a certified physical therapist or athletic trainer who has access to an electrical stimulator. Electrical stimulation can prevent the profound weakness that occurs sometimes with nerve injuries and can speed recovery. It is best to seek a physician's advice before doing this, though.

If there is no muscle weakness, all of the exercises in Chapter 13 are quite safe as long as they do not aggravate the nerve injury and cause pain.

Fascial Injuries

One of the structures most commonly injured in athletics is fascia. Yet very few athletes or lay people know what fascia is or have even heard of it until they injure it. Fascia is a fibrous membrane that covers, supports, and separates muscles, and unites the skin with underlying tissues. One of the reasons that skin can slide back and forth is that the layers of fascia slide on each other. Fascia is the basic packaging tissue of the body. All of our muscles are enclosed within sheets of fascia. It is the stuff that binds us together and holds our shape.

Fascia is important because in some parts of the body it is actually stronger than ligaments. Problems can arise when fascia is stretched, either by repeated pulling or by one acute stretch, or when it is torn by a direct injury or blow. In many cases it will heal completely and be fine, although in the healing stage the area of injury becomes inflamed as part of the natural healing process. This inflamation can be painful if stress is put upon the fascia by use of the area of injury, especially in the case of the fascia that covers the bottom of the foot (the plantar fascia). If this becomes inflamed, every step can be painful. When the healing is complete, the inflammation goes away. But in some cases the fascia heals incompletely, causing a chronically inflamed condition (fascitis) that will remain painful until it is treated or rested for a prolonged period of time—usually months or years. Incomplete healing can also lead to the development of a hernia. When a muscle contracts, the fascia is supposed to hold it in place. If the fascia has a weakened area where a hernia could occur, the muscle can bulge through and get caught, causing pain each time the muscle is used. There are only two satisfactory treatments for this type of problem: Taping, which may not be very successful, and surgery to repair the hernia or to make it larger so the muscle can't get caught.

Another major problem with fascia occurs when a muscle has been bruised or partially torn. The fascia may be too tight to accommodate the resultant muscle swelling, and it may cause additional muscle damage by cutting off the blood supply to the muscle. This is what is called compartment syndrome, and it happens whenever the fascia becomes too tight, for whatever reason. An acute compartment syndrome occurs when there has been an injury, usually with bleeding, and there is marked swelling within the compartment, causing severe pain (called ischemic muscle pain) because of the decreased blood supply. In athletes, however, the compartment syndrome is usually a chronic condition where the enlargement of the muscle caused by vigorous exercise causes a mild decrease in blood supply to the muscle, and the resulting pain leads to decreased performance. For either of these conditions surgery is the only satisfactory treatment. In an acute compartment syndrome, the surgery should be performed as an emergency, but for the chronic type it is elective.

Once fascia is injured, there are no exercises that will foster its healing. Rest from the activity that caused the injury and time are the only cures. In fact, virtually nothing is known about how to make fascia stronger. It is thought (but no one knows for sure) that with exercise and increasing activity, fascia becomes stronger. Therefore, the only preventives for fascia injuries are protection from injury, such as wearing a flak jacket, or pads, and through graduated training so that inappropriate swelling will not develop in muscles during training and exercise. Clearly the prime treatment is prevention. Fascial injuries can be prevented by the training outlined in Chapters 16–19. These training routines will condition and train your body to avoid many of the positions that may lead to injuries of the fascia.

COMMON INJURIES

Foot Injuries

Many foot injuries are the result of wearing improper shoes. After recovering from such an injury, it does not make sense to return to your old shoes. It is well worth the money to purchase good shoes that will prevent further injury. And you must be sure that you have the proper shoe for your sport and that you have regained your strength before you return to any type of running activity.

In addition, prior to returning to any running or jumping activity, you must follow the "hard–easy" principle: After exercising the foot, give it a day of rest before running on it again. The reason for this is that the bones, ligaments, muscles, and joints will take time to recover their strength and must be given a day off to recover.

Downhill skiing is probably the easiest sport to return to after a foot injury because the modern ski boot is so protective of the foot and ankle. While we do not recommend it, you may find that it is possible to return to downhill skiing before your foot injury is completely healed.

The most difficult sport to return to after a foot injury is distance running. It is foolish to attempt to run before complete recovery, because you will run abnormally and injure something else, aggravate the foot injury, or both if your foot is not fully rehabilitated. Remember the concept of serial distortion discussed in Chapter 3.

In the foot, arch strains (which are really small tears of the planteur fascia, the strong tissue that supports the arch) and heel spurs are usually the result of running and jumping repeatedly and extensively on feet that have not had stabilization strengthening.

There are four layers of muscles on the bottom of the foot, all of them important. These muscles help support the arch and contribute to toe motion. If they are weak they will fatigue easily, or tear when you land from high jumping. When the muscles are fatigued or torn, the plantar fascia has to do the whole job of supporting the arch. It too will fatigue and gradually stretch, producing the painful condition called arch strain. In the back of the heel this constant stretch will eventually lead to painful heel spurs. There are exercises that will strengthen the arch and the tendons that come around the ankle to help support the arch. These exercises are not in vogue at present and have been largely ignored for the past twenty years or so. The proper strengthening of the small muscles in the feet and legs that help control the arch will prevent these painful foot conditions.

If an athlete has excessively flat or pronated feet (feet that tend to roll outward), the arch may need extra support that the muscles cannot provide. In these cases, the athlete is well advised to see his orthopedic surgeon or sports podiatrist for consideration of custom-made arch supports, orthotics. These will help to support the arch and hold the foot in a stable position to prevent serial distortion and permit the rigors of athletic competition. Orthotics have proven helpful in distance running, and they are also quite useful in maximum-performance training of jumpers and runners in other sports.

Since the foot is the base from which we begin most of our athletic maneuvers, a stable foot is extremely important. It is for this reason that we recommend training the foot with the exercise routines we cover in Chapters 15–19.

Ankle Sprains

Most ankle sprains occur when the athlete comes down on a rough or hard surface and the foot turns under and in, tearing the ligaments on the outside of the ankle joint. This can occur from landing on a rough spot on the ground, landing on an opponent's foot, or simply coming down with the foot in poor position. With proper training and strengthening, it is possible to teach your body to land with your foot in the proper position. Training can also give your foot sufficient strength to recover quickly and return to the normal stable position, even it you do land on an uneven surface or someone's foot. After a sprain, simply walking or gently running over rough ground may be enough to reinjure your ankle if the leg muscles have not been trained to be strong enough to prevent stress on the ligaments.

The ankle is a joint that normally depends on bones and ligaments for its stability. Basically the ankle is a square peg in a square hole, a configuration that is usually quite stable. As long as the ligaments are tight, there is no weakness in the ankle. However, if the ligaments have been stretched by ankle sprain and do not heal up tight, there will be some looseness in your ankle. Once the ligaments have healed and you have been successfully rehabilitated, we usually recommend taping before returning to vigorous play. It is possible with the techniques outlined in this book to strengthen your ankle and make up for weakness of the ligaments by vigorously strengthening the muscles and tendons that go around the sides, front, and back of the ankle joint.

The easiest sport to return to after an ankle injury is downhill skiing, because the modern ski boot takes many of the stresses off the ankle joint. The most difficult sports to return to are the high-agility sports where the players wear spikes, such as baseball, soccer, and football. Basketball also has a high injury rate because of its constant jumping and risk of landing on someone else's foot. So before returning to any high-risk sport, it is best to fully rehabilitate your ankle and, if there is any question, to tape it prior to all competition.

For most people, walking on smooth surfaces is an effective way to gradually strengthen the ankle. Jogging on a smooth track and then running is probably the simplest way to rehabilitate an ankle. It is important in the rehabilitative phase to avoid running on rough ground because of the stress this puts on ankle ligaments. Stress must be avoided until you have fully recovered and rehabilitated your ankle. This simple rehabilitation is not enough to allow a return to high-level athletic performance, however.

Shin Splints

"Shin splints" is the lay term for pain along the front of the leg between the knee and ankle where the muscles that move the foot and ankle attach to the tibia (shinbone).

True shin splints are thought to be the result of muscles of the leg (usually in front, but at times the ones in back) pulling themselves away from their attachment to the bones of the leg (the tibia and fibula). Shin splints are most common in the middle-distance runner and the poor runner who tries too vigorously to run. Proper strengthening and balancing of the muscles in the front, back, and sides of the leg, coupled with learning proper foot control and foot strike while running and landing, will decrease the severity and frequency of true shin splints. Working on the O-beam and K-board will help you train the proper muscles to minimize shin splints.

Leg Injuries

There are no devices that will guard the leg from injury during the rehabilitation phase, whether the injury is a broken leg, a torn calf muscle, or a ruptured Achilles tendon. The only safe way to recover is to gradually work through the graded exercises that we will outline. Exercise in a swimming pool may be quite beneficial, as might gentle bicycling. But early resumption of the stress of running should be avoided until you have recovered strength in the bones, muscles, and tendons. Don't forget the hard–easy principle: that is, go easy on the day after a hard workout. Even in the final rehabilitative phase when you are permitted to run, begin by running every other day rather than several days in a row.

Knee Injuries

The most common severe knee ligament injury is tearing the anterior cruciate ligament, which is one of the most important ligaments in the knee. Located in the center of the knee, it prevents the leg from shifting forward on the thigh, and it is essential for proper rotational movement of the knee. Rotational abnormalities are common after a tear of the anterior cruciate ligament.

In spite of the fact that a tear of the anterior cruciate ligament is the most common and serious ligament injury, it is also the most difficult to diagnose and thus it is the most frequently missed injury. When it is torn, the athlete often has the sensation of his knee going in and out of place. Sometimes when this ligament tears, something pops within the knee, but it still feels normal to examiners; then, over the next few days, the knee fills up with blood.

A torn anterior cruciate ligament can occur in both contact and noncontact sports. The most common noncontact way for it to occur is while the athlete is running, coming down from a jump, or sprinting slightly out of control. The leg will stick on the ground and he will feel something pop in his knee. This ligament can tear completely without any contact at all.

Once this ligament is torn the other ligaments around the knee will gradually stretch and the knee will loosen up over a five-year period. This will have a profound effect on the athlete's ability to function and it will significantly increase the risk of meniscus injury (cartilage tear). Obviously the best way to prevent such an injury is for the athlete to train himself to not come down from a jump or run and land out of control. It is possible to teach this type of control. This is one of the reasons that we stress training on the O-beam, K-board, mini-trampoline and jump box. With these training techniques, you can significantly minimize your risk of sustaining this kind of serious knee injury.

Injuries to the knee cartilage (meniscus injuries) can occur from changing directions (cutting) or pivoting on the knee without adequate control and from playing with fatigued muscles. Proper strengthening and training can minimize your chance of sustaining these injuries as well. Since it takes a rotation force to tear a knee cartilage, we emphasize rotation training to minimize your chance of meniscus injury.

Knee injuries are rightfully feared by athletes because they are the most common cause of permanent disability and shortening of athletic careers. However, this does not have to be the case. Proper rehabilitation can return many athletes to their sport at peak or near-peak capacity. The important thing is to get proper strength and motion prior to returning to the pounding of running. If you must run, it is best to do it supported by water in a pool until you have fully rehabilitated your knee.

It used to be thought that the quadriceps muscles (the strong group of muscles in the front of the thigh that straighten the knee) were the key muscles in knee rehabilitation. Quadriceps conditioning was emphasized, and the other muscles in back (the hamstrings) and along the sides of the thigh were ignored. There is no question that quadriceps strengthening is an essential part of knee rehabilitation. But if you have an anterior cruciate ligament injury, strengthening the quads alone will aggravate and put stress on that healing ligament. The proper group of muscles to strengthen first is the hamstring muscles. Strengthening these will take strain off the cruciate ligament and prevent the abnormal motion that the cruciate ligament also prevents.

It is very important in rehabilitating the knee to know which ligaments were injured, especially if it was your anterior cruciate ligament. You must work on your hamstrings first and then your quads. Be patient—don't resume running too soon. After any major knee injury we strongly recommend that you read Chapter 22, on knee rehabilitation.

Hamstring Pulls, Hamstring Tears, and Thigh Muscle Pulls

No football or track season goes by without headlines reporting some high-school, college, or pro player who has sustained a significant hamstring or thigh muscle pull. The majority of these muscle tears are a result of improper or imbalanced strengthening of the thigh muscles. The muscles in the front or back overpower the opposite group and, with fatigue, tear the weaker group of muscles, causing this preventable, painful, and disabling injury.

Another frequent cause of such injuries (especially hamstring pulls) is over-vigorous stretching exercises. It is quite common to hear athletes say, "I don't understand why I pulled my muscle. I spent more time than usual stretching them out first, before I worked out." This over-vigorous stretching can lead to weakness in the muscle–tendon unit, as well as in the fascia, and can set it up for a hamstring pull.

To make matters worse, some athletes do not do any strengthening exercises after they have recovered from hamstring muscles tears, and end up tearing the hamstrings again and again. The hamstrings are weaker once they have been torn, and the stronger quadriceps muscles in the front of the thigh continue to overpower and tear them. There is no question that our method can minimize your risk of hamstring and thigh muscle pulls because we emphasize training all of the muscles in your thigh rather than one group or another. In addition, we emphasize strength through your full ROM and this, combined with the balancing of strength, is your best insurance policy against hamstring pulls.

Hip Pointers and Groin Pulls

One of the causes of what is commonly called a "hip pointer" (any severe, painful injury to the front part of the hip joint region) is a tear of the sartorius muscle, which begins at the prominent point and front of the hip. This can be prevented with proper strengthening of this muscle. (See Chapters 13 and 15 on sartorius isolation.)

The same is true of groin pulls. Proper strengthening throughout the full range of motion of all the muscles will help decrease these nagging, painful injuries. However, the most important thing to do to avoid groin pulls is to stop doing the hurdler's stretch and other harmful stretching maneuvers.

Lower-Back and Spine Injuries, and Herniated Discs

One of the tragedies for modern athletes has been the rapid increase in the frequency of a painful, disabling, chronic back condition called spondylolysis. Spondylolysis is a true fatigue fracture of one or both of the supporting pillars of the lumbar spine, called the pars interarticularis. This fatigue fracture is the result of hyperextension caused by repetitive, forceful backbends. These are most frequently practiced by female gymnasts, but the position assumed by interior linemen in football at the line of scrimmage also involves this harmful hyperextension. The third group of athletes who most often assume this posture are swimmers who emphasize the butterfly stroke. If there are fatigue fractures on both sides of the spine at one level—what is called a bilateral spondylolysis—the spine is unstable and this can lead to the shifting forward of the entire spine, called spondylolisthesis. Both spondylolysis and spondylolisthesis can be painful and preclude all athletic maneuvers. Fortunately, if spondylolysis is recognized early, three months of rest from athletics will frequently lead to healing of the defect. With the American mania for playing with pain, however, this condition is rarely rested and that is the reason it often goes on to become spondylolisthesis. Occasionally a ruptured or herniated disc can result from performing some of the harmful back-strengthening exercises and weight-lifting techniques. To avoid such injuries, you must keep your back in the stable position we discussed in Chapters 2 and 3, on the core and stabilization.

Neck Injuries

Everyone agrees that strengthening the neck muscles decreases the severity and frequency of neck injuries to both ligaments and discs. In fact, many professional football players are able to land directly on their head and neck because of the intensive strengthening exercises they have done. In addition, these exercises, combined with shoulder-girdle strengthening exercises, may help prevent the painful nerve stretch that occurs across the shoulders and down the arms, most commonly in football and wrestling. Such nerve stretches are often called "stingers" or "burners." The recommended exercises and training are listed in Chapter 14.

Upper-Back and Shoulder Injuries

Since the arms and shoulders are attached to the muscles of the upper back, it is frequently difficult to separate upper back injuries from shoulder injuries. We must treat the two together.

The single most destructive activity in sports is throwing. The forces on the muscles, tendons, and ligaments of the arm and shoulder in throwing a ball are four times as great as the forces on a leg kicking a ball. Although the arm is significantly smaller in muscle, tendon, and bone size than the leg, it is subjected to these more powerful forces. This is why baseball pitchers have the shortest careers and most troubles of any group of athletes. Because many throwing problems are a result of improper throwing techniques, it takes careful evaluation by a coach to ensure that the pitchers are not "arming" a throw but instead are using proper body mechanics and throwing techniques. In addition, many throwers fail to do any arm strengthening exercises at all, or if they do, they strengthen only one group of muscles rather than properly balance the muscles on all sides of the shoulder and arm. It is for this reason that resumption of throwing must be the last thing done in the rehabilitation of the arm and shoulder. Not only do throwers have to strengthen their arms and shoulders, they must also strengthen their core. We believe this is essential in training throwers and is the aspect of training most frequently neglected. People with arm and shoulder problems should read Chapter 2, on the core, and do the exercises in Chapter 14, Training the Core. Also, read Chapter 3 on stabilization.

A second group of athletes who have a high percentage of shoulder problems is swimmers. Swimming is the only sport that depends primarily on the arms for propulsion. The yardages that modern swimmers swim, and the stresses involved, seem to account for the fact that at one time or another approximately one-half of all competitive swimmers will have shoulder troubles or complaints. Ironically, for most other athletes (that is, nonswimmers and nonthrowers), swimming is a nice, effective, and gentle way to help in the rehabilitation of many shoulder and arm injuries.

There are some shoulder injuries that will not heal without surgery, no matter how effective the strengthening exercises have been. This is because the shoulder joint is inherently unstable. The socket is no deeper than a saucer, and with the full motion required in sports, the ball part of the shoulder joint can easily roll out of this saucer-shaped socket once the strong ligaments and cartilage in the back of the shoulder have been stretched or injured. Muscle strength alone cannot make up for this weakness, and it takes surgery to tighten things up again if the injury has not healed perfectly.

Surgery may be the only answer for the problems of the thrower or swimmer who has continued to perform in spite of pain for several years. The changes and damage done over a long time can be severe enough that without surgery full rehabilitation is impossible. While return to competition is usually possible for swimmers, this is not necessarily the case for professional pitchers.

Elbow Injuries

After the shoulder, the elbow is the joint most commonly stressed by throwing athletes. "Little League elbow" and "tennis elbow" are probably the two lay terms most commonly heard in sports medicine. Both are the result of overuse, improper training, and inadequate rest. Both conditions could be avoided with proper strengthening and proper throwing techniques.

The elbow probably gets stiffer faster than any other joint in the body. After a severe elbow injury, it is unfortunately common not to regain the full motion that the athlete had prior to the injury. This need not be a significant problem, however, since with proper rehabilitation, adequate motion can usually be obtained.

While it is common for shoulder ligament injuries to heal loose, it is rare for this to happen in the elbow if the injury is permitted to heal properly. Unfortunately, in athletes with high degrees of flexibility, primarily gymnasts and swimmers, a serious elbow injury that is not rested properly can heal with an unstable elbow joint that will give trouble on a permanent basis even with otherwise proper rehabilitation. So it is as important to let ligament injuries heal in the elbow as it is in the shoulder.

Tennis elbow is most commonly caused by inadequate strength in the forearm muscles. This weakness, combined with a poor backhand, results in tennis elbow. Everyone agrees now that proper strengthening of these muscles plays a significant role in preventing or decreasing tennis elbow. It is also essential to have proper form on backhand, or use a two-handed backhand.

Inadequate strength also causes the elbow problems that plague pitchers from too much throwing. Such problems are similar to, but more serious than, tennis elbow. In tennis elbow the problem is usually tearing of the tendons and muscles on the outer side of the elbow, whereas in pitching it is on the inner side. Strengthening exercises can be done to help prevent the painful overstretching and tearing of these muscles.

The comprehensive training system outlined in Chapters 13 and 15, ROM Training and Bands, will help you strengthen your upper extremity for tennis and baseball. But don't forget your core training as well.

8

How to Survive on Exercise Machines

We are in an era of exercise machines. Pro athletes, American beauties, and health clubs all extol the virtues of various exercise machines. In this book we want to teach you how to train inexpensively, but more important than that, to train properly and avoid injuries. If we are to do this, we must include a discussion of the various exercise machines: which ones specifically to watch out for, and how to properly use any that you may come in contact with.

One of the major problems in discussing exercise machines is that there has been very little objective evaluation of the pros and cons of any machine or machine system. We Americans have slavishly accepted the value of certain brand-name machines without comparatively testing them.

We have spent a chapter on the dangers of exercise without a machine, with and without weights, but now we must warn you that exercising with machines can be dangerous as well. What are the facts, and what are our warnings?

Machines based on lever systems fit the average athletic build.

Those of you familiar with the bell curve realize that only about two-thirds of us fall within this average range; one-third of us would have to use lever-system machines that do not fit us properly.

Most of the expensive exercise machines are fixed in one plane of activity so that you do not get rotational training and training of the midcourse correctors. You are only exercising your muscles in one plane without the need for stabilizing the weights. This is an incomplete way to train. Remember the importance of the stabilizer muscles that pop on and off like the course-correcting rockets of a space ship and give you dynamic stabilization.

Most machines have increments of five or ten pounds. These are about twice as high as the increments we frequently recommend as ideal.

It almost goes without saying that no machine can train you for everything—just think about the variety of athletic maneuvers performed in even the simplest sports. In fact, most machines are mainly for arms and legs. Very little core exercise can be performed on any of the commonly available machines.

You may have a tendency to exercise in an unsupervised fashion because machines are so easy to use and are assumed to be safe. It is quite easy to exercise in an improper, unstable fashion on machines because you need not fear that the weights are going to fall on you.

You must always remember the principles and techniques of stability that we outlined in Chapter 3. Do not fall into the trap of thinking that with the machines you can somehow strain and groan and use bad form and not be hurt. Quite the opposite is true. For example, you *must* keep your back in a stable position. You should not strain overmuch, and do not arch or bend your back and lose your body's natural protection.

The other point to remember with regard to machines is that if you bend one joint, you are changing the motion in another, so to properly train the muscles that move one joint you must hold the other joints still. This action of one muscle upon another is called concurrent contraction or cocontraction. The best example of this is in trying to strengthen the muscles around the knee. Bending your hip in any way makes it impossible to get full motion about the knee joint.

UNIVERSAL AND PARAMOUNT

The commonly available exercise machines use basic levers and pulleys, as in the popular Universal and Paramount machines. The only significant difference between the Universal and the Paramount is that with the Universal, you have to use both arms or both legs while doing your exercises, whereas the Paramount advertises the fact that each limb can be exercised independently. There is an advantage in this because in the recovery phase after injuries there is a tendency to cheat and do most of the work with the good side.

These large machines have the advantages of being difficult to steal, of not being messy (there are not a lot of weights lying around free), and of looking nice and shiny and impressive. Their disadvantages are that they exercise almost exclusively the arms and legs, providing few core training benefits, and they function on only one track, so you do not get any rotational training or training of midcourse correctors. Learning synergy—the joint operation of many muscles—and balance is essential for proper performance.

Following are some cautions for those using Universal, Paramount, and other basic lever-and-pulley machines.

Seated Press

We highly recommend that you do not perform the seated press in the Paramount Sports Trainer. In this position, the athlete has a tendency to go into the unstable banana-back position or the hyperextended back position, placing great strain on the back.

Knee Extension and Thigh-Curl Machines

Some of the most readily available lever training machines in most gyms are knee extension and thigh-curl machines. The problem is that they must be used properly. We strongly recommend that you read about structural integrity and stability in Chapter 3 to learn proper form. When doing either the leg extension or the leg flexion, do not arch your back and strain. Never throw your whole body into it. You must maintain good position. The basic rule of thumb is *train, don't strain!*

More importantly, do not bend or hike your hip up when using the thigh-curl or knee flexion part of the machine, because doing so

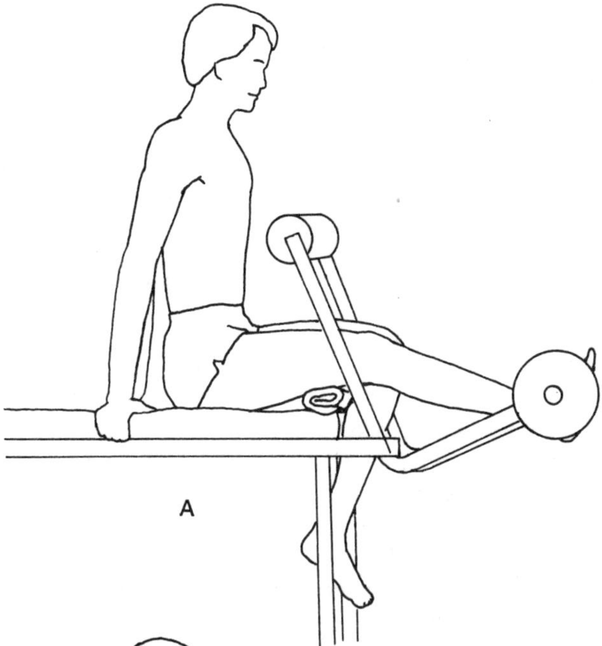

A

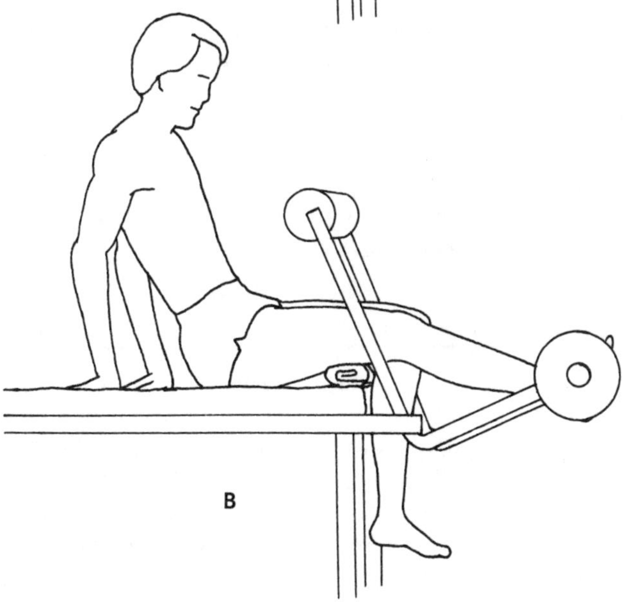

B

Knee extension *Figure A shows the proper way to do a knee extension—with the knee coming fully straight and the hip bent at a proper position for the back. Figure B shows an incorrect posture and illustrates concentric contraction. By putting your back in poor position, then leaning back and straining, you change your hip and knee position and fail to train either of these joints properly.*

defeats the purpose of the exercise by making it impossible to properly exercise your hamstrings. Hiking your hip up causes concurrent contraction or cocontraction of the muscles in the leg, which allows only one-half of the possible range of motion of the knee. There is no way to maximally train your hamstrings for athletic performance by doing this.

NAUTILUS

Nautilus machines were developed in an attempt to overcome some of the difficulties of the Universal and other weight machines. Since they use cams (rather than levers), they are intended to provide training throughout the full range of motion of the joints. This is obviously beneficial. Unfortunately, everyone does not fit the norm, and Nautilus machines still suffer from the fact that they only train you in one plane and so do not train rotation or what we call essential synergy; Nautilus machines just don't train your midcourse correctors at all. We do, however, completely agree that it is essential to train both flexion and extension, or what are called eccentric and concentric contractions (Nautilus calls these movements positive and negative). There are Nautilus machines to exercise every one of the common joints.

Here are some cautions and warnings for those using Nautilus machines.

Pullover Machine

Do not get your elbows higher than your forehead when using the pullover or else you will force your shoulders beyond their normal range of motion. We have seen injuries occur from doing this.

Pectoralis Machines

The end point of the load from pectoralis machines will probably cause stretch marks over the front of your shoulder. Also, we believe that the ten-pound increments are too large an increase in load for each training session.

Nautilus Arm Abduction, Nautilus Shoulder II, and the Nautilus Overhead Press

These machines could benefit from a rib-stabilizer belt or a belt around the waist. When doing these exercises, you must avoid elevating the rib cage if you wish to get the benefit from this machine.

Nautilus Leg Press

Using the Nautilus leg press, you should avoid the backward snap of the knee and also backbending of the knee. Do not raise your pelvis off the seat or you will not get the full benefit from this machine.

Nautilus Neck Machine

"Nautilus eye," an infection which sometimes follows use of the Nautilus neck machine, is an ill-deserved name. Actually it is a superficial eye infection caused by sticking sweaty pads on one's face, and can be quite painful. We strongly recommend that you put a clean towel over the face pads before exercising on this machine; this will prevent Nautilus eye. We believe the machine's ten-pound increments are too much, too soon for the average person. We have seen people get neck strain and spasms in the neck muscles from these large increments; we only recommend them for highly trained athletes.

HYDRAULIC MACHINES

The hydraulic exercise machines are tough and may be used in training elite athletes. We are particularly concerned about use of the adduction/abduction machine and the squat machine. In the squat machine, you tend to increase the lordotic curve, or swayback position, of your back. Some people encourage athletes to throw themselves into the squat machine and strain, but doing this can strain and sprain the back or the muscles being exercised.

The hydraulic machines are only for the advanced training of athletes and should not be used by anyone who is out of shape or recovering from an injury. Most people should use other machines or the control-training methods in the back of the book rather than the hydraulics, which require a great deal of strength and fitness.

ISOKINETIC MACHINES: THE MINI-GYM AND THE CYBEX

The Mini-Gym is an inexpensive isokinetic ("same motion") machine. We agree with the concept pushed by isokinetic advocates that you must exercise through your full range of motion. Unfortunately, even on the Cybex you only exercise in one plane. These machines can be set for exercise at different speeds. The resistance does not change through your full arc of motion. This is done through the use of a centrifugal plate so that the faster you move, the more resistance you get while exercising. Unfortunately you can only exercise concentrically and there is no eccentric (extension) load in the coming back position, so you can only train in one direction at a time. The isokinetic machines are useful in training, but they are not the complete training devices that some claim them to be.

Isokinetic Leaper

One isokinetic machine that if used improperly can cause problems is the isokinetic leaper. When using this machine, you must maintain your spine in the facet lock position (see Chapter 3 on stability). If you arch your back too much or bend your back in a banana-back position, and then try to jump, you put inordinate strain on your back. If you use a poor position and overdo it, it is possible to develop a stress fracture in your spine, which can be a chronic cause of back pain.

LEVER-BAR ROWING

One apparatus we do not believe should ever be used is the lever-bar rowing device. This apparatus is most often used in body-building gymnasiums. It can be very damaging to the lumbar spine because at the low point, or the starting position, you are forced into an unstable banana-back position. This puts a great deal of strain on your back while you are trying to get the load lifted. This is even worse than the Jefferson lift, which we condemned in the exercise section. The argument that one can lift more weights with this and get added training benefit out of it is crazy. Don't ever use this apparatus.

WORTHLESS EXERCISE MACHINES

In some spas and health clubs, you can see other vibrating exercise machines that jiggle you, wiggle you, and even move you at times. All of these machines are worthless for training. While they may make you feel good and pass the time, they are certainly of no training benefit whatsoever. Remember, you must put out to get back.

9

Healing

"Healing takes time," said Hippocrates. Despite all the medical advances in the more than two thousand years since his observation, that fact still remains true. So, because it is often impossible to speed up the healing process, one of the aims in rehabilitation is to avoid the complications that are often caused by rest and inactivity. Besides preventing these complications, rehabilitation also promotes a safe return to full activity, with the goal of minimizing the potential for further injuries.

It is also important to remember that inflammation is the normal first stage of the healing process; it is the body's reaction to injury. If there is proper rest, inflammation will disappear with the normal healing process. This period of rest varies according to the injury. It may take less than one day, or it may be weeks, months, or even a year before normal activities can be resumed.

If healing takes time and rest permits healing, then why don't we simply rest all athletic injuries until full healing has occurred? The reason is that there are eight serious and significant complications of complete rest.

First, rest leads to joint stiffness. Joints are lubricated and nourished by joint fluid, which is distributed by the movement of the joint. Holding a joint stiff for long periods of time will decrease the health of the joint surface cartilage and the beautifully gliding motion of the normal joint will be lost.

Second: Ligaments, muscles, and tendons all become stiff with rest. This combined with the joint stiffness, leads to a marked decrease in flexibility.

The third complication is poor circulation. Blood is returned to the heart and lungs by way of the veins. The main force that returns the blood is muscle action. During rest the muscles are inactive, and this can lead to what physicians call poor venous return which is, in fact, sluggish and poor circulation. Rest also leads to loss of the normal tone of the blood vessels, which aggravates the blood flow in the veins. The effect of sluggish circulation can lead to pooling or puddling of the blood in the veins, so that they stay full, and this will eventually cause swelling of the inactive part. If the rest continues, blood clots can actually form. When activity is begun later on, these blood clots can break free and move to the lungs, causing a serious complication called pulmonary embolism—which can even at times be life threatening. This is rare in an athlete who is up and active on crutches during rehabilitation; it usually happens to people who have been on prolonged bedrest or in traction.

A fourth complication of rest is decrease in the strength of the bone. Bones become softer because the calcium that makes them hard is washed out. Bone is constantly being turned over (formed and broken down by the body in a normal process); it becomes harder when it is active and when there is stress put upon it. When the stress is removed and the activity is lessened, the body naturally makes the bone softer by taking the calcium out of it. So the bones themselves actually become softer and weaker when they are rested for long periods of time.

The fifth and usually most obvious complication of rest is the dramatic decrease in muscle size and strength that comes after any period of rest. This is the thing that horrifies athletes the most, and causes them the greatest concern. Loss of muscle size and strength can be dramatic and really begins to occur in a matter of just a few days. Certainly by two weeks a definite decrease in size of muscle mass can easily be seen.

The sixth complication of rest and inactivity is one that most people are not aware of: Pain tolerance decreases. After rest, the injured part is more sensitive because the nerves in it are more sensitive to pressure and pain-stimulating activities.

The last two complications of rest are a definite decrease in aerobic capacity, which occurs gradually, and a rather dramatic decrease in anaerobic capacity, which occurs rapidly.

From this impressive list of eight complications you can see why the answer is not absolute rest, but resting only the injured part of the athlete. We try to maintain muscle tone, range of motion, and conditioning by using all the other, uninjured parts of the body. If we do that, then we can dramatically minimize the complications of rest and, in addition, encourage return to activity in the shortest period of time.

RESTING LIGAMENT INJURIES

If resting injured parts is generally desirable, there is one case where it is absolutely crucial, and this is when ligament injuries are involved. If an injured ligament is not rested, if frequent stress is put upon it and it is continually stretched, this leads to increased lengthening of the ligament, with the result that it will heal looser. This in turn leads to joint instability, which leads to insecurity and decreased ability to function with the joint. Arthritis is a common complication of unstable joints that have been used over a period of years. This is especially true for the knee joint. The best research available shows that a completely torn knee ligament takes one year to heal to normal strength. But no matter how long it takes, a ligament injury must be protected and rested as long as is necessary. Ligaments should return to function only when they are safely healed and the muscles are strong enough to provide the extra support necessary to prevent the later complications of what is called ligamentous instability.

When to return to activity is the most difficult question of all. The athlete is the worst person to answer this question, because he or she always wants to return too soon. A physician or an experienced trainer will give the best answer. Follow that advice!

PAIN

No other word seems to dominate a sportscast or a discussion of athletics as much as the word *pain.* No matter what the sport, the issue of pain comes up. But "pain" can mean many different things. And there are at least twenty different terms used to describe pain. Almost everyone knows what pain is, and no one can adequately define it to suit everyone.

Unfortunately, the three most commonly heard phrases regarding pain are all extremely damaging to athletes in America. These are, "Playing with pain," "He/She can play with pain," and "Without pain there ain't no gain."

What we often fail to realize is that pain is a result of too much, too soon. We prefer the quote, "Train, don't strain."

Pain is nature's warning signal that we are doing something wrong or that we have been injured. If we ignore pain and continue, some harm is going to come to us. As for research, there is almost none at all being done on pain tolerance. While there is very little written in medical textbooks about the subject, one of the first things a young doctor learns from treating several patients is that there are great differences in pain tolerance. What is a severe and disablingly painful injury in one person can be a minor nuisance in another. Experienced, good coaches also recognize that their players have differing degrees of pain tolerance. Nurses know it, and even parents who have at least two children recognize that each child has a different degree of pain tolerance. But despite what everybody knows, there still is virtually nothing useful written on this topic. The reason for this, of course, is that it is impossible to measure pain in any way that is meaningful.

Ethnic differences are significant in pain behavior. The American Indians are famous for their stoic attitudes toward pain. They show a lack of apparent reaction to obviously painful stimuli. On the other hand, many Middle Eastern cultures are quite vocal and dramatic in their responses to what can be relatively minor painful conditions.

Many women feel that women who have given birth have higher pain tolerances than men. The argument they use is, "You men don't know what pain is until you have borne a child." However, any obstetrician or nurse who has seen several births knows that there are tremendous variations in the behavior of women who are in the act of giving birth. While many women show very high pain tolerances, many others have low pain tolerances. Obviously, the same is true of men.

A few children are cursed by the fact that they do not suffer any pain at all. Their nervous system seems entirely normal and all the common tests are normal, yet they can burn themselves and not react to it. They can have serious infection and fractures and not respond. Of course, this is the "cursed" part of it. They do not have the normal protective sensation that pain provides, and they can suffer severe bodily injury before their parents become aware that they have even been injured. At times they can even suffer severe permanent injuries to joints. In adults, the most common medical problem that can lead to a lack of proper pain sensation is diabetes. The diabetic effect on the nerve can eliminate the deep protective pain sensation that helps prevent serious joint injuries.

Unfortunately, it seems that several of our famous professional athletes may have incredibly high pain tolerances, as evidenced by the injuries that they play with. This has led to some famous, very short careers by gifted athletes who should have rested their injuries and prolonged their careers.

Pain relief, on the other hand, has received a great deal of research. This has led to the discovery of endorphins, which are substances normally released in our body that give us relief from pain. Endorphins, a kind of internal morphine system, are increased with stress and injuries, just as cortisone is released initially during stress.

This research has revealed that in the animal world, the camel has extremely high endorphin levels. Anyone who has worked with camels will tell you how mean and how difficult to discipline they are, and what high pain tolerances they have. One of the reasons camels are so hard to discipline is because it is difficult to do something that truly hurts the animal. It may very well turn out that the differences we see in pain tolerances in patients are, in fact, due to the differences in the endorphin levels that our bodies can develop in reaction to injury.

One of the first things an athlete must learn is to listen to painful stimuli, because they are the body's warnings. To ignore pain is to ignore a danger signal. Play is not play if it is painful, and an athlete playing with pain is an athlete who is at risk.

However, athletes must also learn the difference between *pain* that is a warning sign of injury and *soreness* (often called "pain") from exercise, indicating a lactic-acid buildup in the muscles. This soreness from exercise is a natural occurrence, and it is what the coaches are referring to when they say, "Without pain there ain't no gain." It is true that to improve you must stress your muscles. You must exercise them sufficiently hard for them to be a bit sore. (Weight lifters call this sensation "Burn.") But you must learn to differentiate this from the pain that is a warning of too much stress, or the pain of an injury. The dangerous part is that the young athlete may not have enough experience to separate the two types of "pain." So just as he has been badgered into ignoring the soreness from exercise, he may think he must ignore the pain that is a warning signal—and risk further, more severe injury. To add to the confusion, fifteen years ago it was in vogue to talk of the pain or agony of the long-distance runner. Now, in the midst of our running explosion, we talk of the ecstasy or the high of long-distance running; we no longer talk of the pain of running at all. And people are running longer distances and training harder now than they did ten or fifteen years ago.

One of the most interesting aspects of pain is the fact that young children, until they enter adolescence, rarely complain of pain unless they have been taught to by their parents. If they sustain an injury and it is serious they will come home and say, "Mom, I've broken my arm"; or, "I hurt my knee"; or they will simply limp around for days until the injury is healed. Frequently an active, athletic child will say to a parent, "I'm not interested in playing," and will sit around reading or watching television when this is totally out of character. What the child is probably doing is listening to his or her body and instinctively resting an injured part long enough for it to heal before resuming activities. The only way a child can be forced to ignore an injury is through heavy parental or coaching pressure to "rub it off" and play, or to "play with pain," or "get tough." So we need to be more like children, to get in tune with our bodies so that we listen to nature's warning signal—pain. And we must learn to differentiate that from the discomfort and soreness caused by training.

Furthermore, if you can, try to develop sufficient insight into your own tolerances, and evaluate whether you have a high, average, or low pain threshold or tolerance. This is extremely difficult to do. It is also difficult for parents to evaluate in their children unless they have more than two children. We say this because most people who think they have a high pain tolerance or say they have a high pain tolerance do not. People with high pain tolerances are usually relatively unaware of pain and don't talk about it, much less brag about their levels of tolerance.

A discussion of pain is important in any discussion of rehabilitation because after an injury, there seems to be a decrease in pain tolerance. The bones become softer. The ligaments, tendons, and muscles become stiff. Just lifting a leg once or twice may require a major effort. Bending an injured joint may be impossible because of adhesions or scar tissue. Whereas pain is your friend when you are injured because it warns you that something has gone awry, it may be your enemy in the rehabilitation process. Rehabilitating an injury requires work. If the injury has been severe, there will probably be some discomfort. And what would have been an effortless motion before the injury may be a major athletic achievement during the first few weeks of the rehabilitative process. Simply moving a joint once or twice may completely fatigue a muscle so that it becomes quite sore. As always, you should be alert to the difference between the normal muscle soreness of exercise and the pain that is a warning signal of trouble. Rehabilitation might be uncomfortable and it is hard work, but it should not be excessively painful. If, however, you always had a low pain tolerance and the injury has lowered it even further, or if you are in the healing phase of a nerve injury, you may need the help of a therapist to help you work through your pain and learn to ignore it and overcome it. Or you may need a TNS (transcutaneous nerve stimulator) unit or other modality to help you.

ATTITUDE AND EMOTIONS

Being injured is a downer! It is depressing to be injured; it is depressing to hurt. After three months of pain of any sort, even the most emotionally stable person will show definite signs of depression. Psychological testing will reveal an obvious increase in depressive tendencies as well as what psychologists call hysteria and hypochondriasis. An injury that is three months old and still hurting will change you. You will be depressed, irritable, more interested in yourself, and talk more about your injury (that is hypochondriasis).

Fortunately, these changes are temporary. They last only as long as you are still disabled from injury and still hurting. Once you have recovered, even the psychological tests will revert to what was normal for you before the injury.

One of the best treatments for depression is exercise of any sort. Exercises are good for your specific injury, but they are also the key to your mental as well as your physical recovery.

Depression can be a major problem, and there are many different forms it can take. It may simply be a sensation of feeling "blue" or "down in the dumps." Or you may have thoughts like "I'll never play again," or "I'm getting older." There is also the realization that your body is not perfect and not indestructible, and that you are not infallible. You will be aware that "it can happen to me, and you may even wonder, "What did I do wrong to deserve this?" It is normal for any or all of these thoughts and feelings to occur to an athlete who has been injured. They are an indication of at least mild depression.

Next comes the double-edged sword. Depression definitely increases pain. What might be a mild pain when you are feeling good can be magnified tremendously by depression. So what might be a minor injury can become a severe and major problem in an even mildly depressed state. Depression decreases your pain tolerance.

Furthermore, depression is aggravated by pain medications. Physiological depressants like codeine, Demerol, morphine, alcohol, and Darvon are all effective pain medications of varying strength but they are also psychological depressants. If you are in a depressed state these medications may not give you much pain relief and may depress you still further, starting you on a vicious downward cycle. One of the reasons physicians, therapists, trainers, and coaches vigorously try to get their athletes off pain medication as soon as possible is that it takes more and more pain medicine to deaden the pain, and it is easy to become mildly addicted psychologically to these medications.

In a depressed state, it is difficult to get going and it is much more difficult to get yourself to do exercises. But exercise is the best treatment for depression, for your lowered pain tolerance, for your weakened state, and for your injury.

Hypochondriasis is an abnormal anxiety about your health; it is a frequent symptom of depressed states. You usually are not as concerned with others as you were before the injury. You worry about your athletic career and that you might reinjure your body. In addition, there is an increased concern with what would normally have been ignored or considered minor symptoms, the minor snaps and cracks that your muscles make while moving your injured joint. All of these concerns and changes do decrease as your recovery progresses and you become more convinced that you are indeed going to get better.

The final major emotional hurdle is fear of reinjury. This is a natural fear; any athlete who has ever had a significant injury has experienced it at some point; but you must get over it. Any athlete who goes back to participation fearful that he or she is going to be reinjured, probably will be reinjured. This is especially true in a collision sport such as football. There is nothing that will cause an injury as much as a fear of injury or reinjury. This is why the last goal of rehabilitation is to convince you that you have recovered sufficiently and that you are good enough to perform without being reinjured. You must have solid control of your arms and legs to have this confidence. You must have faith in your doctor, trainer, and the exercise program, and that you have done the best you can to recover and are now ready to perform.

Nothing that we can say or do will give you the desire to recover. If you do not care about recovering and do not want to play again, then your life will be very easy: You simply do nothing. But without the desire and the will to recover, you will never return to your pre-injury performance levels.

EARLY MOTION

We have already talked of the benefits of rest, the trap of rest, and the complications of rest. Much of the same can be said about motion. In fact, we believe one of the reasons for the popularity of stretching is because people have confused the benefits of stretching with the benefits of early, gentle motion. Early motion involves *moving* the injured part with your own muscles rather than simply stretching. Early motion discourages the formation of scar tissue and adhesions while encouraging healing. If the injury is protected, early motion that is graduated and prescribed by your physician promotes the healing of broken bones. In fact, the proper healing of *any* type of injury is benefited by early, gentle, active motion. One of the arts of treatment, of course, is knowing when to prescribe early motion; it is a question of timing.

MASSAGE

Massage is potent medicine; it has been for centuries and continues to be. There is no question that proper massage can relax tense muscles, decrease the pain of a muscle in spasm, enhance sleep, and increase performance through proper relaxation. In fact, it may very well be that the proper massage enhances performance far better than the proper warm-up and certainly is far superior to the stretching that most athletes do.

In rehabilitation of injury, massage can increase blood flow, both arterial and venous. It improves lymph drainage, decreases swelling, and can help break up scar tissue and decrease adhesions. Properly applied to sore muscles, it decreases pain. An experienced masseur has the ability to find muscles that are in spasm and, with proper massage, relax the spasms. Recently we have seen tremendous interest in acupressure, which is really an ancient form of massage.

If massage does all these things, why isn't it practiced more? Probably for the same reason that Americans insist on using machines for exercise: We are in love with machines. We use TNS machines. We use Dyna-Wave machines. We use all kinds of therapy machines. It is more time-efficient and a lot less work to put a machine on an athlete than to administer massage. Both authors have traveled overseas and around the country with United States teams and can speak from experience. The trainers are often the hardest-working people on the team. They exhaust themselves massaging athletes all day long. Massage is a "hands-on" type of therapy; it is hard work and it is not efficient. But there is nothing like properly done massage; it is a masterful form of therapy.

MODALITIES

"Modalities" is the medical term for varieties of physical treatment, either with machines or temperature. Usually it is the delivery of heat with varying waveforms to deep structures to aid healing and decrease pain and inflammation.

Cryotherapy, or Treatment Using Cold: Ice, Cold Packs, and Ice Whirlpools

Ice can be considered the universal drug of choice for athletic injuries. In a healthy, conscious athlete I have never seen an injury or complication from ice treatment. Ice decreases bleeding, promotes healing, and decreases pain. It decreases swelling by closing down the blood vessels, and also by preventing the chemical reaction and inflammation that occurs as a result of an injury.

Ice is the safest and most effective pain reliever for most minor athletic injuries. It is usually applied in a form called ice massage. An easy way to administer it is by first freezing water in plastic-foam cups; then tear the rim off, and rub the sore area for 10 to 15 minutes. This should be done 3 to 5 times a day.

Ice increases healing in two ways: First, it prevents the complications of a lot of swelling and bleeding, and this in itself will promote and speed up the healing process. In addition, when ice is removed, blood vessels that were narrowed and closed down will open up and react much as they do when heat is applied. This seems to encourage the healing process without causing excessive bleeding. With any new injury, ice is the best treatment. It is also a very safe treatment for a healthy athlete.

The only problem with ice is that it does temporarily increase stiffness in tissues, so it is best not to apply it to a crucial area of function right before an activity. This is why trainers will at times alternate heat and ice. This problem is not a reason to avoid using ice; we mentioned it just as a warning that you should use it properly.

While ice is the cheapest, safest, and most effective way to apply cold, first-aid cold packs are also available commercially. When the two chemicals in a cold pack are mixed (by breaking a bag within the bag), an endothermic chemical reaction occurs, producing cold.

This pack is almost as effective as ice in cooling. Cold packs have the advantage of being convenient, since they do not require refrigeration. They are obviously much more expensive than ice.

One big warning: Many of them are not safe to reuse, so never refreeze a cold pack. They are capable of getting much colder than ice, and can actually freeze the tissue. While complications of ice in athletes are almost unknown, frostbite can occur from a refrozen cold pack.

Another way to use cryotherapy is with an ice whirlpool. While it takes a courageous and hardy athlete to submerge an injured arm or leg in an ice whirlpool, it is an extremely effective way to apply cold. Obviously it cannot be tolerated for more than 10 to 15 minutes, but with proper supervision a healthy athlete who has normal sensation can use it without much trouble.

Just remember: Of all the ways to apply cryotherapy, ice is the cheapest, most effective, and safest.

Heat

Heat is commonly used in the treatment and rehabilitation of athletic injuries. Applied heat increases circulation to an area. It dilates blood vessels (widens them), so that more blood flows in. Heat does increase the flexibility of tissue and can combat the stiffness that cold may cause.

The problem with heat is that if it is applied too early to an injury, or if too much of it is applied, it will increase swelling. In addition, if it is applied while there is bleeding or less than 72 hours after bleeding has stopped, it may increase bleeding or cause further bleeding, thus delaying healing. Though heat applied to the skin does not penetrate as deeply as cold applied to the skin, it must be used cautiously for a new injury.

Since heat does decrease muscle soreness it is a proper treatment in rehabilitation, but it is only rarely applied to new athletic injuries.

For muscle stiffness and soreness during rehabilitation, heat can safely be applied by standing under a hot shower or using a heating pad, a whirlpool, or a warm tub bath. The main difference between moist and dry heat is that water is a good conductor of heat, making moist heat more effective than dry heat. Also, dryness permits a little bit of air between the heating pad and the skin, interfering with the heat transfer. Water conducts the heat to the skin and the deeper tissues more effectively.

Whirlpool

Many athletes feel that they have not had proper rehabilitation if they have not used a whirlpool. All that a whirlpool does is surround the injured arm, leg, or body with swirling waters of varying temperatures. An ice whirlpool can be used if there is swelling or the injury is new. This will frequently decrease the severity of the injury and cut down the swelling, although, as we said above, it takes a hardy, courageous person to submit to this treatment.

When most people think of whirlpools, they think of warm water. This is an effective way to warm an extremity, and in the rehabilitation of injuries, this warming will decrease stiffness and muscle soreness and increase flexibility. If properly combined with exercises, it can speed up recovery. Properly supervised by a therapist, a whirlpool can be an effective aid in the rehabilitation of an athlete.

However, if you have an injured hand, elbow, ankle, or knee and simply soak it in the whirlpool without exercises, this can cause more swelling and delay recovery. The whirlpool or any soaking in warm water is not a treatment in and of itself, but must be combined with proper exercises.

Deep Heat, Ultrasound, Dyna-Wave, Medcosound

Heat-wave therapy machines make it possible to get the healing effects of heat to the deep tissues. They get heat to penetrate more deeply than can be done with a heating pad or hot packs. They should be applied by a trained therapist. Properly utilized, these can be very helpful ways of treating and rehabilitating various injuries.

TNS (Transcutaneous Nerve Stimulator)

Some of you may be familiar with the little black boxes that various pro and amateur athletes have worn to decrease pain and permit function. These little black boxes are called transcutaneous nerve stimulators, and are a way of blocking pain from a chronic, painful injury without the use of drugs or injections. Although science does not understand precisely how the TNS works, it stimulates the skin with a mild electric sensation that somehow blocks nerves from feeling pain. It usually is quite effective for the first thirty days, and in some people for much longer than that. For most athletes who have a condition in which pain is the prime problem preventing rehabilitation, a TNS unit may be the answer, though it should be prescribed only by a physician.

Other than an allergic reaction to its tape, we know of no complications that occur from it. It is safe, effective, and at the present time is not believed to be habit forming. In many instances it is preferable to drugs or injections for treating pain.

Electrical Stimulation

For a long time physicians knew that the proper type of low-voltage electrical stimulation of muscles could minimize the atrophy and weakness that occur to muscles at times of illness and injury. But when this did not prove very effective in the treatment of polio patients who had permanent paralysis, the method seemed to fall into disrepute and was not used for many years. However, it has come back into favor since it was learned that the Russians are using electrical stimulation to enhance and increase strength in normal muscle. While this has not been fully studied, it appears that properly supervised electrical stimulation may be an effective way to speed up the recovery of an athlete and help him or her regain strength in the muscles of an injured arm or leg. It should only be prescribed by a physician and administered by a certified therapist or trainer.

MEDICATION

There are only a few medicines that should be necessary in the rehabilitation of injured athletes. While it is generally good policy to avoid medications, there are times when your physician may feel it necessary to prescribe some.

Aspirin

For the treatment of inflammation, swelling, stiffness, and the pain caused by most common athletic injuries, aspirin (acetylsalicylic acid) is still the standard drug of choice. If taken properly, which means (depending upon the weight of the athlete) two or three 5-grain (325 mg) tablets of aspirin three, four, or five times a day, aspirin will decrease swelling in an injured joint or extremity, decrease stiffness, speed up healing of cartilage and tissue, and prevent further damage to injured cartilage by inhibiting the enzymes that destroy cartilage. It will also decrease inflammation and adhesion formation. Many experts feel it is our most effective pain reliever.

There are two big problems with aspirin. First, it increases bleeding tendencies; therefore, in a new injury if there is bleeding (less than two to three days old), aspirin may cause continued bleeding and should not be used. Ice is a much safer way to control the bleeding and swelling in that instance. Second, anyone with a sensitive stomach or colon, or who has a history of ulcers, should not take aspirin because it can cause ulcer symptoms or even bleeding ulcers in a susceptible person. This is usually not a problem in a young, healthy athlete, but if he or she continues to take high doses of aspirin on an empty stomach, this can become a significant problem. If continued use of aspirin is necessary, I recommend that it be taken three or four times a day after meals. This will have a protective effect on the stomach and intestinal tract without decreasing the effectiveness of the aspirin.

Acetaminophen (Tylenol, Datril)

Acetaminophen is an effective, safe pain reliever in the doses recommended—two or three tablets, three or four times a day. In a healthy athlete it should cause no problems at all when pain medication is indicated. It has no therapeutic effects other than relieving pain.

Controversial Drugs

ORAL CORTISONE

Cortisone is an essential naturally occurring hormone. All of us have cortisone circulating in our blood stream throughout the day.

Levels are higher at some times than at others, but it is always there. Because cortisone occurs naturally there is no reason for young and healthy athletes without medical problems to ever require cortisone in pill form. If oral cortisone has been prescribed for a young, healthy athlete without other medical problems, get a second opinion!

CORTISONE INJECTIONS

Cortisone shots can at times be the appropriate treatment for a large variety of painful athletic conditions that have failed to respond to all other kinds of treatment. This is much more common in the mature adult and very, very rarely necessary in a teenager. There are very few complications from cortisone injections that occur away from the area that is injected. A cortisone injection will markedly decrease inflammation in the area where it is given. It will usually decrease swelling dramatically. It will weaken scar tissue and adhesions, and after the first day it will usually decrease pain and swelling in the area. Some of this decrease in pain will be due to the decrease in inflammation and swelling and the weakening of the scar tissue, but there is also a direct effect on the sensation nerves in the area where the injection has been given, making them less sensitive to pain.

However, at the same time, the cortisone will decrease healing of ligaments and tendons in the area where the injection is given, and it will weaken the strength of a ligament or tendon. For the first three weeks, the ligament or tendon in the area injected may be as much as 50 percent weaker, and it takes up to six weeks to regain full strength. So there is a definite increase in risk of a ruptured ligament or tendon during the first month after a cortisone injection is given.

Doctors use cortisone injections cautiously in the young athlete because their bodies' healing capacities are so great that rest will usually solve the problem. In the more mature athlete, who does not have the same healing capabilities, there are times when a cortisone injection may be necessary—but there are always risks involved.

Cortisone is very seldom injected into the joints of injured athletes. A second opinion should always be sought before you permit an injection into a joint. Cortisone in joints, especially the knee, may cause permanent damage to the joint surface cartilage. It will dramatically decrease swelling, and may mask a serious problem in the joint.

DMSO

The lay press has become fascinated by dimethyl sulfoxide, a simple, easily made, and inexpensive drug. When applied to an inflamed area, DMSO often seems to have the ability to decrease the pain and inflammation. DMSO also has the unusual property of carrying into the circulation any chemical compound or drug that is on the skin, so it should never be applied over a salve or chemical compound, but only to normal, clean skin.

At this time, DMSO has not been released by the FDA for general use. The only DMSO readily available in most of the United States is not medical grade, but veterinary or chemical grade and not meant to be used on humans.

Although DMSO has many famous proponents who recommend it highly, and there have been dramatic testimonials to its effectiveness, since at the present time it is not legally available for human use (except for the treatment of interstitial cystitis) in most states we cannot recommend it.

ANABOLIC STEROIDS, TESTOSTERONE, DIANABOL, MALE SEX HORMONE, ETC.

Many weight lifters and people on strength training, both in this country and across the world, are taking hormones on a regular or irregular basis. They take them because they notice an increase in strength while they are on the drugs. While there is little good scientific evidence available on the effects of these drugs, their widespread use is made possible through a drug black market.

In males and females, steroids increase hair formation, raise anxiety and irritability levels, and increase aggressive behavior. Anyone who knows someone taking these drugs will soon notice that he or she is more irritable, jumpy, and aggressive. And they look a little bit different while they are taking the medications.

There seems to be no question that athletes are stronger while taking these drugs. But so far the best evidence indicates that it is not the hormones that make the athletes stronger; it is the increased mental aggressiveness induced by the hormone that permits the athlete to be more physically aggressive and vigorous in weight training. This greater effort in turn leads to the increased strength; there is no direct effect of a magic strength pill that is making the muscles stronger!

The risks of taking these medications are still unknown. However, it seems quite likely that men who take them increase their chances of developing high blood pressure and cancer of the prostate and liver. Effects upon potency and sterility are still unknown.

Females who take these drugs increase their risk of hair formation that is usually considered unfeminine and unwanted. Also present is a significant increase in the risk of infertility, an unknown risk of cancer, and certainly the chance of high blood pressure as well.

One of the reasons that we do not yet know all the risks is that the athletes who have been taking these drugs will only in the next ten to twenty years be reaching the age where we would expect them to "reap the harvest" of the complications of the abuse of these extremely potent drugs.

If we can get athletes to believe the best scientific opinions—and believe them enough to act on those beliefs—then the abuse of potent hormones will cease. Athletes must realize that the hormones do not increase strength; they just make them work harder and more aggressively at their strength training. But the risks of serious medical complications and fatal diseases that may result from prolonged use of hormones are significant.

VITAMINS

There are no miracle vitamins that are going to make you stronger or heal you faster. However, vitamin C is an essential vitamin in the healing of all injured tissues. If you are eating a balanced diet with plenty of fruit in it, then you do not need any additional vitamin C. If there is some question as to whether your diet is well balanced, then an additional 500 to 1,000 mg. of vitamin C a day, especially during the recovery phase after an injury or in intense heavy training, may be helpful. Anything more than that will be passed out of your body in the urine, so it is a waste to make your urine expensive with very high doses of vitamin C.

HOW TO PICK A DOCTOR

The person who can probably best evaluate an orthopedic surgeon and his results with both surgically and nonsurgically treated patients, is an experienced, certified trainer who has worked with more than one physician. This is because they have seen different doctors treat different injuries and they, more than anyone else, know the results with a large group of patients. If you don't know a certified, experienced athletic trainer, then your next best bet is to ask a coach you trust whom he would recommend. If you have friends who have had surgery themselves, it certainly would be wise to consult them as to who has a solid reputation in your community as well. If none of those tips are helpful, then you need to go to the most experienced orthopedic surgeon you know or can find who treats a large number of athletes.

The most difficult question for us to answer is what to do if surgery is recommended. If one orthopedic surgeon recommends surgery, it is usually possible to find another who won't. So shopping around may keep you from having surgery, but it may not be the best treatment. The reason for this is twofold: First, surgery is frequently the most conservative method of treatment; performed by an experienced orthopedic surgeon it will lead to the best result in certain instances. Second, most ligament injuries are best treated surgically within the first ten days to three weeks maximum. After two to three weeks, the results of surgery usually are not as good, and often are no different from surgery performed at a much later date.

So the same orthopedic surgeon who might recommend surgery if he sees you within the first week of your injury might not recommend surgery if he sees you three or four weeks after that injury. Our best advice on what to do if surgery is recommended is, if you have confidence in and trust the advice of the orthopedic surgeon you have consulted, then follow his recommendations. If the recommendations sound too radical to you, and deep down you do not believe that you require surgery, then get a second and even a third opinion. Most athletes instinctively know if they have sustained a complete ligament rupture. They may not want to admit it; they may not want to face the fact that they require surgery; but deep down they know "something is gone" or something has completely torn. If you have that feeling and surgery is recommended, then we would advise you to go along with that surgical recommendation. However, if you don't have confidence in your surgeon, then we would advise you not to let him operate upon you, since confidence plays an important part in proper rehabilitation after any surgery.

Therapists

One of the purposes of this book is to help the injured athlete understand the importance of rehabilitation and the types of exercises he or she should be doing. We do not want to replace the therapist. But unfortunately there is a shortage of therapists to treat injured athletes, and so frequently once the injury itself has healed, the rehabilitation is left to the athlete and his own devices. However, it is far better to have a therapist supervising rehabilitation. The question is, if someone is available, who should supervise it?

M.D.'S

Orthopedic surgeons are trained to evaluate and treat injuries, including athletic injuries. Other physicians besides orthopedic surgeons are also experienced, and some have training in the diagnosis and treatment of athletic injuries. But few, if any, physicians have training in or are experienced in the day-to-day supervision of the rehabilitation of an injured athlete. This is an extremely time-consuming process, and almost all physicians have delegated the authority to supervise the rehabilitation process to a therapist or group of therapists with whom they are familiar. Behind every successful and prominent orthopedic surgeon who has good results in the field of sports medicine is a therapist or trainer who has mastered the art of progressive training of the injured athlete. While all physicians in sports medicine realize and appreciate the value of rehabilitation, they also know that the results of their treatment hinge upon good rehabilitation. Few doctors know the exact specifics of the number of pounds lifted, the number of times it is done, and the gradations in the process. If you ask them to write a prescription for you, they will usually write "knee rehabilitation" or "ankle rehab" or "lower extremity rehab" and send you to their therapist. So if you want to know their program, you had best talk to their therapists.

REGISTERED PHYSICAL THERAPIST

Unfortunately, most physical therapists receive little specific training in the rehabilitation of injured athletes. They are extremely well trained in rehabilitating other injured patients, paralyzed patients, and severely handicapped people; but for most therapists a triumph is the ability to walk, and a huge success is the ability to walk upstairs without holding onto a railing. A few, through practice and exposure to athletes, have mastered the art of taking an athlete beyond these goals to athletic competition. But while a physical therapist may be essential in the first stages of rehabilitation, most of them can only get you started; then you will have to either follow the program in this book or find someone who is more familiar with the complete rehabilitation of injured athletes.

Those physical therapists who have had exposure to athletes and are familiar with the demands of athletic competition constitute one of the groups of therapists we would highly recommend you have supervise your rehabilitation when the time is right. They are trained in the use of whirlpool, transcutaneous nerve stimulators, electrical stimulation, Dyna-Wave, ultrasound, medcosound, and all the other modalities that we discussed earlier. These treatments can be quite helpful at times, and in many communities physical therapists are the only ones who can administer these modes of treatment to you.

CERTIFIED ATHLETIC TRAINERS

Behind every successful team physician who gets consistently good results from his treatments, both surgical and nonsurgical, is a good certified athletic trainer. They are specifically trained in the rehabilitation and treatment of athletic injuries and are quite familiar with the demands of the various sports. Once it is time for your rehabilitation, especially after you have graduated from physical therapy, we would highly recommend that you have a certified athletic trainer supervise you. Unfortunately, athletic trainers usually do not have access to all the modalities available to physical therapists, but they probably will have access to the essential ones.

OTHER THERAPISTS

There are correctional therapists, some physiologists, and other "trainers" who have vast experience in the rehabilitation of athletic injuries. The reason we stress experience is that the road to rehabilitation is usually not a smooth recovery process, but has its ups and downs. Experienced therapists can be a great help in judging whether a setback or pain or swelling is to be expected or is out of the ordinary and requires reevaluation by a physician. They know from experience when to push harder and when to back off on exercise, when to apply heat, when to apply ice, and all of the subtleties an inexperienced person would not be sensitive to. If there is no one in your community with this experience, then be sure to read the training program outlined in Part Two of this book, because you still need the rehabilitation, even if you have to struggle and go it alone.

10

Children and Training

The exercises in this book are all safe for children to do, and the training methods outlined are superior educational tools.

There has been little research on exercise programs for children, probably because many people do not realize that children are not merely "little adults." Their soft tissue behaves differently and indeed they behave differently than adults do. Children have an innate common sense and are also more in tune with their bodies; they will not perform harmful exercises or maneuvers if left to their own devices. Unfortunately, many programs have been wrongfully forced upon children. For example, stiffness is not a problem in children. In fact, the problem is an opposite one, of looseness or laxity. So there is no need for children ever to do stretching exercises of any sort.

We strongly believe that children can and should be taught proper weight-lifting techniques. This is different from children doing weight lifting training. It has been clearly established that if children are taught proper techniques, they will use those techniques for the rest of their lives. This is true of tennis strokes and golf swings, and it is also true of proper weight lifting in stable positions and postures.

Prepubescent children do not benefit from weight-lifting training because they lack the presence of hormones that permit the increase in strength with resistance exercises.

After an injury, most orthopedic surgeons will not refer children to physical therapists because they know that stretching and exercises frequently do more harm than good. Stretching can be injurious to stiff joints in children—and stiffness is not a long-term problem in children after injury except in extremely rare, major, and severe injuries.

Even though resistance exercises are safe for children to do—no harm will come to their bones or their growth zones—we do not advocate resistance exercises for children. Most will find these exercises boring, and they will rebel against an activity that is not fun to perform. Since resistance exercises are one of the keys to proper rehabilitation and improving athletic performance in later life, we do not want to destroy this useful tool for future athletes by having them become bored with them at an early age.

The only injuries from weight lifting we have ever seen were those in young boys who tried to lift barbells or weights that were too heavy for them. These children lost control and dropped the weights, sustaining wrist fractures that were not serious.

We recommend that children learn basic tumbling and falling techniques, since knowing how to fall and land softly is one key way to prevent injuries.

In addition, beams, boards, and boxes (see Chapters 16, 17, and 19) are useful tools in training children and will help teach balance, coordination, and especially that long-forgotten virtue, good posture.

11

Playing Yourself into Shape—The Myth

Depending upon the sport, many athletes feel they are able to play themselves into shape or rehabilitate themselves merely by gradually increasing the intensity with which they play. Many athletes who are out of shape and out of condition frequently will use this method instead of a rehabilitation program, thinking it is the safest and most reasonable way to condition themselves.

A variation of this is for athletes to pick a sport that looks like it is "good exercise" and use this sport to rehabilitate their injury, to play themselves into condition, or to improve their performance. An example would be a football player who decides he is going to play racquetball or jog to get himself into condition for football or rehabilitate his injured knee.

Does either of these methods work? We will now discuss some of the common sports, and how useful (or dangerous) they are for "playing yourself into shape" or playing to rehabilitate your injury.

BASEBALL

Major-league baseball players are probably responsible for originating the idea of playing yourself into shape. They would show up six to eight weeks before the season in a nice warm location, where they would run around the outfield two or three times and take batting practice for half an hour a day to gradually "get themselves into shape." Since baseball traditionally does not require great physical condition, this routine was effective for players to retain their timing in fielding and hitting. But baseball is essentially a game of timing and coordination, with very short bursts of activity. Since the players were only honing natural skills, this routine was effective in helping them regain timing and polish up those skills. When age diminished players' reflex time and slowed them down, they simply retired.

Since baseball is a game of standing around between short bursts of intense physical activity that mostly involves twisting maneuvers or sprinting with spikes across a rough outfield, their is no conceivable way that playing baseball as your only method of training can rehabilitate any injury below the shoulder. Baseball is an anaerobic sport, and the maneuvers required in baseball are those of maximal performance for short periods of time. These short periods of time are not long enough to confer any training benefit. In addition, they require some extremely difficult athletic maneuvers, and one should be completely rehabilitated before even attempting them.

We can only speculate on how long some players' careers could have been extended had proper training and conditioning been utilized.

An exception to this, of course, is the pitcher. Training and strengthening of the pitching arm is still a complex, poorly understood issue. Pitchers did require the six to eight weeks to bring their arms into throwing condition. However, it was quite rare for any baseball club to use strengthening exercises for pitching arms which were specifically designed to avoid injury and shoulder problems.

BASKETBALL

Basketball does require a high degree of aerobic physical conditioning, and it is possible by playing full-court basketball to "play yourself into shape." If, however, you are recovering from an injury (especially an ankle or knee injury), the stresses of basketball are too great for you to risk playing before full rehabilitation and recovery. To return to basketball you must be ready for maximum performance.

Basketball requires long bouts of running. This puts enormous strain on the ankle, knee, and hip joints. Since one of the common injuries in basketball is the sprained ankle, it is illogical if you are just recovering from a sprained ankle to go back and try to play before the ankle is fully rehabilitated. (See discussion of ligaments in Chapter 7.)

In addition to running, basketball requires jumping, which produces even greater strains. If you have a knee that has not been fully rehabilitated, rebounding can certainly reinjure knee ligaments because of the weakness of the muscles around the knee. Actually, it isn't the jumping that is hard on the knees; it is the landing. That's why basketball is extremely difficult to play without a functioning anterior cruciate ligament, which seems to be essential in landing. Athletes who have torn their anterior cruciate ligament feel insecure in their landing and have difficulty playing basketball for this reason. Because of the enormous stresses on this ligament in basketball, we don't recommend your playing basketball until you are fully recovered from any knee injuries you have.

Finger injuries are also quite common in basketball. One cannot rehabilitate hand and finger injuries by playing basketball, although it is frequently possible to continue playing basketball with an injured hand if fingers are properly taped and splinted for the contest. Your treating physician and trainer are the best ones to work out the method of protection.

As we have already emphasized, it is extremely important that you train in a stable fashion to maintain structural integrity. The final lesson in this book is on proper jumping and proper landing techniques. Unfortunately, most people who jump land on one leg or the other, not on both legs. If you are recovering from an injury, this will put either enormous strain on your good leg or far too much strain on your bad leg. (Even when you are healthy, landing requires a great deal of strength for the braking effect.) You must be trained to land in a structurally stable fashion. To return to basketball without this essential training is begging for a recurrence of your old injury or the development of a new one.

VOLLEYBALL

Volleyball is no longer the gentle, coed game we used to play at picnics. It is an extremely difficult and demanding sport. It is roughest on fingers, knees, and occasionally ankles. We do not recommend that you play volleyball to play yourself into shape; it is better to train yourself to play volleyball. Until an ankle or knee injury has been fully rehabilitated, you run a serious risk of aggravating the injury—or causing another one. Volleyball is basically a game of spurts and jumps. These sprints and dives put tremendous strain on the ankle and the knee. The jumping upward itself does not put a great deal of strain on the knee, but landing does. Landing slightly out of control and alignment can cause quite severe ankle- and knee-ligament injuries. This is why it is unsafe to go back to volleyball until you are completely rehabilitated and have regained full strength in your legs.

While it is impossible to rehabilitate finger and hand injuries by playing volleyball, it is frequently possible to play or train with a finger injury if the finger is taped. But since splints may be illegal, it is best to consult with your coach and check the rules carefully before you decide to compete with taped or splinted fingers.

High-level competitive volleyball puts enormous strain upon the shoulders and the shoulder girdle. You must maximally train your shoulders to perform in a structurally stable fashion prior to returning to competition from any shoulder injury. There is no conceivable way that playing volleyball is going to rehabilitate any shoulder injury. In fact, quite the contrary is true. We strongly recommend that you read Chapters 13, 14, and 15 before considering returning to volleyball after a shoulder problem.

FOOTBALL

Football is a game that combines bursts of running with collisions. In the past several years we have seen a definite improvement in the training of football players, with the result that they are now in better condition than ever before. High-school football players today are bigger and stronger than many pros were twenty years ago. Because of this increased strength and the frequent collisions that occur, it is unsafe to return to football before one has fully recovered from an injury.

There are two reasons for this: First, if you do not have full strength, there is a definite risk of making the injury worse and sustaining a tremendous setback. Second, if you know that you are not fully recovered, you try to protect yourself from reinjury. And there is no surer "kiss of death" than playing football while fearing and trying to avoid injury. The athlete who is injured in football is always the one who is most afraid, and this unquestionably becomes a self-fulfilling prophecy.

It is important here that we replace the slogan "If there's no pain, there's no gain" with the more sensible "Coax the development by training and not straining."

All coaches and players know that injuries are part of the game; the big football programs have ample numbers of "bodies" to substitute for injured players, so there is often no great external pressure to return. The exception to this is the superstar, whose very presence can make a difference even if he is in an injured condition. There is enormous pressure on this type of player to return too soon, prior to satisfactory rehabilitation. Unfortunately, if he does this, the superstar can end up with an abbreviated career, jeopardizing his entire future in football. It is the truly great coach who will let the superstar rehabilitate his injury fully before permitting him to return to duty.

The other problem situation occurs in the small football program, where there are a minimal number of "bodies" and three or four injuries can jeopardize a team's season by simply leaving insufficient numbers to play. The unfortunate players pressed into action by this combination of events run exactly the same risks as mentioned above.

Coupled with these problems is the great American myth of playing with pain, the unfortunate belief that good players are the ones who can play with injuries and play while hurt. This misunderstood concept has shortened many more careers and permanently disabled more athletes than led teams on to victory.

Since the risk of injury in football is so high, it is extremely difficult to avoid injury in the rehabilitative phase. One should be fully and completely recovered from an old injury and in top condition before returning to play. The same is true of touch football, since many severe injuries can occur in that seemingly "harmless" sport. So, be sure to rehabilitate yourself and get into condition before you attempt to play football; never use it as a way to get yourself into condition!

SOCCER

Soccer players around the world typically try to play themselves into condition. In fact, we have heard of several United States professionals who said they were going to play themselves back into shape to rehabilitate their injury to a leg or knee.

If you are out of condition, either aerobically or anaerobically, there is no question that playing soccer will gradually improve both your aerobic and anaerobic capacity. Since the average soccer player is said to run about six and a half miles per game, that much aerobic conditioning and training is bound to improve aerobic capacity. But if you are in very poor condition, so much running will cause a great deal of fatigue, and fatigue greatly increases your risk of injuring muscles, tendons, or even knee cartilage (the meniscus), and knee and ankle ligaments. If you are trying to recuperate from an ankle, knee, or hip injury, the demands of soccer are far too great to safely use it to rehabilitate an injury. It is foolish to return to that much running without full prior rehabilitation of your lower-extremity injury.

If, however, you have a wrist or hand, elbow, or even shoulder injury, and have kept yourself in condition during the acute phase of the injury, it is possible to play with such an injury. But you must always be aware of proper falling techniques. Trips do occur in soccer; diving is part of the game, and if you land slightly out of control on your wrist, arm, or shoulder, you clearly could undo any healing that has occurred. In fact, it could greatly aggravate your injury. This is why we strongly recommend you *not* use soccer as a means of playing yourself back into shape or attempting to rehabilitate an injury.

BICYCLING

Bicycling, especially on a stationary bicycle, is an effective and safe exercise form. The stationary bicycle is quite helpful in rehabilitating hip, thigh, and knee injuries since it builds both strength and endurance without putting marked force on the joint surfaces of the knee or hip. By altering the height of the seat, you can dramatically change the amount of exercise and motion required in the hip or knee. There is some exercise benefit for the ankle as well, but the stationary bicycle is much more effective for the knee and hip. One word of caution: On an exercise bicycle, if you do not place your foot over the middle of the pedal but instead put all the pressure on the toes, you can develop Achilles tendinitis. If there are toe plates and your foot does not slide into them well, you should get longer toe plates.

Bicycling outdoors is an equally effective way to exercise the joints, but you face the obvious risk of falling and the occasional need to step off the bicycle. So if your leg is not rehabilitated enough to withstand great forces, it is not wise to risk bicycling outdoors. The same is even more important in bicycle racing. Until your leg is fully rehabilitated and can take the stress of a bad fall, it is very foolish to risk undoing the healing of an injury by resuming racing too soon.

Bicycles with downturned handlebars may look as though they would cause a great deal of strain on the lower back and be quite uncomfortable, but this is not the case. The important thing is to get a bicycle frame in which the seat and handlebars are proper for your height. I speak from personal experience. My old bicycle was the traditional three-speed with handlebars upright, but my new one had the larger frame with the downturned handlebars and was actually more comfortable because of the bigger frame. If you have a tendency to get backaches, it is well worth your while when you buy a bicycle to have it properly sized and fitted by an experienced bicycle dealer.

Bicycling outdoors places some pressure on the shoulders, elbows, and wrists. This should not be ignored if you have an upper-arm or shoulder injury. Check with your physician before you begin any bicycling as a means to stay fit while you are recuperating from an upper extremity injury.

Bicycling should never be the sole method of rehabilitating any injury, since it only trains in one plane, and there is also a tendency to rely on the machine. There is virtually no training in bicycling for the spin functions or twisting rotation movements, nor are any of the stabilizers stressed significantly in this form of exercise.

RACQUETBALL

Racquetball has been one of the boom sports. It became popular because it is very easy to learn and you can play well enough to have fun with only one or two lessons at most. It is a good form of exercise and you can work up a sweat without too much difficulty. If you were to play racquetball three or four times a week for one to one and a half hours each time, you would eventually achieve a reasonable level of aerobic fitness. However, if you are quite unfit, your knees and calves might become too fatigued during those first weeks of playing and you would be vulnerable to a muscle or tendon injury, or even a knee-cartilage injury if you twisted too suddenly. Shoulder tendinitis is an extremely common problem if you hit the ball incorrectly, and wrist tendinitis is common even if you hit the ball correctly. We strongly recommend the training system outlined later in the book prior to trying to play yourself into shape with racquetball.

There is virtually no athletic injury that can be benefited and rehabilitated by playing racquetball. The stress on the ankles and the Achilles tendons is far too great to risk playing racquetball unless any injuries to them have been fully rehabilitated, and the same is true of any knee or thigh injury. It is foolhardy in the healing phase of an elbow, wrist, or shoulder injury to play racquetball if the injury is on the side you hit the ball with, because hitting the racquetball itself can cause injuries to these joints. Moreover, there is no conceivable way that playing racquetball will rehabilitate your wrist, elbow, or shoulder injury. And racquetball involves a great deal of twisting and bending, which puts a great deal of stress on the spine. Any back problem or injury you had should be fully recuperated and rehabilitated prior to resuming the game; racquetball itself cannot be used as a way to rehabilitate your spine injury.

Racquetball is a high-performance activity which places inordinate demands upon various body segments. It is an excellent sport, but it is not a rehabilitative activity.

TENNIS

The tennis boom is over, yet many people still use tennis as a way to play themselves into shape or improve their overall conditioning.

Actually you have to be at least a very good "B" player and play primarily singles three or four days a week to really get any conditioning and aerobic training out of tennis. If you are at this level and playing singles, there is no question that it is an excellent form of exercise. There is a great deal of running, cutting, and use of the upper extremities. If you are an experienced player who has not gotten too out of shape, it is possible to play yourself into shape by going back judiciously. However, it is far better to go into an exercise program and develop the proper strength and mobility before trying to play tennis than to use tennis to achieve aerobic and anaerobic fitness.

If you have an injury, the stress of tennis is too great for you to resume playing until you have rehabilitated the injury. This is especially true for any injury of the wrist, elbow, or shoulder on the side that you use to hit the ball. Shoulder and elbow problems are extremely common in tennis. There is no conceivable way that hitting a tennis ball is going to rehabilitate an injury, and it can tear it down, delay healing, magnify the problem, or create other problems.

Ankle, knee, and hip injuries should be fully rehabilitated prior to returning to the stress of cutting in tennis because there is too great a risk of reinjuring these areas while running or stretching for a ball.

The same is true of spine injuries. One needs good spinal and abdominal musculature and a pain-free back to play tennis with any degree of vigor at all. The twisting motion to properly hit and reach for a ball puts a great deal of stress on the discs, muscles, and ligaments in the lower spine, so these areas must be in tiptop shape before you resume playing tennis.

We cannot think of any way that playing tennis could be effective or safe for rehabilitating injuries.

SWIMMING

Many authorities consider swimming the ideal form of exercise and rehabilitation. The point is debatable, but swimming is certainly quite a beneficial form of exercise. One of the reasons for this is that it eliminates gravity, so the normal strain of gravity is not present on your body. But moving yourself through water puts a different set of demands on your muscles, joints, and ligaments than moving on land does. Most of the exercise benefit of swimming is to the shoulders and upper body, except in the case of the breast stroke. The breast-stroke kick (frog kick) puts a great deal of rotation strain on the ankle and a great deal of ligament and cartilage strain on the knee.

Swimming is almost the ideal exercise for people with back troubles —as long as they avoid the butterfly stroke, which is extremely stressful to the lower back and can cause a severe structural abnormality in the lumbar spine by the repetitive nature of the force that it puts upon the back. Anyone with a back problem should never attempt the butterfly stroke. And competitive butterfliers who have back pain should not swim the stroke until the pain has disappeared. If pain is a persistent problem, we strongly recommend consultation with an orthopedic surgeon.

If you have been injured and want to try swimming, you should check with your physician regarding the specific nature of your injury, but there are very few injuries in which swimming cannot be an aid in the rehabilitative process. On the other hand it is virtually impossible to fully rehabilitate any injury exclusively with swimming, because sooner or later you are going to have to put gravity upon the injured part or lift weights if you have injured upper extremities. So while it is impossible to fully rehabilitate an injury with just swimming, it is possible to maintain or increase your level of aerobic fitness and at the same time facilitate rehabilitation with a fair degree of safety for most injuries.

SPEED AND FIGURE SKATING

Ice skating, both speed skating and figure skating, is a quite demanding sport and form of exercise. Upper-extremity injuries sometimes occur from falls after jumps or from being "wiped out" on turns, but other than that they are fairly uncommon. Skating does demand strong muscles in the legs and thighs and around the hips. Because of the demands on these muscle groups, if you are a skater it is recommended that you thoroughly rehabilitate and strengthen any injured lower extremity before you return to the ice.

If you have injured your knee ligaments seriously, you may have difficulty with some of the twisting, spinning, and jumping maneuvers. After any knee-ligament injury, do not return to these stressful maneuvers until you have fully and completely rehabilitated your injury, or you will certainly magnify your present problem or injure something else.

ROLLER SKATING

Roller skating has become another of our boom sports. Unfortunately, the injury rate in roller skating is still quite high. This is because many skaters fall, and injuries result from a skate's hitting ruts or cracks in pavements. Roller skating is an excellent form of exercise, but it should not be considered as a form of rehabilitation for any type of injury at all.

CROSS-COUNTRY SKIING

Cross-country skiing is probably the best single form of aerobic exercise known to modern man. It puts enormous energy demands on both the upper and lower extremities. The most fit athletes in the world are competitive cross-country skiers on an international level. But cross-country skiing can be an extremely mild form of exercise if you do it slowly and gently. It is much easier on the knees, ankles, and hips than running. In many respects it is similar to cycling: It puts weightbearing stress on the arms and shoulders, and is not too stressful for the spine. Cross-country skiing is an excellent form of exercise that is gentle, yet can be quite vigorous.

However, because it puts weightbearing stress on both the upper and lower extremities, we do not recommend it for rehabilitation of any injury. Furthermore, cold air increases the stress on the heart, so if you have heart trouble, it is not recommended.

DOWNHILL SKIING

Downhill skiing is a good form of exercise. There is, however, significant risk of injury to the knee ligaments, especially since it requires deep squats on one or both legs, with a force of from 200 to 400 pounds when jumping small hills or holes. Broken legs also are a risk. The common upper extremity injuries are injuries to the thumb ligament or the shoulders.

There is no injury that can safely be rehabilitated by downhill skiing. However, modern ski boots are so good that it is quite possible to ski even in the presence of an ankle injury. The boots provide almost as much protection to the ankle as a cast does.

It is quite possible to return to downhill skiing after most injuries if there has been intensive rehabilitation. Downhill skiing is possible after most athletic injuries with proper training and conditioning, but it should never be used to rehabilitate an injury.

GYMNASTICS

Most experienced gymnasts realize that it is impossible to work one's way into condition by just doing gymnastics. Early on they recognize that they need appropriate training and strengthening prior to doing gymnastics maneuvers; the maneuvers themselves are not sufficient as a method of improving their strength, full range of motion, and agility.

If that is true for a healthy gymnast, it is doubly true for an injured gymnast. I can't think of an athletic injury that can be safely rehabilitated by doing gymnastics alone. Even minor finger injuries are stressed in gymnastic maneuvers, as are minor toe injuries and every injury in between. You must fully rehabilitate your injury prior to returning to gymnastics rather than using gymnastics and its maneuvers as a form of rehabilitation.

RUNNING

Before the running boom in this country began, many physicians and trainers looked upon running as a form of rehabilitation and therapy rather than as a goal. With football and baseball as the primary sports, there never was need to run any great distance, and the stress of the repetitive pounding of distance running was not appreciated.

The emphasis then was on the ability of the athlete to run a figure-eight, or "cut," as a test for rehabilitation rather than on his ability to run in a straight line. However, that was only for a distance of yards, not miles.

But when athletes began to run significant mileage, it became obvious to everyone treating athletic injuries how stressful running is on the knees. In fact, long distance running is an extremely demanding activity that puts enormous stress on the knee and all its structures and on the ankle-joint surface. It is both difficult and dangerous to run long distances with any type of abnormality within the knee or in the joint surface of the ankle joint. If you are not structurally stable, distance running will almost inevitably lead to some type of injury.

Running, therefore, is a goal of rehabilitation rather than a form of rehabilitation. It is one of the *last* things an athlete is permitted to do. Even after arthroscopic surgery, the most minor of surgeries in the knee, running is discouraged for a minimum of six to eight weeks; after knee-ligament surgery, it may be discouraged for as long as six months. And there are some injuries that may require a year of healing before running can be resumed. The repetitive shock of running puts enormous stress on the ankle, knee, and hip joints; the bones of the lower leg and thigh; and on the muscles, ligaments, and tendons. If they are not in top shape, these structures will react with pain and inflammation; you will have created a new injury situation rather than rehabilitated an old injury.

One of the most difficult problems in the rehabilitation of athletes is teaching them to accept a certain degree of disability. Even in the case of a significant knee or ankle injury, it is often possible—with good rehabilitation and hard work—for the athlete to return to many of the sports we have listed here, including tennis, racquetball, football, baseball, volleyball, bicycling, swimming, roller skating, and skiing. However, after any serious knee or ankle injury, it is very rare that an athlete can return to long-distance running. Long-distance running puts maximal strain on the knee and ankle, so a joint that is good enough for most other sports simply won't hold up under the pounding and stresses of what many people mistakenly believe is an easy sport. It can be very difficult for someone who has fallen in love with long-distance running to accept the fact that there are limits to the mileage that they will be able to put on their knees and ankles, and that those limits are usually much lower than they are happy to accept. So while rehabilitation can get them back to almost any other sport, they may very well have to give up long-distance running. If they like endurance-type sports, they should consider switching to bicycling, cross-country skiing, or swimming.

PART TWO

THE TOTAL BODY TRAINING PROGRAM

12

Progression

Milo of Corinth, so the ancient story goes, carried a baby calf on his shoulders every day. You can guess what happened—as the calf grew, so did Milo's muscles. Finally Milo amazed all by carrying a bull on his shoulders around the amphitheater floor. The secret? Milo grew with his weights.

But a modern Milo wouldn't have such great success. He would have a sore foot and not practice, he would forget, or maybe the baby calf would get sick. The end result is that the modern Milo would not grow with his weight. But then Milo would probably decide to make up for lost time and pick a bigger calf to work on, or perhaps he would want to test how good he really is by trying to lift an entire bull. The result would be injury and setback, and the fame of our modern Milo would not reach any record books.

This tends to be the American habit: We try to measurably increase every day. Our goal is more and more; our progress (or lack of it) can make us fatigued, excited or depressed. We train as if we are trying to peak every day. Europeans, on the other hand, use a system of cycles and percentages. For example, your goal is that at the end of six weeks you will be able to lift 105 percent of the weight you can now lift. So you set up a progression. Your first step is to establish your one-time maximum. Using correct form, you measure the maximum weight that you can lift one time only. (If you can do it twice, it is not your maximum.) The first week you would do five reps at 70 percent of your maximum; the next week, three reps at 90 percent; and the third week, ten reps at 70 percent. For the fourth week, do five reps at 80 percent, followed the next week by three reps at 90 percent and finally one rep at 105 percent the sixth week. Then begin your program all over again with a new one-time maximum. With this system you would never try to do the entire weight in one pop.

There are sound reasons for adopting a progression system. For one thing, your body is stressed if your workouts are done properly in the correct form. Even workouts on the O-beam and K-board can be quite strenuous, and workouts on the soft down jump box (see Chapters 16, 17, and 19) are quite vigorous. We recommend heavy workouts of any type on no more than alternating days, in order to let your body recover and maximally benefit from your training routine.

We discussed how lactic acid builds up in each muscle when you use anaerobic energy, and how it must be buffered to take away the acidity. Since no one cell or group of cells contains a buffer level high enough to fully neutralize the acid built up in performing, blood circulation must take the acid across many cells in order to neutralize it. Heavy workouts only on alternating days will train the buffer levels to increase to the needed amount, with the result that the pain won't be great but the gain will be there.

Most athletes are chomping at the bit to get on with their training and rehabilitation. They always want to push things. While one of the gratifying aspects of treating athletes is that most of them are highly motivated and intent upon maximizing their performance potential, it is important that they progress in an orderly fashion from one phase to another, not attempt to leapfrog and take short cuts.

We insist that: 1 You take no short cuts. 2 You do each exercise properly, using proper form to maintain structural integrity. 3 You don't progress to the next level until you have completely finished the level you are at. 4 You progress only according to the formula that we outline in each chapter on exercise routines.

Whether you are simply out of shape and trying to get back into form, or recovering from an injury, the progression is the same. That is, you must first do the dynamic range of motion exercises. You should not progress beyond the D'ROM routine for any joint or series of motions until you have at least 75 percent of the possible range of motion for that joint—and preferably the full ROM. Second, you progress to exercises using bands; then you progress to those using beams and boards. Only when you can do full routines of D'ROM, bands, beams, and boards may you progress to boxes and maximal-performance training and activities.

If you shortcut these steps or attempt to run or play too soon, you will have not completed your training or rehabilitation and will instead risk aggravating your old injury and even creating new ones.

SOME SIGNIFICANT DEFINITIONS

Before we get into the specific exercise routine, we must define some basic terms so that everyone knows what we are talking about.

Reps Reps is short for repetitions. The term is commonly used in exercise routines by weight lifters and athletes. To do five reps of an exercise would be to perform that exercise five times in a row without resting in between.

Sets A set is one complete exercise routine. We often recommend doing three sets of a routine per workout although a key to successful training is to vary the number of sets you do, the speed with which you do them, and the amount of resistance you apply.

Concentric A concentric action of a muscle is the contraction or shortening of the muscle while it is doing work. (In the Nautilus system, this is called a "positive" muscle action.) A good example of a muscle's concentric action is when you "make a muscle" in your upper arm by flexing your biceps as you bend your elbow.

Eccentric An eccentric action of a muscle is a detraction or lengthening of the muscle while it is doing work. (In the Nautilus system this is called a "negative" muscle action, which we believe is a confusing term.) An example of an eccentric muscle action would be the reverse of "making a muscle" in your upper arm; if you held a weight in your hand that forced your elbow to go from bent to straight, the lengthening of your biceps as you resisted that force would be an eccentric muscle action. It is important to realize that the muscles continue to work in both directions, whether you are bending the arm or straightening it.

Acceleration and Deceleration A muscle works by making something move or by slowing something down. The action of a muscle in making something move is called acceleration; the action of braking is called deceleration (or negative acceleration). Muscles work in both directions and we must train them in both directions.

Strength Strength is the ability to move something that resists being moved. For example, the ability to lift fifty pounds one foot off the ground would show a certain amount of strength.

Stamina Stamina is the ability to move something that resists being moved for a certain amount of time; it is the ability to do reps. For example, being able to lift fifty pounds a foot off the ground, let it back down, and repeat this action for several minutes requires more stamina than lifting the fifty pounds once.

Power Power is the ability to very quickly move from one point to another something that resists being moved. In other words, power enables you to move something fast. You are more powerful if you can lift fifty pounds one foot in one-hundredth of a second than if it takes you one second to move it. Most trainers think that increasing strength directly increases speed. Actually, you need to train for power to increase speed. You obviously need strength to train for power, but to increase speed in any activity, you must specifically train for power.

Terminal Flicks Terminal flicks are repetitions of the last few inches at the extreme of any exercise. You just flick through the last 10 to 30 degrees of motion. Terminal flicks build up stamina and strength.

ROM "ROM" is short for range of motion, which is the arc through which a body part moves. The limits of a joint's range of motion depend upon the actual anatomic construction of the joint, the ligaments around the sides of the joint, the tendons that connect the muscles to the bones that move the joints, and the muscles themselves that move the body part.

TRAIN SMART

If you do your exercise routines properly, they will help get you into shape and will definitely enhance your performance in all competitive and recreational sports, including dance. In addition, you will probably strengthen all of the muscles in your arms and legs. In walking, and even more so in running, twisting, and jumping, we use all of our muscles. Many muscles function as midcourse correctors, stabilizers, or brakes, rather than as prime movers. The failure of most training systems is that they only increase strength in the "prime movers," the obvious large muscles in front and back, and they fail to train all muscles completely. For peak performance, you must train all of your muscles.

Here are some basic guidelines for all forms of resistance training—weights, power bands, machines, springs, pulleys, isokinetics, or even gravity.

First, train smart—don't strain. By training smart, we mean train with knowledge. You must know what you are doing and the reasons behind it. You must know the benefits and the liabilities and limitations. You must keep the overall system in mind and use order in your progression. The second part, "don't strain," may sound almost heretical. But we are firmly convinced that there is no physical benefit in pain. We want an athlete or individual to build up, not tear down, and pain is usually a sign of breaking down. If your system of training is orderly, you should be planning for balanced development, which means that you won't overpower any group of muscles. Look at the following four basic guidelines and see how the balance is maintained. This is the order we recommend you follow for any exercise routine, illustrated on the following pages.

1. Flexion followed by extension. First bend the joint, then straighten it out.
2. Protraction followed by retraction. This is especially important for the shoulder, where protraction is pulling the shoulder blades forward; retraction is pulling them together and back.

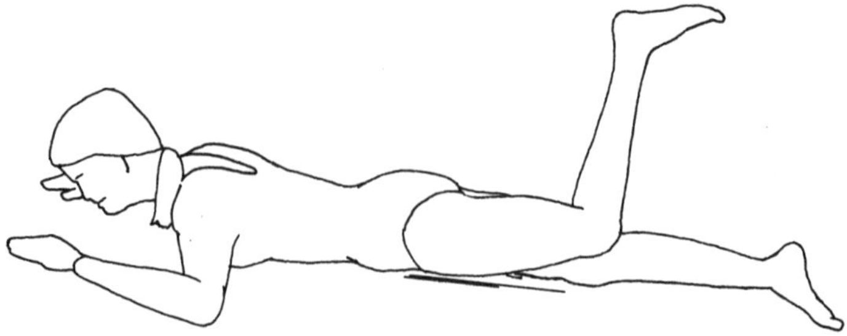

Flexion–extension *In this example, the knee is flexed while the hip is extended.*

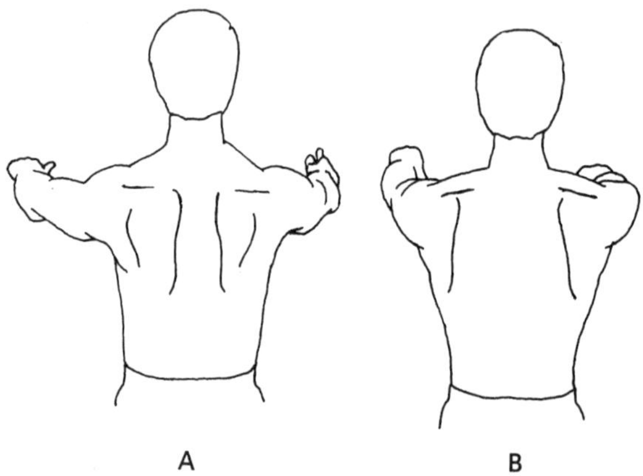

Protraction–retraction *Figure A shows shoulder or scapular retraction. Figure B shows scapular protraction.*

3. Elevation followed by depression. This applies to any of the core and shoulder muscles, as well as to the hips and ribs. Moving the shoulders toward the ears is elevation (this is sometimes called "the shrug"). Depression is seldom done because the weight of gravity does it constantly.
4. Outward spins followed by inward spins (rotation). This is an important practice that is often ignored. In the hand it would be supination followed by pronation, which is palms up, then palms down. At the shoulder, it is outward then inward spins. At the hip it is likewise outward and then inward spins.

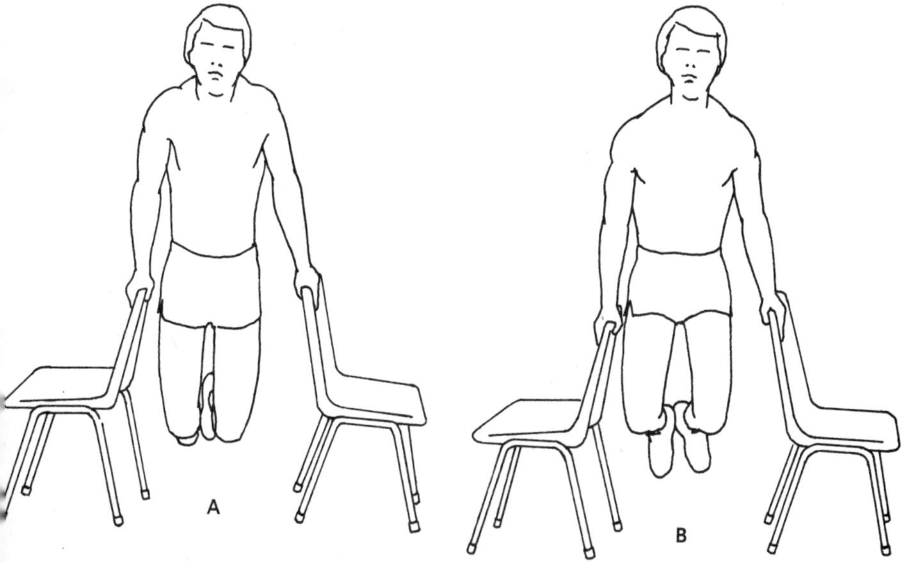

Elevation–depression *Elevation of the shoulder blades, or scapulae, is shown in figure A. Depression of the scapulae is shown in figure B.*

Spins or rotations *Figure A shows outward or external rotation of the knee; figure B shows inward or internal rotation.*

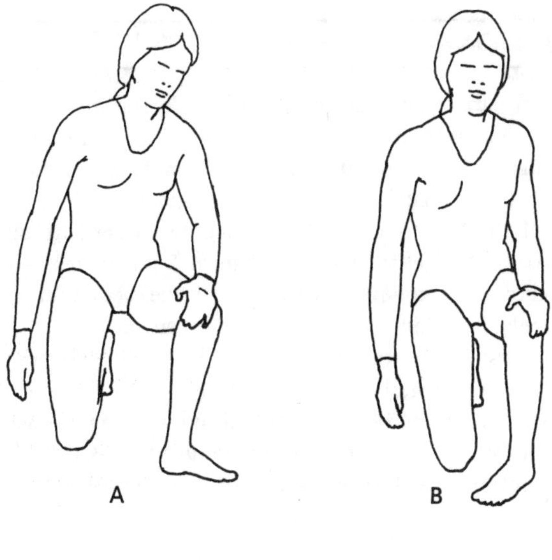

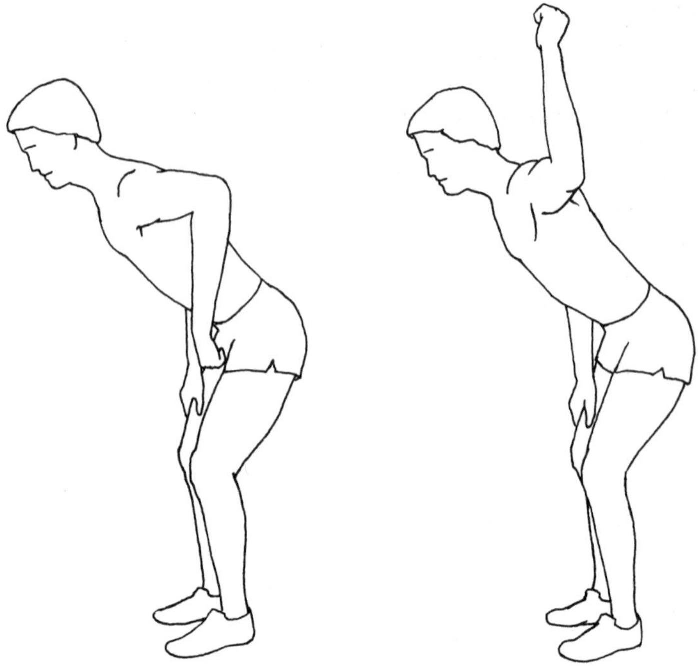

A B

Shoulder rotation *Internal (A) and external (B) shoulder rotations.*

REPETITIONS

The second part of any plan is how often do you do the exercises. Think in terms of complete repetitions, which are full trips over the whole range of motion, from full extension to full flexion. It is possible in doing repetitions to do only a quarter, a half, or three-quarters of the trip. But usually you should concentrate on a full range of motion to get the complete benefit from the rep.

In talking about training smart, one of the significant advances you can make is to think up sets of varying exercises that use different muscle groups. By exercising continually but with different muscle groups you can get the best of two worlds.

First, you will get aerobic training because your body will be continually exercised. Remember, aerobic training means that you must exercise continuously for at least two minutes before the "with oxygen" system kicks on. Also remember that even though your sport may be primarily short performance, you still need the aerobic training to allow you to better handle the built-up lactic acid produced by any performance.

The second benefit of this system is that you would not overstrain one muscle group or several groups by doing high reps, which could be damaging. By combining exercises you would also compress your workout time, since you won't need the rest period between sets of the same exercise.

SUMMARY

Beginning programs usually include three sequences of six exercises each done for one set. Repetitions should follow this rationale: Use six to ten reps for small muscle groups like the arms, and fifteen to twenty for legs and other large groups.

Remember that a muscle cannot be forced into growth. It must be coaxed gradually. If you are using weights, start with light weights and build up reps, then reduce reps and add weight—after which you start the whole rep increase program over again. You can also increase the number of sets to three. It may be more important, however, to think in terms of increasing sequences once you reach a certain point. Remember the principle of balance!

13

Dynamic Range of Motion Training

As you will recall from Chapter 4, dynamic range of motion, which we abbreviate D'ROM (pronounced *D-prime-R-O-M*), is that part of a joint's potential range of motion over which you have active muscular control. D'ROM training helps you realize fully your potential range of motion, with full muscle control throughout it.

D'ROM training is the basis of rehabilitation of all athletic injuries, and it is used as the basic warm-up prior to vigorous training. We use the D'ROM routine instead of stretching exercises, since it gives all the benefits that stretching exercises are supposed to give without causing any of the injuries that often happen to those who stretch.

An easy way to remember your D'ROM routine is to start at your hips and knees; work down to the feet and ankles; then do your shoulders, which will also work your elbows. Then proceed to the core training routine. To remember the sequence of exercises for each joint, just keep in mind the fact that all joints bend and straighten (flex and extend); some joints also either bend sideways or rotate; and some joints are capable of all three kinds of motion. For example, the hip and shoulder flex and extend, they bend to the side (abduction/adduction) and they also rotate. So the D'ROM routine begins with flexion and extension and then proceeds to sideways bending and finally rotation, covering as many of those movements as are possible for each joint. This will warm up all of the muscles that move your joints and improve your performance potential immensely.

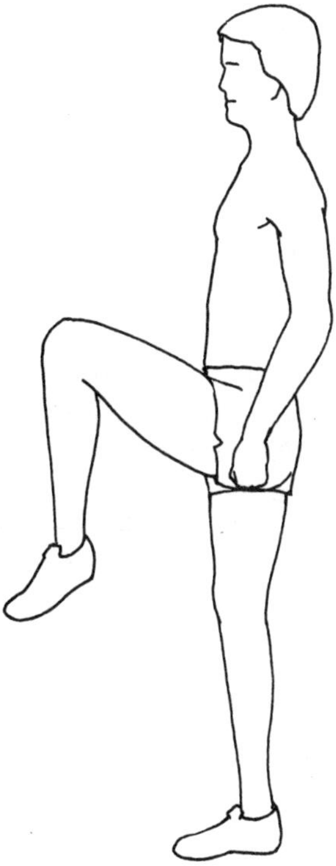

Hip flexion *Rom: 0 to 120 degrees. Standing with knee flexed or extended, do 5 to 15 reps, followed by a short burst of terminal flicks.*

Hip flexion *Rom: 0 to 120 degrees. Lying supine with knee extended, you may either dorsiflex foot (bend foot up, as shown here) or point toes. Do 5 to 15 reps, followed by a short burst of terminal flicks.*

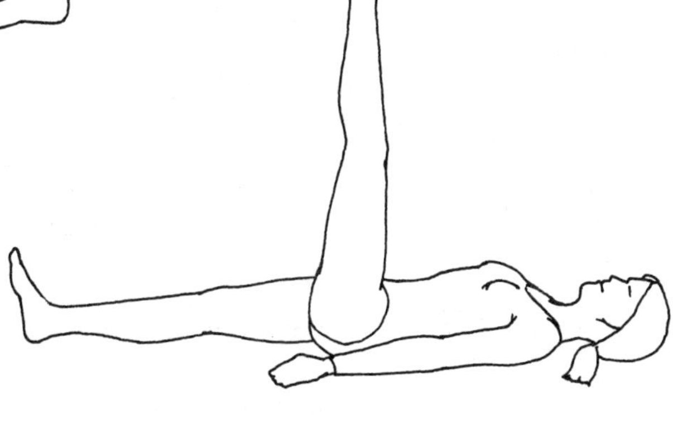

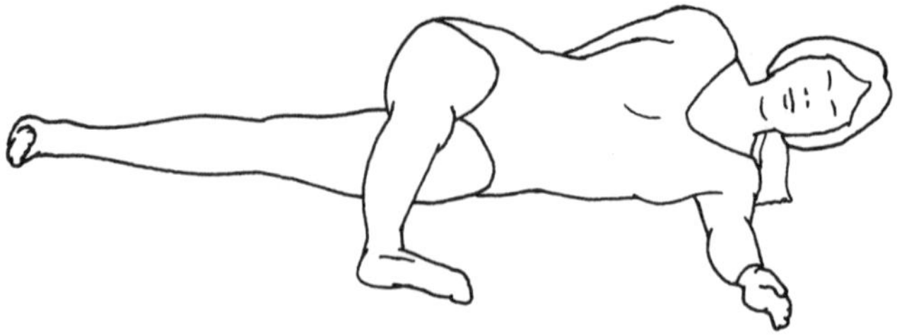

Hip flexion *ROM: 0 to 120 degrees. Side-lying, with knee straight, do 5 to 15 reps, followed by a short burst of terminal flicks.*

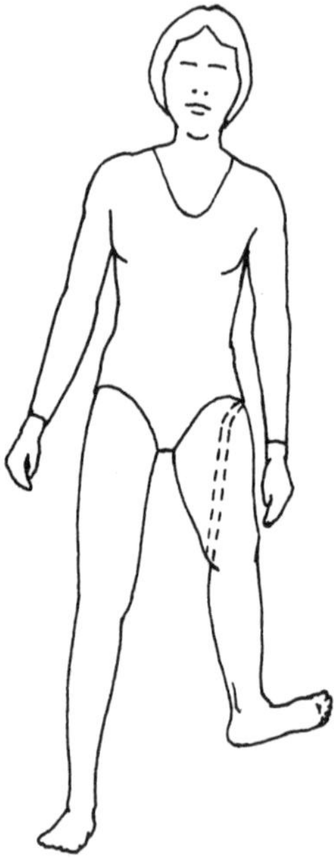

Sartorius isolation *The sartorius muscle crosses the front of the thigh, approximately where the dotted area indicates. In a standing position, flex the hip and rotate the entire leg outwards approximately 45 degrees. Then flex the hip from 0 to 90 degrees. Do 5 to 15 reps with a short burst of terminal flicks.*

Hip hyperextension *In prone position (face down), bend knee; then extend hip by raising leg off the ground from 0 to 15 degrees. Do 5 to 15 reps with a short burst of terminal flicks.*

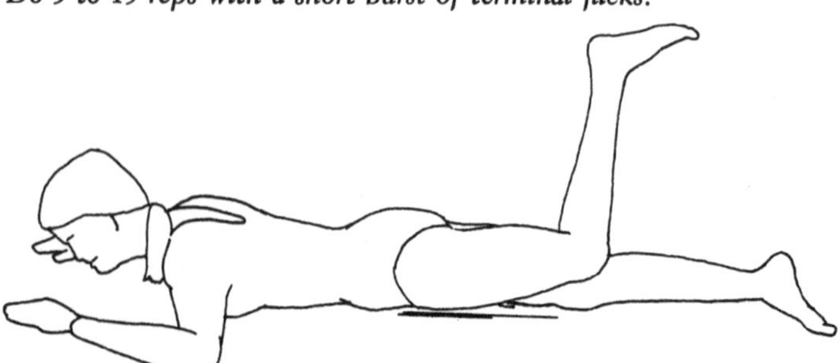

Hip abduction ROM: *0 to 45 degrees. This can be done either standing or lying. Do 5 to 15 reps, then do a burst of terminal flicks.*

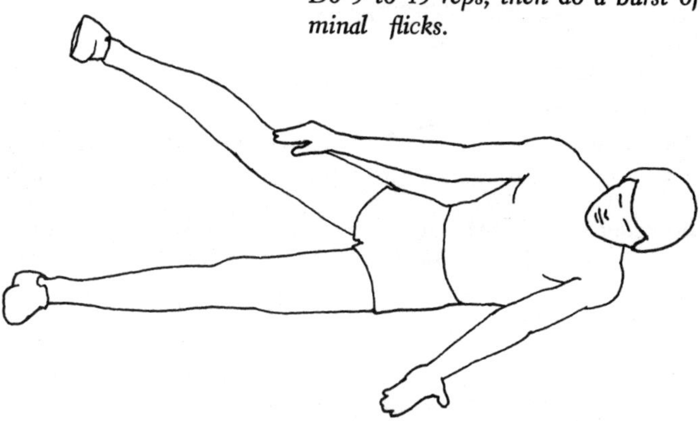

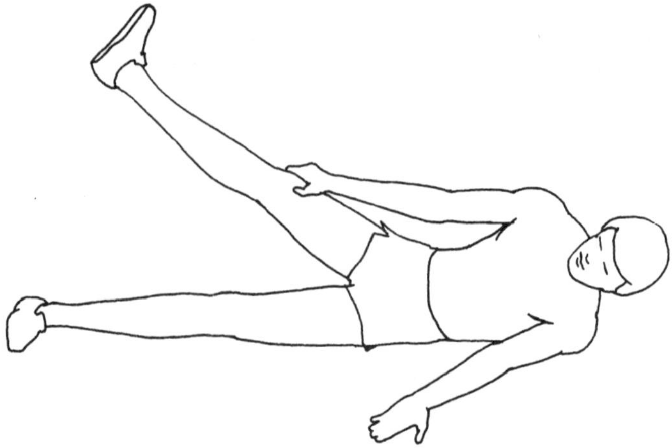

Improper form for hip abduction *When the hip is externally rotated, it is not appropriate for either hip flexion or hip abduction. This is a hybrid and will not accomplish the training goals.*

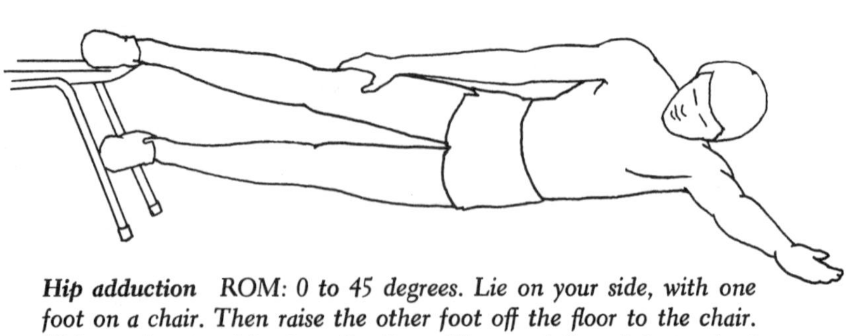

Hip adduction ROM: *0 to 45 degrees. Lie on your side, with one foot on a chair. Then raise the other foot off the floor to the chair. This motion is adduction. Do 5 to 15 reps, followed by a short burst of terminal flicks.*

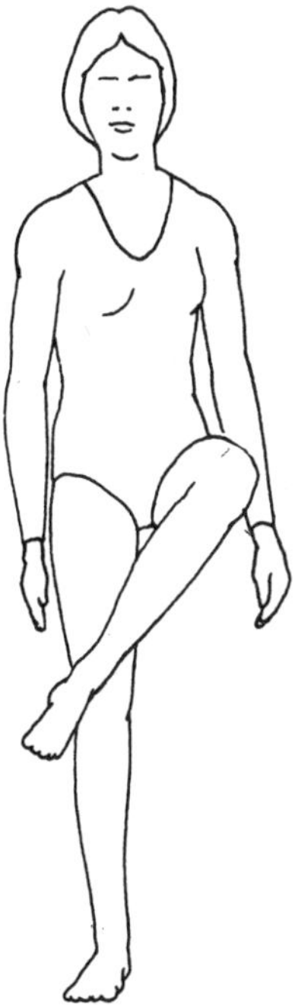

External rotation of hip ROM: 0 to 45 degrees. *This is done in a standing position, with the knee flexed 90 degrees. Move the foot inward; this rotates the hip outward. Do 5 to 15 reps, followed by a short burst of terminal flicks.*

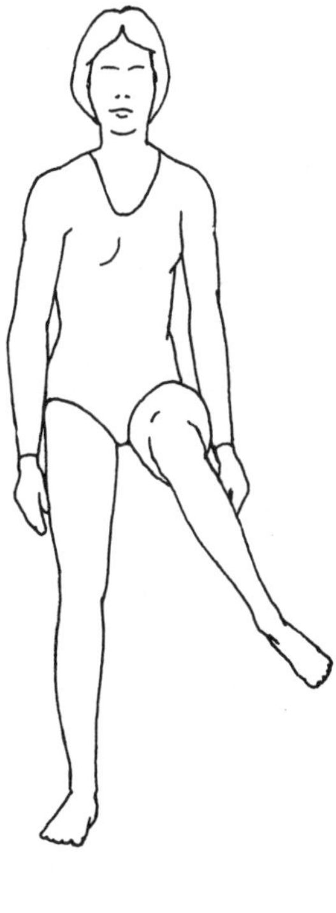

Internal rotation of hips ROM: 0 to 45 degrees. *Done in a standing position, with the knee flexed 90 degrees. Note that moving the foot outward rotates the hip inward. Do 5 to 15 reps, followed by a short burst of terminal flicks.*

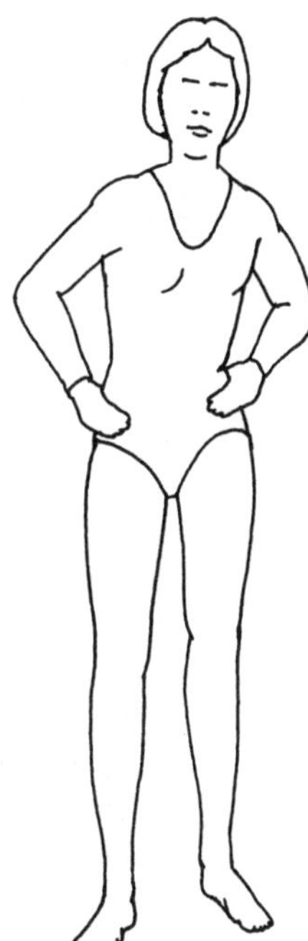

Hip hiker ROM: 0 to 15 *degrees. Raise the leg off the ground by hiking the hip. Do 5 to 15 reps.*

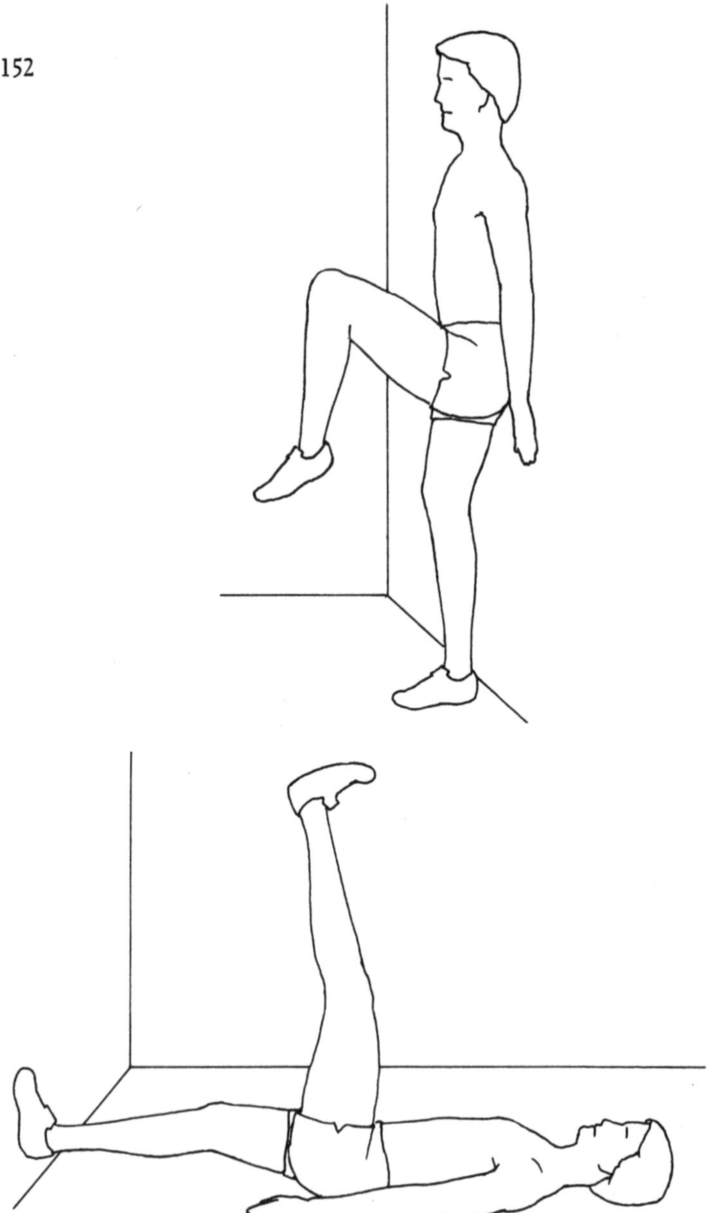

Knee extension and flexion *ROM: 0 to 120 degrees. Can be done either lying or while standing and leaning against a wall. Do 5 to 15 reps with short burst of terminal flicks at the extreme of the extension (when knee is straight) and flexion (when knee is bent).*

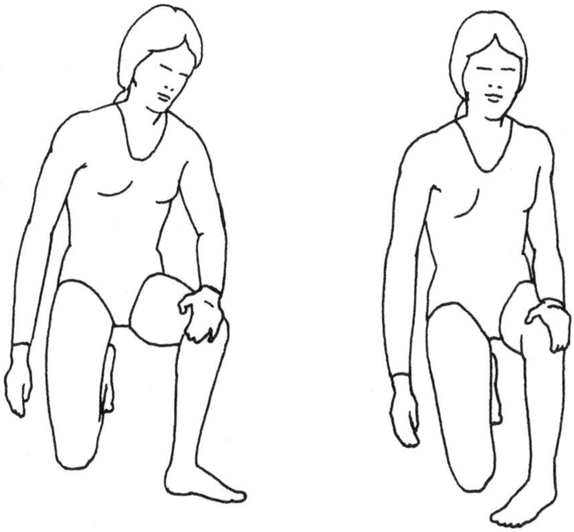

Internal and external rotation of the knee *Kneel on one knee and rotate your foot outward and then inward. Do 5 to 15 reps with a burst of terminal flicks at the extreme of outward (external) rotation and inward (internal) rotation.*

Plantar flexion (heel raises) ROM: 0 to 60 degrees. *Do 5 to 15 reps with short bursts of terminal flicks.*

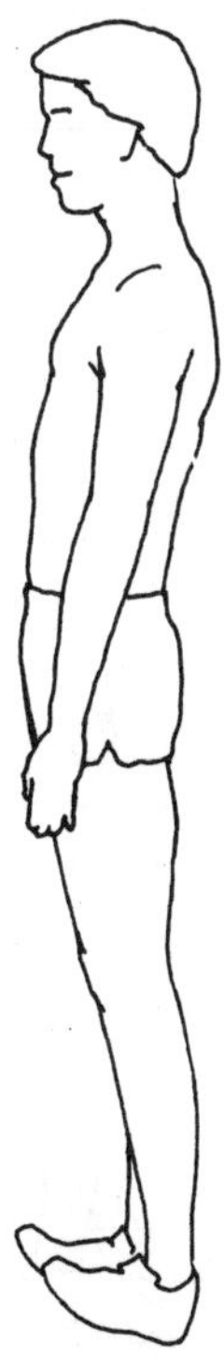

Dorsiflexion (toe raises) ROM: 0 to 45 degrees. *Stand on your heels with toes up. Do 5 to 15 reps, followed by a short burst of terminal flicks.*

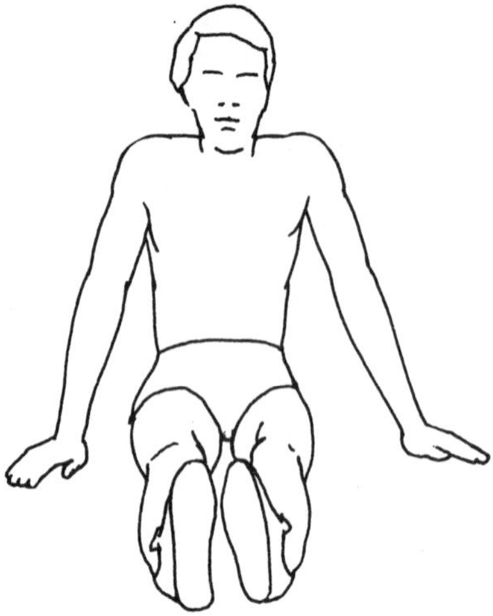

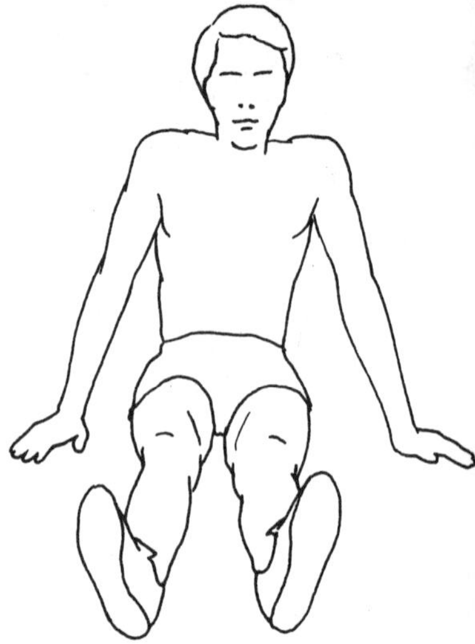

Supination *ROM: 0 to 45 degrees. Rotate heels and foot inward. Do 5 to 15 reps followed by a short burst of terminal flicks.*

Pronation *ROM: 0 to 25 degrees. Rotate heels and feet outward Do 5 to 15 reps followed by a short burst of terminal flicks.*

Shoulder girdle internal and external rotation *Complete internal rotation of the shoulder girdle (glenohumeral joint) with elbow flexed is shown in figure A. Do 5 to 15 reps followed by short bursts of terminal flicks. Figure B shows complete external rotation; again, do 5 to 15 reps followed by short bursts of terminal flicks.*

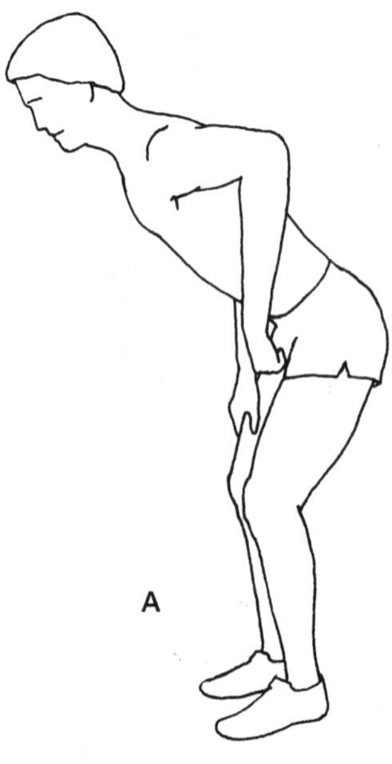

A

B

Abduction and forward flexion of shoulder girdle with internal rotation *Turn arms with thumbs out for external rotation. Do 5 to 15 reps followed by short bursts of terminal flicks.*

Scapular elevation and depression This *can be done as illustrated or simply by shrugging your shoulders and then depressing them. Doing it as illustrated uses your body weight for greater training. Do 5 to 15 reps followed by short bursts of terminal flicks at both maximum elevation and maximum depression.*

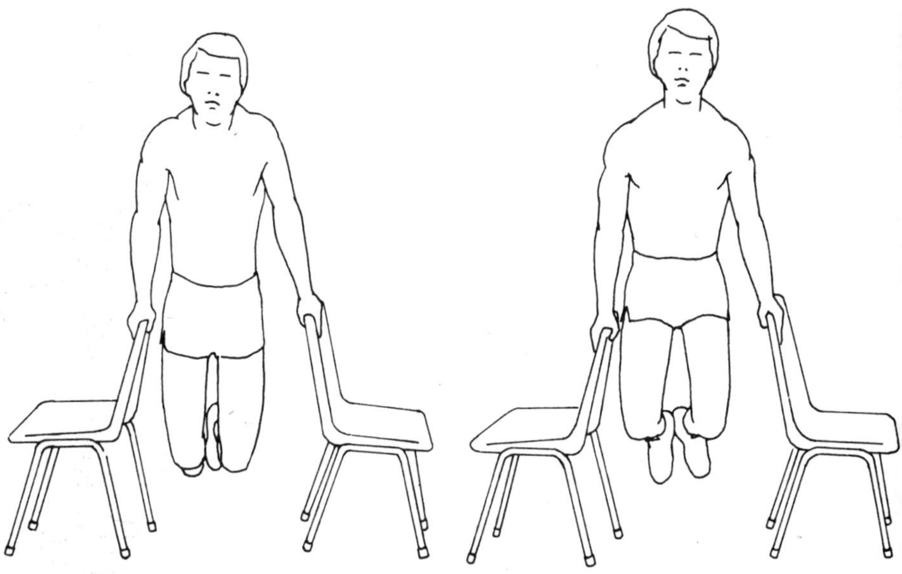

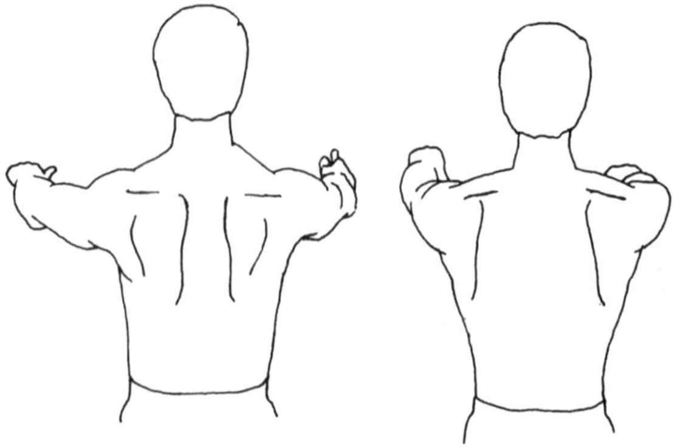

A B

Scapular protraction and retraction *Marked scapular retraction is shown in figure A, protraction in figure B. Do 5 to 15 reps followed by short bursts of terminal flicks at the ends of the motion in both protracted and retracted positions.*

You now have completed a full D'ROM training routine. Of course, you should have exercised both the right and the left sides. You will note that you are completely warmed up and you have not wasted ten to twenty minutes by stretching. Instead, you have already had the beginnings of a good workout. Now advance to the core training routine.

14

Training the Core

Most commonly used exercise programs emphasize the development of arm and leg muscles. The design of exercise machines such as the Paramount and Universal also implicitly emphasizes building up the peripheral "show muscles" of the arms and legs. In contrast, we believe that if you want the best performance you are capable of producing, you must make development of the core muscles a top priority.

The core muscles are centrally located in the body. We all know that the body's center of gravity is not located in a leg or an arm; it is in the core. Stabilization of the center gives the extremities freedom to move, and allows both the arms and legs to be much more efficient. If you want ultimate control over your extremities, you must develop a stable, strong core that can meet any movement stress.

The core muscles are those muscles that act to stabilize the body while it is being maintained in an erect, antigravity position; while one of your arms or legs is being propelled or slowed down; or while you are doing activities like squatting, jumping, shoveling snow, or lifting weights overhead.

The core muscles control the head, neck, ribs, spine, and pelvis. Control of the core is the sum of controls of each one of these components. Thus, in training the core, we are particularly interested in developing those muscles that connect the head to the neck and those that connect the torso to the pelvis.

As we noted previously, development of the muscles of the core provides a significant guard against injuries. The emphasis in most exercise programs is to make one stronger, bigger, or faster, or to foster cardiovascular improvement along with flexibility and endurance. Focusing on these goals is usually done at the expense of learning how to effectively stabilize the center of the body in the most efficient manner for minimizing injury and optimizing function.

SPECIFIC SKILLS TO BE DEVELOPED WITH CORE TRAINING

Neck Lock

The neck-lock action consists of tucking in the chin to elevate the head and elongate the cervical spine. Merely tilting the head either backward or forward fails to introduce the lock action. Centering the head should become a reflex.

Rib Lock (Depression)

The rib lock involves depressing your ribs by contracting the upper abdominal muscles—as if preparing for a blow from the middleweight champion. You'll want to develop this control so that rib depression can occur while lifting your arms overhead, withstanding a blow, performing basic movement actions like walking and running, and bending forward, sideward, or backward—whenever your upper body is not directly upright.

You will note that this action is uneducated in most humans because rib depression is a passive process, performed without muscle action during both quiet and deep respiration. Muscular rib depression occurs only during forced breathing, so it is an ability that will improve only through training.

Full Rib Elevation

Rib elevation is another action that most people never develop. Being able to elevate and fix the first two ribs, thus allowing for the raising of the lower ribs, will obviously aid greatly in respiration. Practicing rib elevation will also help you develop your feel for rib lock, the opposite training.

Development of Full Spinal Mobility

The five major directions in which the spine moves are bending forward (flexion), bending backward (extension), bending to both sides, and rotation. These happen either individually or, more often, as combinations. Certain of the muscles usually function only as balance correctors, and so do not come into play unless there is some movement. Since sports activities involve so much strenuous movement, adequate training is imperative, both for performance and for injury prevention.

Control Over the Pelvis

The curve of your lower back (called the lordotic curve) will become greater as you squat and will become less pronounced in actions such as easy standing. It is the tilting of the pelvis that allows these motions to occur easily. The pelvis also provides the base for all movement of your legs, so providing a stable, efficient base of action is extremely important.

Scapular Retraction

Scapular retraction is the ability to control the shoulder assembly. Most people have developed the pull-forward part of the shoulder much more fully than the pull-backward part. This creates an imbalance in body control and endangers the shoulder during throwing motions, especially during the shunt or slowdown portion of the motion.

HOW IS CORE TRAINING DONE?

Remember that these core muscles are made of slow-twitch red fibers. They are capable of generating a slow, sustained contraction. Thus they are perfectly suited to continually supporting the body against movement shocks, gravity, and heavy weights.

To train these muscles, we need a slow, steady, sustained effort rather than twenty quick reps. Save the fast work for training the arms and legs. If you correctly train your core, your extremity action will also improve because you will have an even better base.

Training begins in the mind. You have to be aware of your ability to put the core in a stable position. This calls for attention to the exercises, with a focus on what is needed and concentration on doing them correctly. Your body, meanwhile, must be taught how each movement feels, so that the movement becomes an automatic correction when needed. Awareness of the tone of the muscles and a sense of where they are constitute important parts of body education.

You will use three types of muscle action. The first is *concentric*, or shortening. When a muscle develops tension sufficient to overcome a resistance so that the muscle moves a body part in spite of the resistance (for example, when a weight lifter performs curls), it is in the concentric mode.

The second mode is *static*. This is a holding at the terminal point, the classic isometric position. In the static state, the muscle effort has changed so that instead of shortening or lengthening, it is balanced in a state of equilibrium.

The third mode is *eccentric*. In the eccentric mode the muscle is being caused by resistance to extend or lengthen.

THE NECK

The following exercises will help you protect and even develop your neck movements. Starting exercises do not use any weight except that of the head.

Basic Neck Development

Mastery of this starting level should be accomplished in a relatively short period. After this period, which is usually no longer than a month, the exercises become too easy.

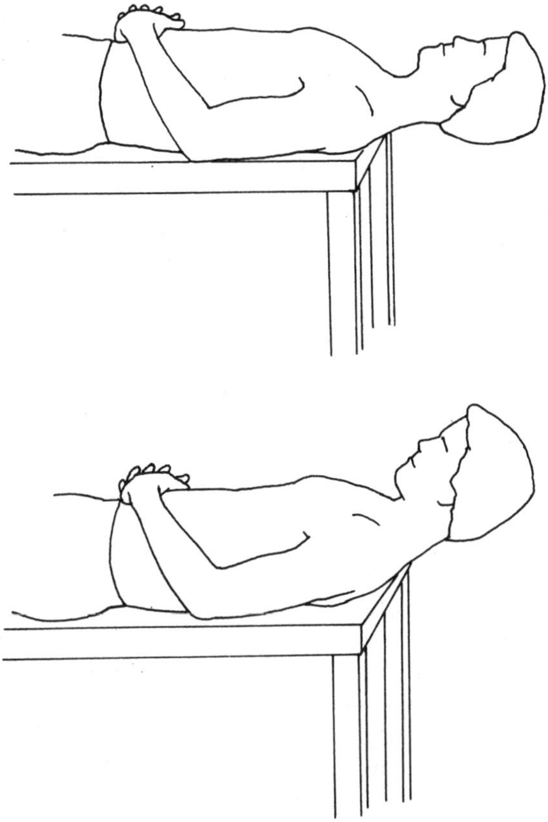

Forward neck bends (neck flexion)   Do 12 reps, 3 to 5 sets.

1. FORWARD NECK BENDS (NECK FLEXION)

Lie in a supine position (facing upward) on a table. Your head should be held over the edge of a bench with your shoulders remaining on the table. Let your head move down and backward toward the floor, but move it down slowly, with control. You are practicing eccentric contraction—maintaining resistance even though the muscles are lengthening. From this position, first tuck chin and move the head upward toward the chest, then continue lifting head as far as possible. Stop just before shoulders lift off the table. Then, slowly lower head, keeping chin tucked. Repeat in a progressive manner, finally getting up to 12 reps for 3 to 5 sets in sequence with all the other exercises in order to get both aerobic and anaerobic training.

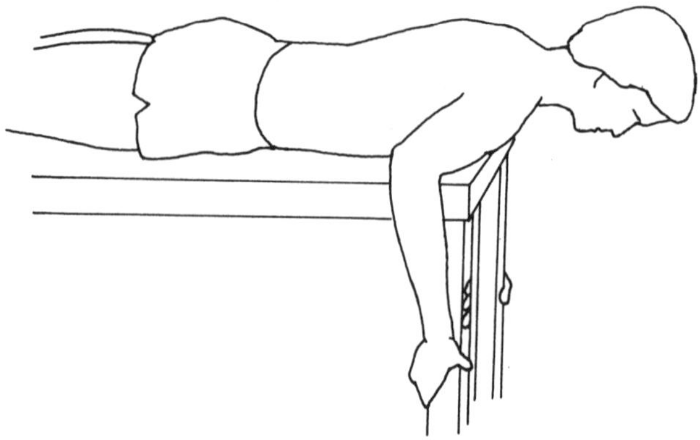

Backward neck bends (neck extension) *Do 12 reps, 3 to 5 sets.*

2. BACKWARD NECK BENDS (NECK EXTENSION)

Assume a prone position on the bench. Let both arms hang straight down over the edge of the bench and grip the bench legs. Move head slowly (with resistance again) down all the way so chin is tucked to chest. First, backward bend or extend head back so chin moves away from chest; then lift head up, extending the neck. Stop before shoulders leave table. Lower slowly until chin touches chest again. Do repetitions in a progressive manner.

3. SIDE NECK BENDS (LATERAL FLEXION)

Assume a position lying on either side. The bottom arm should be placed straight down over the edge of the bench for support. The back should be perfectly straight, the top shoulder pointing toward the ceiling. Your head should be in the neutral position; that is, horizontal to the floor and looking straight ahead. With resistance, lower your head so the bottom ear touches the bottom shoulder, then laterally flex your neck, trying to touch the top ear to the top shoulder. Stop before your shoulder leaves the table. Take care not to forward bend or backward bend, or to rotate your head to either side while performing the exercise. Then lower your head all the way until the bottom ear touches the bottom shoulder. Turn over, and repeat the entire exercise on your other side. You should work both sides equally and in a progressive manner.

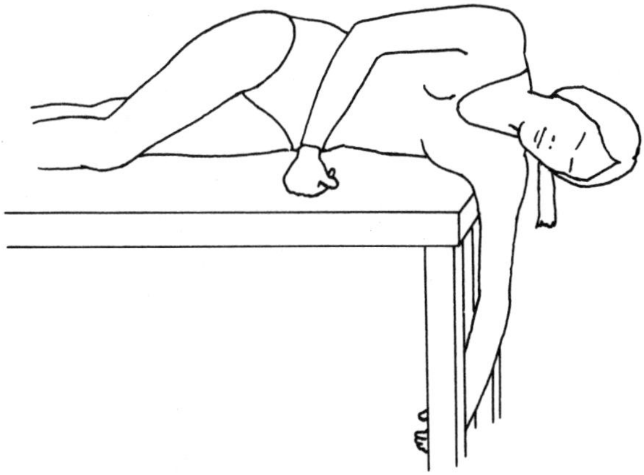

Side bends (lateral flexion) *Note that when you do this you always get more effect on the up side because of gravity. Do 12 reps, 3 to 5 sets.*

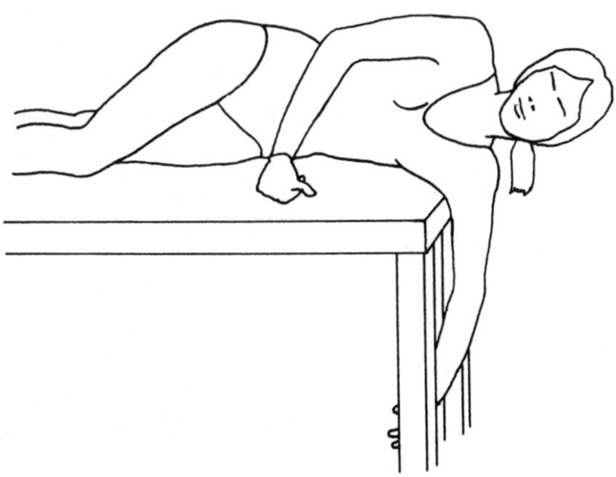

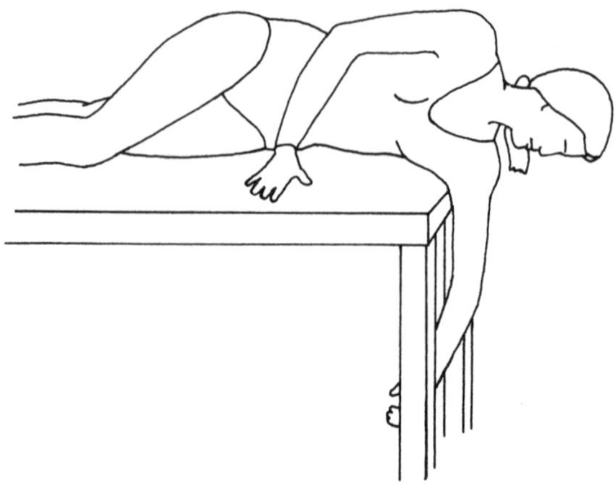

Neck rotation Again, because of gravity you should do this exercise on both sides. Do 12 reps, 3 to 5 sets.

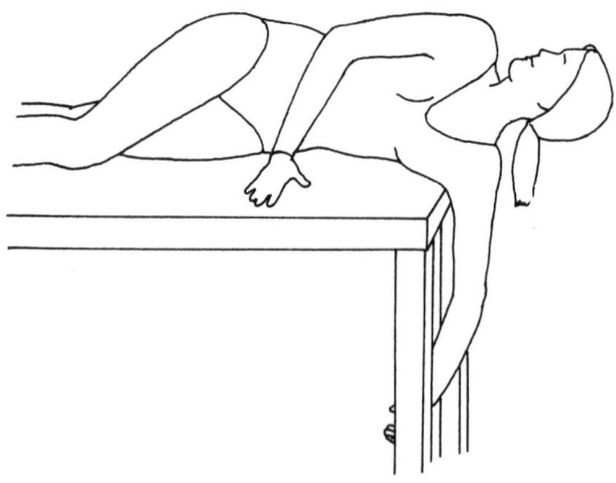

4. NECK ROTATIONS, RIGHT AND LEFT

Assume a position lying on either side as you did with the side neck bends. The bottom arm should be placed straight down over the edge of the bench for support. The head should be maintained in the neutral position. Rotate face around to floor, then back toward the ceiling. Do this in a progressive manner and then repeat the exercise on the opposite side.

Intermediate Neck Development

Once the starter exercises become too easy, you must move on to more challenging training. However, we do not recommend the various neck development machines such as the Nautilus or the Hydraulic for this level. If you are going to use them, do so only after completing the advanced neck training.

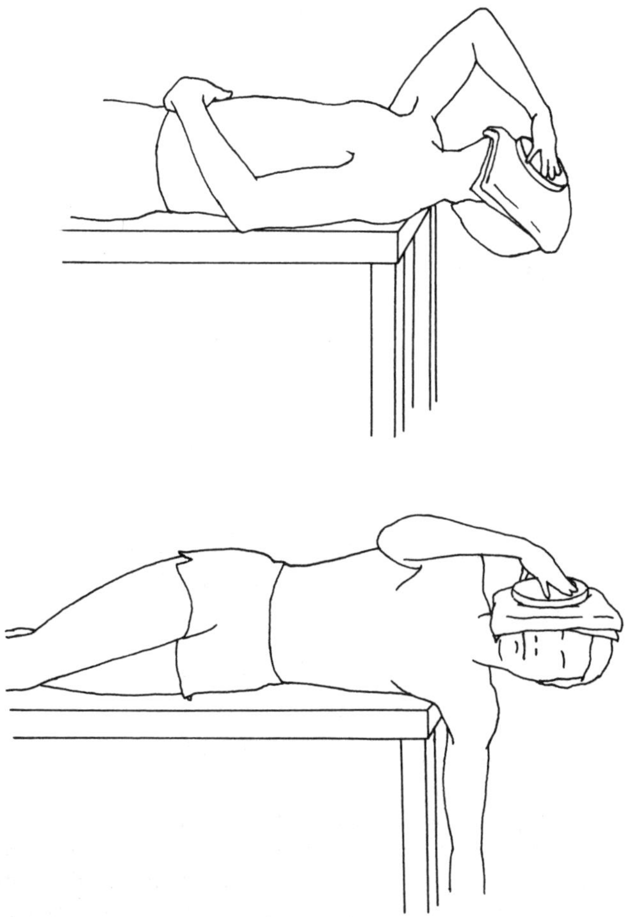

Intermediate neck exercises with weights *Use a towel between your head and the weight. Start with a light weight and build up.*

For some exercises at the intermediate level we recommend that you use a plate from a weight set. Note that you *must* use a pad such as a towel between the weight and your head. Stabilize the weight with one or both hands, holding it just enough to maintain the position of the plate, but not enough to do the actual work.

For the first intermediate neck exercise, lie on a bench facing upward, place the weight upon a folded towel on your forehead, and stabilize the plate with one or both hands. Then do the forward neck bend. Also repeat the backward neck bend, side neck bend, and neck rotations. Continue using these same four exercises, building up the weight increments from very light to much heavier. You'll be surprised about how much greater the training value of these exercises becomes with the weights.

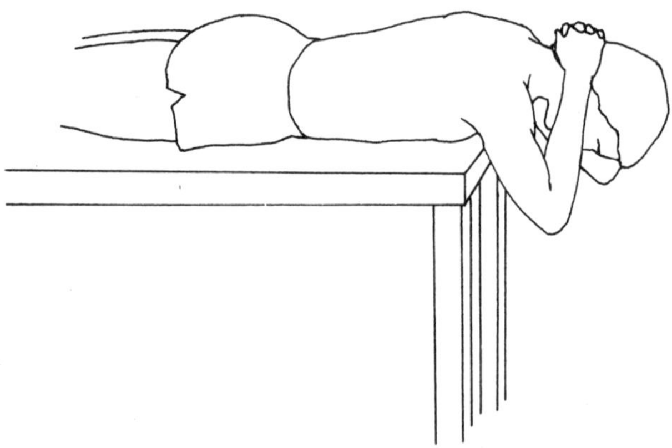

Intermediate neck exercises *The hands can be used as resistance.*

Another set of intermediate-level variations calls for using your hands to exert pressure while you do the four exercises. Your hands will change the angle of bend and provide a different kind of pressure. For forward bending, place your hands in front on both sides of your jaw. For backward bending, place your hands behind your head. For right and left rotations, hold your chin in a locked position. You'll notice the different angle produced and a slightly different stress on the neck muscles.

Advanced Neck Development

While you may wish to spend $2,000 on a neck machine, we have a suggestion for a very effective device that will probably cost you just a few dollars. Take a football helmet—perhaps an old model, because you won't be using it for contact. It must have a chin strap because the helmet is actually a hat for your weights. Then get a threaded flange (a flat metal plate with slots for bolts or nails) that will accept ¾-inch galvanized pipe and mount it on top of the helmet with four small bolts. Use washers on the bolt heads inside the helmet.

Take a six-inch section of ¾-inch pipe and drill holes every half inch along its length in order to hold the weight plates. Then screw the pipe into the flange. Two small bolts and nuts to hold the weight will finish off the assembly. If the plate seems loose, a rubber band on the pipe will secure it better. If you wish to make a more complex helmet, add pipes on the right and left sides of the helmet.

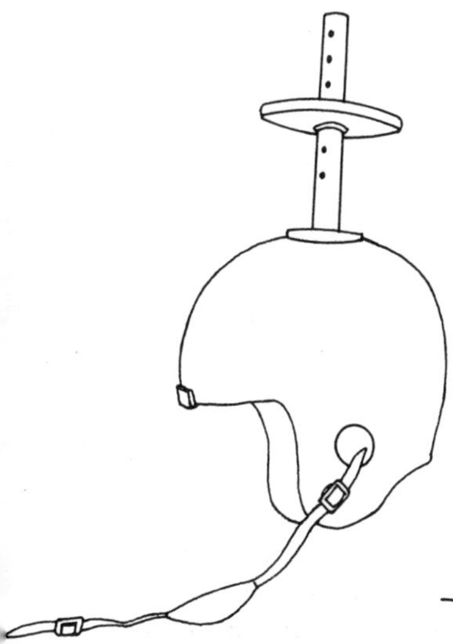

Advanced neck-strengthening device *See the text for how to make this inexpensive but effective neck machine.*

Advanced neck development

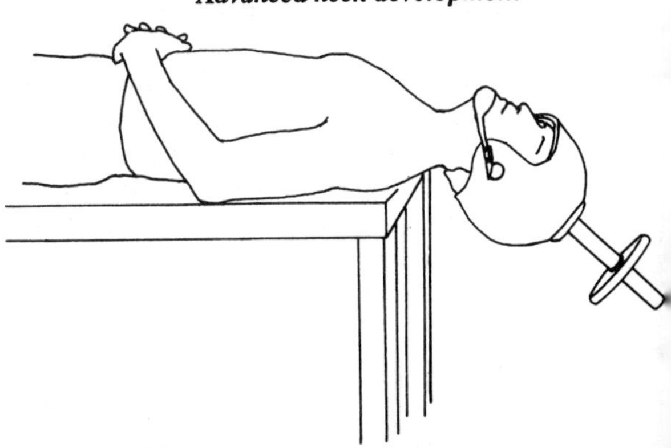

Begin by doing the same exercises you did in the starter and intermediate levels, but this time wear your weight helmet. Start with light weights—a pound or pound and a half, if you have them—then increase the increments gradually. You can change the mechanical advantage and increase the resistance by moving the weight from up against the helmet to the end of the pole. We believe there is real advantage in *gradual* increase in weights. One of the prime difficulties with the commercial neck machines is that the weights start out too big and the jumps are in excessively large increments.

Remember, the idea is not to hold contests to see how much weight you can hold with your weight helmet. The idea is to make slow, steady gains in neck strength. Too much, too soon can do just the opposite because of the danger of tearing down instead of building up.

Begin the exercises with one set per workout for the first month, then add a set a month up to three sets maximum. Continue the three-set program until you have achieved the desired size and strength increase. At this point, return to the one set twice weekly to maintain what you have gained.

THE TORSO

We will use the same directional emphasis in building up the torso that we used with the neck. The first group of exercises will be forward bending, the next group will be backward bending, and the third will be sideward bending.

Torso Curls

The purpose of torso curls is to develop the abdominal muscles and increase the range of motion of the spine.

The abdominal muscles are often weak due to the fact that they are never isolated and worked properly. They are very important muscles in stabilizing the upper body when it receives a blow. The abdominals can never be overdeveloped, and their importance cannot be overemphasized. Unfortunately, the classic sit-up exercises are not only dangerous, but also do not do a good job in building up these crucial muscles.

BASIC TORSO CURLS

Torso curls are best done on some type of inclined board so that you can progressively increase the resistance from gravity by increasing the decline, but you should always begin on a flat surface. Assume a supine position with knees straight and feet anchored in some manner. Use towels or pads to raise the pelvis off the board four to five inches. Put these towels or pads just at the top of the pelvis to prevent irritation of the sacrum. Touch your hands together in front of you, with your arms parallel to your body.

The first step is to tuck chin to chest, then continue coming up, flexing the upper back and progressing down to the lower back, which should be the last part to come up off the board. Stop at the point where the last lumbar vertebra clears the lying surface and don't rock onto the sacrum. Return down slowly, letting the lower back touch first and stopping as soon as it touches. Keep your chin tucked and your upper spine bent forward. Do this exercise in a slow, steady, sustained manner.

The chin must be tucked tightly throughout the exercise. The shoulders and upper back should not touch the flat surface until the exercise is completed. The back should be in a curled position, never straight. If done correctly, at first these will be hard to do. Do not jerk or throw yourself upward.

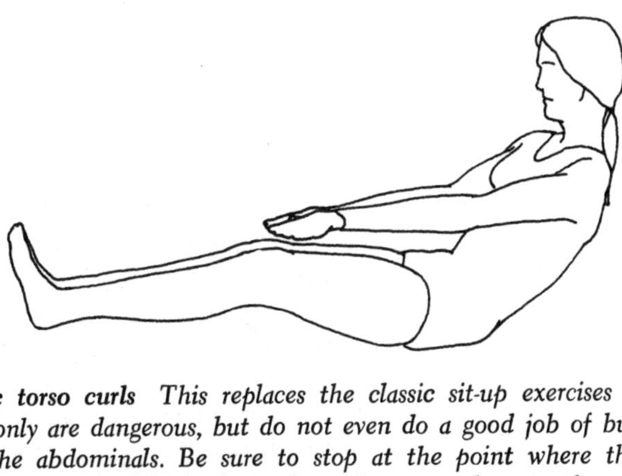

Basic torso curls *This replaces the classic sit-up exercises which not only are dangerous, but do not even do a good job of building up the abdominals. Be sure to stop at the point where the last lumbar vertebra clears the surface; do not rock onto the sacrum. Move slowly both ways.*

INTERMEDIATE TORSO CURLS

Increase resistance by progressively increasing the decline angle of the board. You can also achieve an increase by varying the arm position. Clasp your hands behind your neck for another intermediate variable.

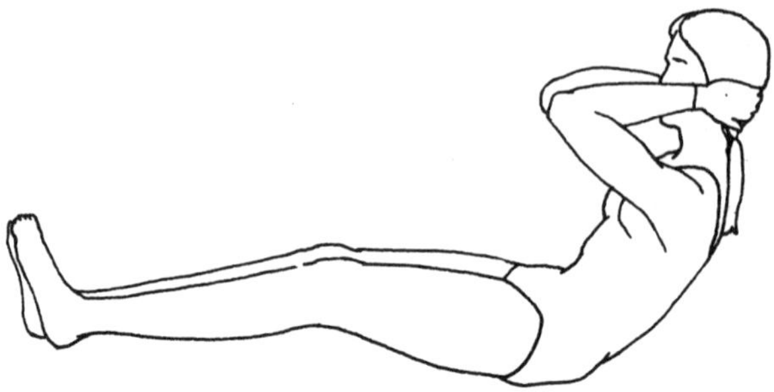

Intermediate torso curl *Note the position of the hands.*

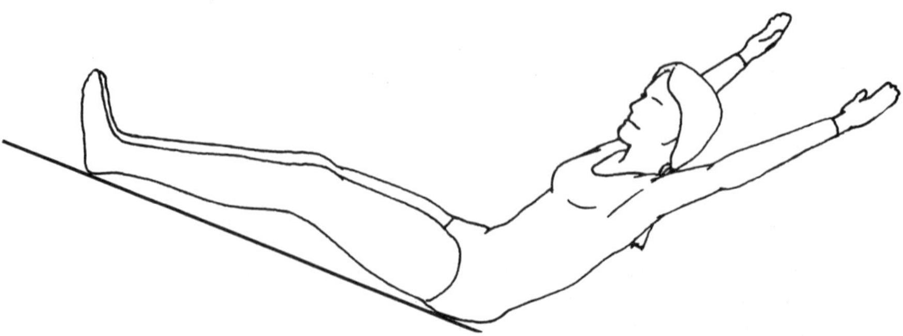

Intermediate torso curl *Hand and arm placement makes the difference.*

ADVANCED TORSO CURLS

The most advanced torso curl is the bent 110° leg torso curl. Anchor your feet so your legs are in the 110° position as shown in the diagram. You will note that this is the only position that truly relaxes the psoas muscle, which flexes the thigh.

Again, start the exercises by clasping your hands behind your neck. Later you can hold your arms over your head. This is an excellent throwing foundation exercise. One further variation of arm position is to hold weights behind your head in a progression from one to twenty-five pounds. And, as we have said before and will say again, the race goes not to the one who holds the most weight behind the head; it goes to the person who does each level and progression the right way.

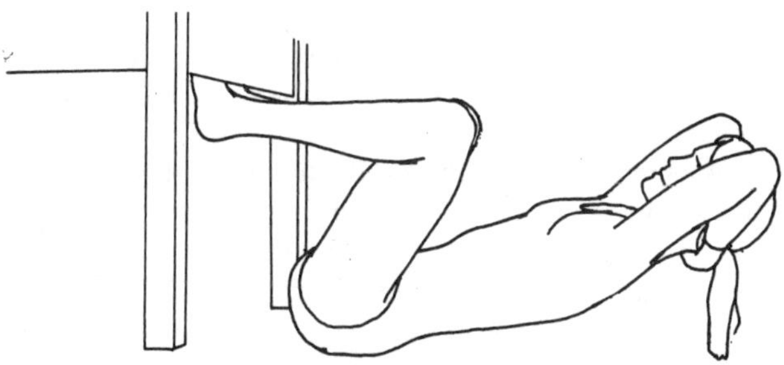

Advanced 110° leg torso curl *This advanced exercise is done lying on your back with your legs up and feet anchored. This is the only position that relaxes the psoas muscle.*

Backward Bends from the Horizontal Position (Prone Torso Hyperextension)

The purpose of backward bends is to strengthen the muscles of the back and hips and to increase the range of motion of the spine.

The back muscles are usually weak and are easily strained in weight training or in sports. Seldom are the back muscles isolated and trained. Strong back muscles are very important, though, in football blocking and tackling and in weight sports, especially for stabilization.

We believe that torso hyperextensions are among the most important exercises you can do. It is essential to practice them if you want to be a high-performance athlete. Unfortunately, they are almost universally performed incorrectly, and far too often they cause strains and spasms of the lower back muscles and fascia. This happens because these exercises are done far too fast, usually traveling too great a distance, and with momentum rather than muscular contractile effort. Do not snap or jerk backwards!

BASIC BACKWARD BENDS

Assume a prone (face down) position on a bench. Use a belt or a bar to hold down the lower legs. If you do this on a mat or a carpeted floor, have a partner hold down your legs. Put your hands down by your sides. First extend your neck fully, then continue to arch your back while elevating the ribs upward. Come as high up above the floor or bench as possible. Look up at the ceiling. Then lower yourself slowly to the beginning horizontal position. Do your reps and sets progressively; your goal is to master the full torso range of motion, which is approximately 45 degrees of torso elevation off the floor or bench.

Back muscles are usually weak; don't strain them by starting out with too much resistance. Be sure to come up as far as possible above the bench while arching the back. Be sure the movement is controlled. What you are looking for is a slow, steady, sustained exercise with a static end point and a return in the same manner. Remember to take your time. After you attain the 45° torso range of motion and can do the exercises well, you can eliminate the leg stabilization for variety.

Basic backward bends (torso hyperextension) *Note the bar holding down the feet, or you can use a strap. Also, by changing the incline of the bench you can make it easier (head higher) or harder (head lower).*

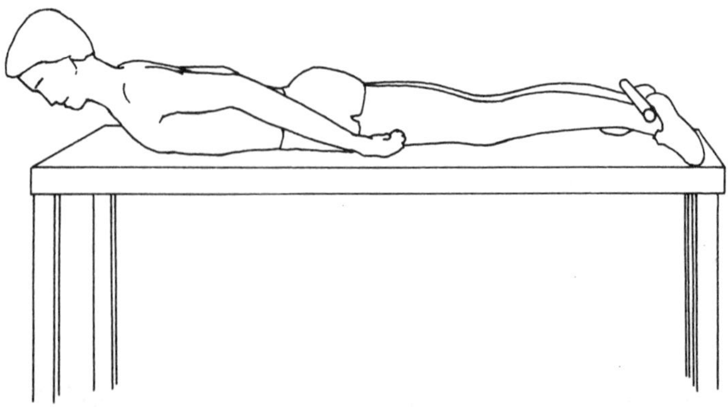

The position of the hands and arms is critical in this progression; they can affect the load or intensity factor almost enough to eliminate the need to use weights. Placing the hands above the head and then raising up in a backward bend is a superhuman feat and should be regarded as very advanced.

How fast one attains the advanced level usually depends on the individual's body type rather than on a group standard. This is an exercise in control, and people with long torsos will advance at a slower rate than those with short torsos. An impatient person would probably be better off not doing this exercise.

Movements involving jerking or snapping the head backward are potentially disastrous. When this exercise is done properly, the spine should never be flexed forward as in the toe touch but rather should begin in extension (straight body line) and then move into hyperextension. This means that the exercise always should be begun with the torso parallel to the floor, no matter whether you are a beginner or an advanced exerciser. Doing the exercise on the hyperextension benches that are commonly available from exercise equipment companies is only recommended with a qualified instructor.

INTERMEDIATE BACKWARD BENDS

The intermediate level of backward bends calls for the same pattern of movement as the starting level. The difference is that when you assume your prone position on the bench, you should

Intermediate backward bends

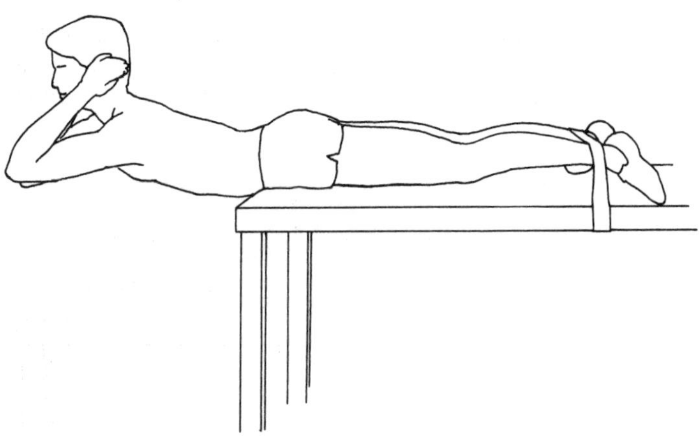

slide forward until the top of the pelvis is at the edge of the bench. You must use a belt or bar to hold down the lower legs. Move the body outward with arm support and maintain the static contraction momentarily while arranging your hand position to accommodate your current strength level. Put your hands behind your head and keep your elbows in close to the sides of your head. Again, extend your neck fully, then continue to arch back while elevating the ribs upward. Come as high up above the bench level as possible. Look up at the ceiling. Then slowly lower yourself to the beginning horizontal position.

When you need extra weight, use small increments of one- or two-pound weights held behind the head. Be sure to come up as far as possible above the bench while arching your back. Be sure the movement is done under control—i.e., with a slow, steady, sustained effort; with a static end point; and with a return in the same manner.

ADVANCED BACKWARD BENDS

The key increment in advanced backward bends is the positioning of the hands. Positioning them straight above your head makes for a very advanced exercise. You can add weights if you need more challenge. But again, remember to maintain a slow, steady, sustained effort with a static end point and a return in the same manner.

Advanced backward bends

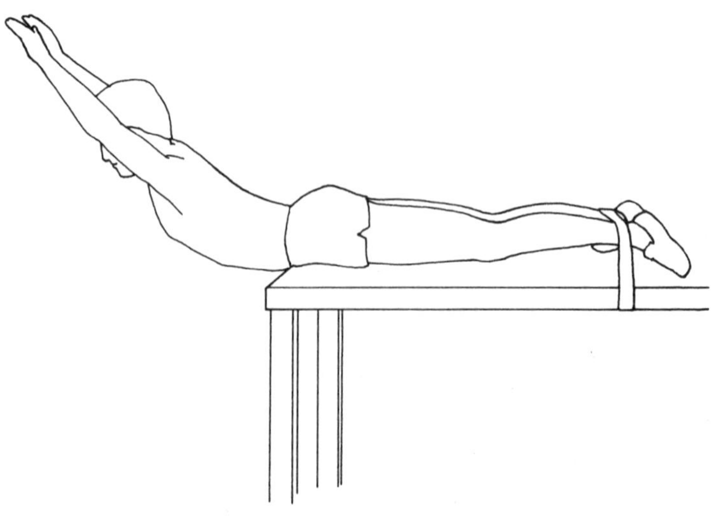

VARIATION OF BACKWARD BENDS

One variation of the backward bend is the only exercise that will develop the upper region of the back (the erector spinae group), which often lacks development. Place the stabilizer belt around the midthoracic region in order to cancel out the action of the sacrospinalis, the large muscle that extends the vertebral column. Place your hands on the back of your head and point your elbows forward. This position of the elbows frees up the blocking action of the scapula which occurs if the elbows are in a side position. From this position, do backward bends as described above.

Side Bends (Lateral Spine Flexion)

Side bends strengthen the lateral spine muscles and increase lateral spine range of motion.

Lateral flexion of the spine is not a common movement in everyday activities. In sports like football, however, it occurs in almost every play, especially for a running back who often gets hit from the side. The lateral spine muscles must be strengthened and trained so they can better absorb blows from the side, expected or unexpected.

BASIC SIDE BENDS

Assume a position lying on either side on a bench. Slide forward so that the top of your pelvis is right on the edge of the bench. Strap down your lower legs or pelvis. Lay your bottom arm across your chest and your top arm down at your side. Let your upper body down over the edge to an angle of no more than 45 degrees. Slowly raise trunk up as far above bench level as possible, taking care not to twist at the waist or bend forward or backward as you come up. Your body should remain in a straight line throughout the exercise. Then lower your trunk slowly back to the starting position. Turn on your other side to exercise the opposite muscle group.

INTERMEDIATE SIDE BENDS

As with the backward bends, the intermediate level of side bends calls for a difference of where the hands are placed. Put your hands behind your head and keep your elbows in close to the side of your head. Be sure the movement is done under control—with a slow, steady, sustained effort; with a static end point; and with a return in the same manner.

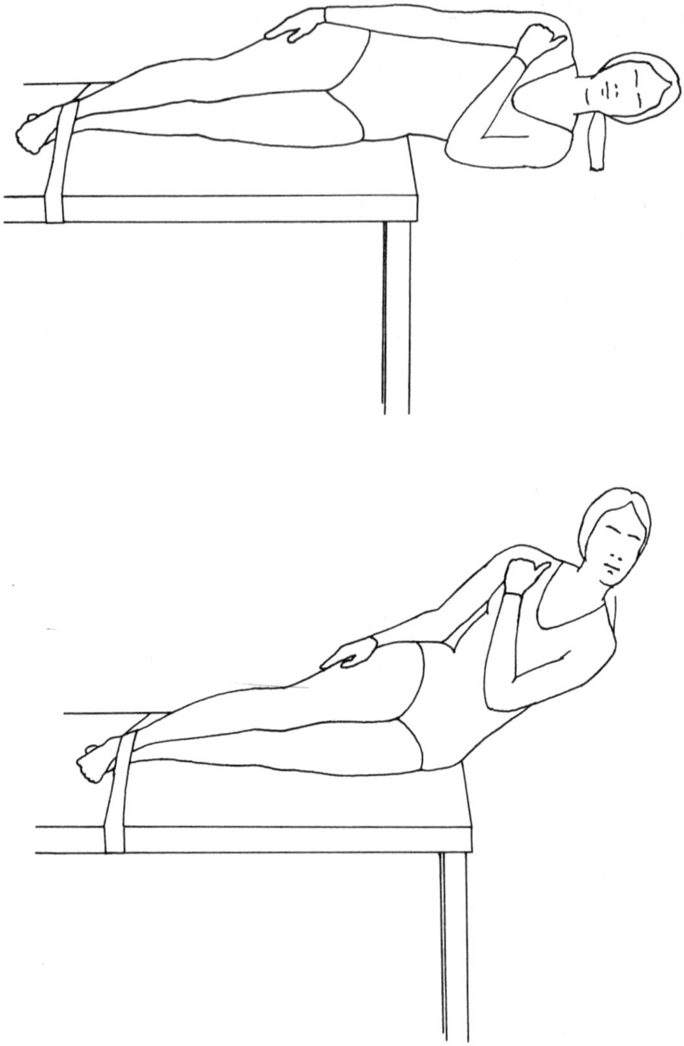

Basic side bends (lateral spine flexion)

ADVANCED SIDE BENDS

Again, the key difference is the positioning of the hands. Positioning them straight above your head is an advanced-level exercise, and weights can be added by holding them on the top side of your head.

HIGH-PERFORMANCE CORE EXERCISES

The exercises just described are the keys to increasing the ability of your core to act as a stable base for your activities. As you do these exercises and both strengthen your muscles and extend your range of motion, we believe you will notice a significant improvement in your performance. It is from a good base, a good foundation, that you can build a better performance.

The following five exercises are high-performance, superadvanced exercises. If you want to train for maximum high performance once you have completed the basic exercises and are able to competently do the advanced core exercises for the upper and lower back, then you can advance to these routines.

High-performance reverse hyperextension *Do this under control, slowly. Don't swing.*

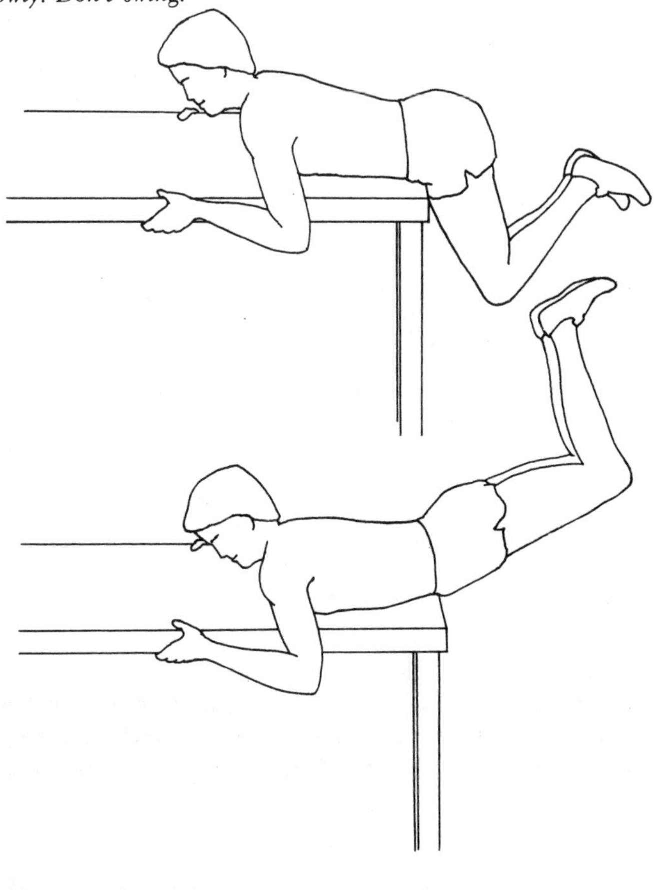

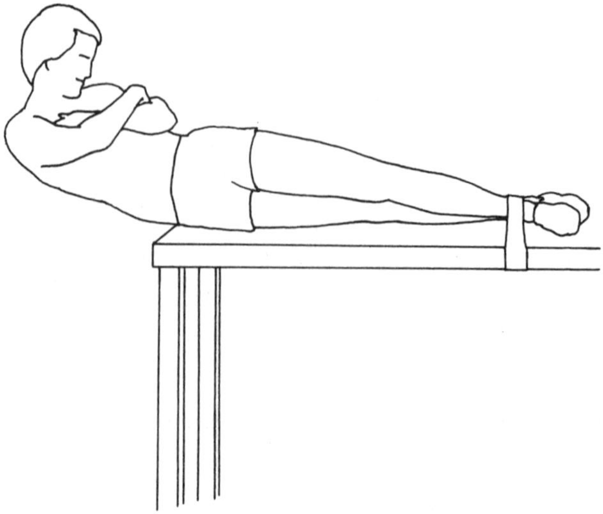

High-performance lateral flexion combined with rotation

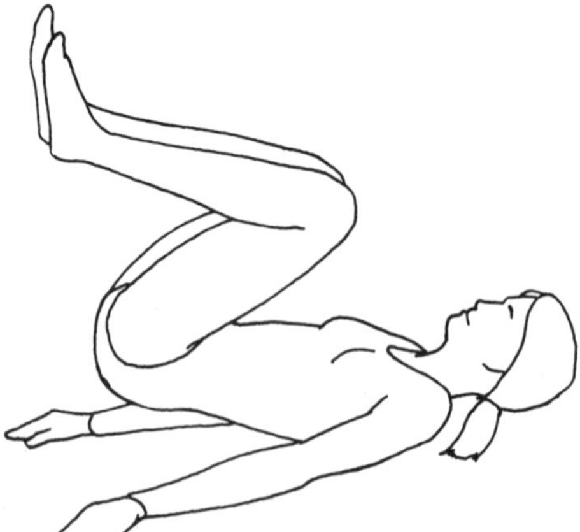

Reverse torso curl *Note that this is the maximum position you should go to.*

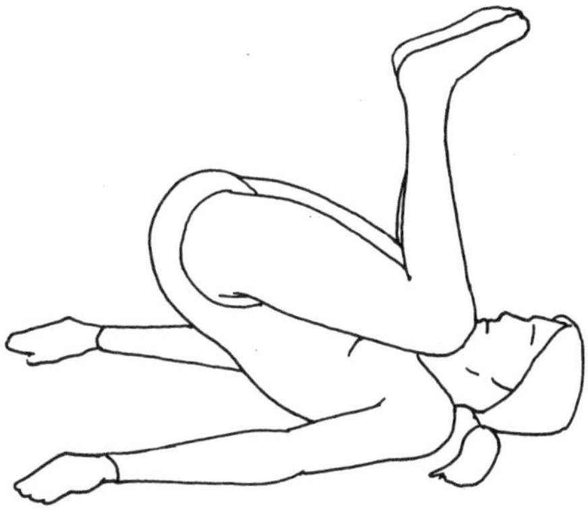

Improper and unsafe position for reverse torso curl *Do not go this far backward; you are then getting into a position similar to the yoga plow.*

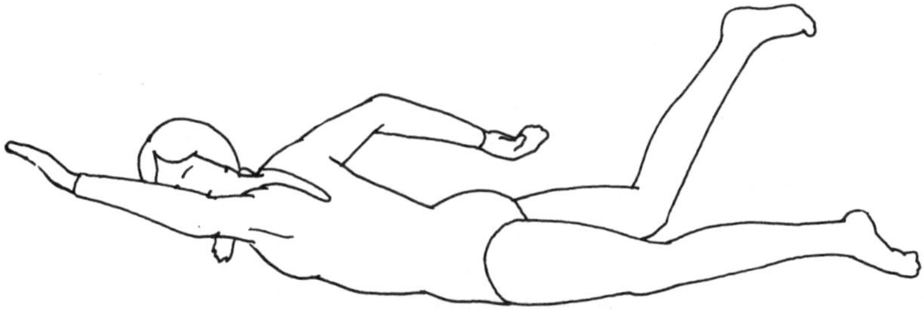

High performance spine hyperextension combined with hip hyperextension, knee flexion, and shoulder rotations

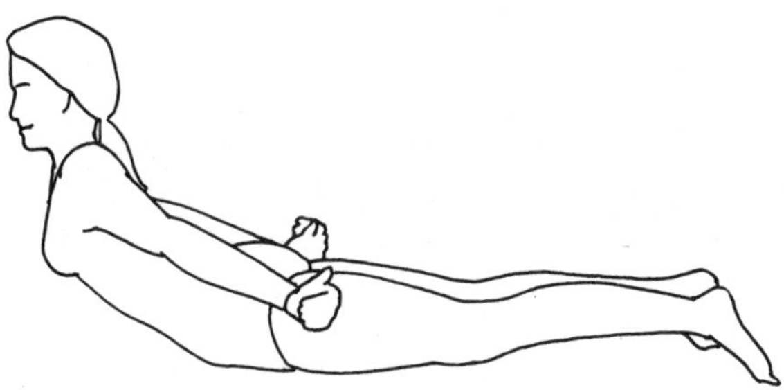

Another modification of advanced spine hyperextension *Note the position of the thumbs, which indicates the direction of rotation of the arms.*

15

Power Bands

One of the best ways to train involves the use of power bands. These look like one- to two-inch-wide overgrown rubber bands, about six inches in length. They are made of natural rubber, so the resistance they offer increases as your power and strength increase. This helps the stabilizer muscles turn on and off and get excellent training.

We expect that as the value of this system becomes recognized these bands will be readily available. The power band is the key piece of equipment you will need for the exercises in this chapter, and you should be able to find one at your local sporting-goods store for only a few dollars. Be sure the ones you buy are made of natural rubber. Power bands last a long time if you care for them properly. They should never be placed on radiators or in sunlight to dry, and after a sweaty workout, it is best to rinse them off in warm water and let them dry because perspiration will also shorten their life. The width and the strength of the power band make it superior for exercising to rubber tubing, but tubing (especially the type of rubber tubing found in medical supply houses) will also work.

One word of caution: As with any exercise, if you are under medical supervision for problems involving areas affected by these exercises, you should consult with your physician prior to beginning the routines outlined here.

TYPES OF POWER-BAND TRAINING

Part of the definition of strength is the ability to move something. It is important to realize that muscles will turn on only when they are operating against resistance or when they are attempting to move something. It often happens that your arm moves in the same direction and distance on two successive moves but that totally different groups of muscles function each time.

For example, first pick up a weight and hold it palm upward at waist level. Put your free hand on your upper arm. As you lift the weight to your shoulder, you will find that the biceps (the muscle in the front of the arm) is on in both the flexion and extension movements. However, the muscles in the back of the arm, the triceps, were not on at all, in either the upward or the downward motion. Next, lean against a wall, facing it, with your shoulders close to the wall and your feet farther away. Put your palms against the wall at shoulder height. Push away from the wall, then lean back toward the wall. As you do these maneuvers, you will feel your triceps muscles working, even though this was basically the same motion as when you picked up the weight. But the resistance was at a completely different place, so your triceps were on and your biceps were off.

Therefore, it is important in strength training to understand where the resistance is. Sometimes you will be pulling against bands in one direction, and other times you will be pulling against bands in the opposite direction while still moving the joint in the same track.

Also, as long as you are moving against resistance, you are working the muscle whether it is getting longer or shorter. A very convenient way to tell which muscles are working is to put your hand on the muscle which you think is being worked and palpate it—that is, feel the muscle. This is the easiest way to tell whether a muscle is on or off.

Developing Strength

As we discussed earlier in the book, strength is the amount of effort or work involved in moving something that resists being moved. For example, the ability to lift fifty pounds one foot off the ground would show a certain amount of strength.

For strength training, you want to go through a full range of motion each time you do an exercise. Remember that the range of motion through which the body part moves is limited by four factors: the construction of the joint, the ligaments that surround the joint, the tendons that link the muscles to the bones and move the joint, and the muscles that move the joint. It is the muscles that usually make the difference between your actual range of motion and your full possible range of motion. As you exercise the particular muscles, you will find that your actual range of motion will increase to the full possible range of motion, if all the other structures are normal.

The key to strength building is slow, steady, sustained effort. Start at one end of your ROM and move slowly to the opposite end of the arc of motion. Once you reach that end, hold that position statically for about two seconds. After the two-second static hold, begin the last half of the exercise: Gradually, slowly, and in a controlled fashion, return to the beginning part of the arc of motion. The return should take about four seconds. This will give you one concentric (shortening) contraction and one eccentric (lengthening) contraction of the muscle as well as an isometric contraction during the static hold. You should repeat this movement for up to three reps, and do three sets of these reps each exercise. Furthermore, we recommend three exercise periods per week, preferably on alternate days.

Developing Stamina

Doing the entire exercise routine without rest trains you for stamina. We also recommend doing terminal flicks to train for stamina. These are important and are usually neglected in most routines. As stated before, terminal flicks are the rapid back-and-fourth movement of the last few inches of the concentric phase, before the static hold, and of the first few inches of the eccentric phase, after the static hold. This rapid flicking at the end of the arc of motion should be performed quickly and repeatedly, beginning with five to ten seconds and gradually increasing until you can do terminal flicks for two minutes.

Developing Power

Power is the ability to move something quickly. If you could initially move that fifty pounds one foot in one second, and after training you can move it one foot in one-hundredth of a second, you have greatly increased your power. In all of our common sports, power is really what you want to train for. But you have to develop your strength before you can train for the power. Obviously you must train for power through the full range of motion, just as in strength training. However, instead of a slow, steady movement, your motion should be explosive, done as quickly as possible from the beginning to the end of the arc of motion. Once you are at the end, you should not let the band pull you back, but resist and perform slowly the eccentric (lengthening) return to the starting point. You must make a conscious effort of braking or decelerating back to the beginning point, just as in the strength-training section. Continue to repeat the power training until you can perform it properly, up to a training session of thirty seconds for each movement.

Note that for any of the exercises you do with power bands, the farther away the band is positioned from the joint being exercised, the more tension there will be. You can start with the bands close to the joint and then gradually move them farther away, increasing the resistance of your exercise. As you do this, you adjust the tension and the training effect.

Also note that the beauty of the power band system is not only the improvement in performance stability you will gain; if you exercise continually by going from one routine to another, you will get an aerobic training benefit as well. It is a mistake to stop the entire exercise session to let a group of muscles recover. Instead, when one group of muscles is fatigued, simply go to another group of muscles which are not fatigued and keep on going through various routines to maximize your aerobic training benefit and the overall conditioning effect of the routine.

SCHEDULE

We strongly recommend only three workouts a week, preferably on alternate days. In addition, since we know that many athletes are addicted to some type of exercise machine, we permit one free-weight or complete exercise-machine workout per week in addition to the three times a week on the power bands. It *is* possible to overtrain. Do not exceed these guidelines!

If you are training for strength, complete up to three reps of the bands routine through a full range of motion. To train for stamina, complete up to three reps, but do at least ten seconds of terminal flicks at the end point of the arc of motion of each routine, and decrease the rest period between sets as much as possible—or even better, go through all three sets without resting in between. For power, build up to thirty seconds of explosive, quick movements. Remember to practice concentric contraction through the full range of motion, followed by a slow, steady eccentric contraction back to the starting point with a conscious braking effort.

Although your goal in training with bands should be three sets, start the first week with only one set. The second week you can increase to two, and perhaps by the fourth week you may be up to the three-set goal. Then you can increase either the distance between the joint and where you place the bands or the size of the bands.

If you are using power bands as supplemental training aids when you practice activities such as dance, football, or basketball, the routine should be done at the completion of practice, not prior to practice. If you do them prior to practice, you run a risk of injuries during practice because of fatigue.

One of the advantages of the bands and our other equipment is that you can work out with them in almost any room. It is of course useful to have a training bench, several strong chairs, or a table to support you.

MENTAL ATTITUDE

Concentrate on the muscles being exercised and the contraction. Form is more important than just getting through the exercise. We believe that a positive mental attitude will enhance your training benefits. Furthermore, there is growing experimental evidence that if you concentrate on the muscle being exercised, you will enhance and improve the exercise benefit of that exercise.

The opposite is also true. Looking at these exercises as a chore will decrease the benefits of your training routines.

A POWER-BAND ROUTINE

Here is a typical power-band routine. An easy way to remember this routine is that the major joints not only bend and straighten (flexion and extension); they also either rotate inward and outward (internal and external rotation) or they bend side to side (abduction and adduction). A few joints do all three, primarily the shoulder and the hip.

So we will begin at the toes, work our way up, and then go from the shoulders out to the hand. Be sure to exercise both the right and left sides of your body, not just the one side shown in the illustrations. Though we have not included them, the same exercises can be performed individually on the fingers and the toes.

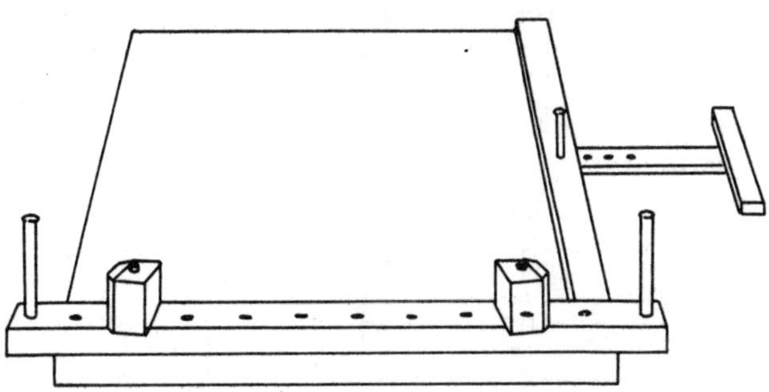

Power-band holder *For proper use of the power bands, you will occasionally need to hook the bands over a peg or a table leg. Or else you can make a holder like this one. The blocks and pegs allow for a variety of adjustments.*

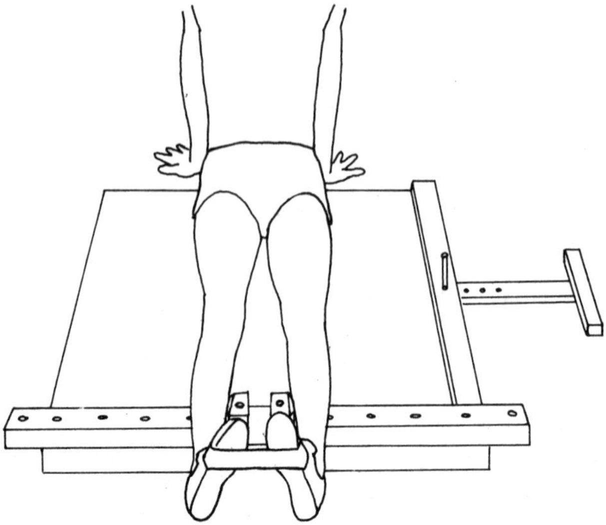

Pronation *Start with the band around your feet. Then turn your feet outward.*

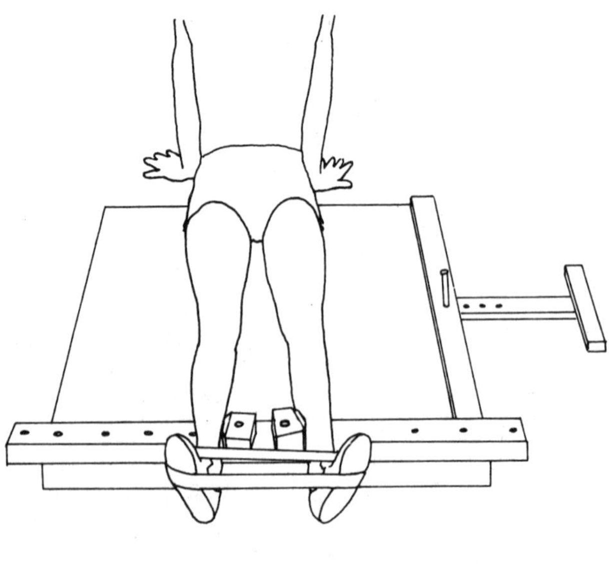

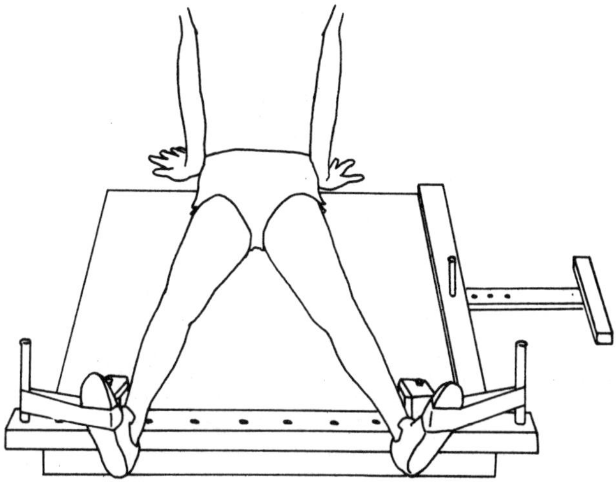

Supination Turn your feet inward as far as possible. Note the position of the ankles.

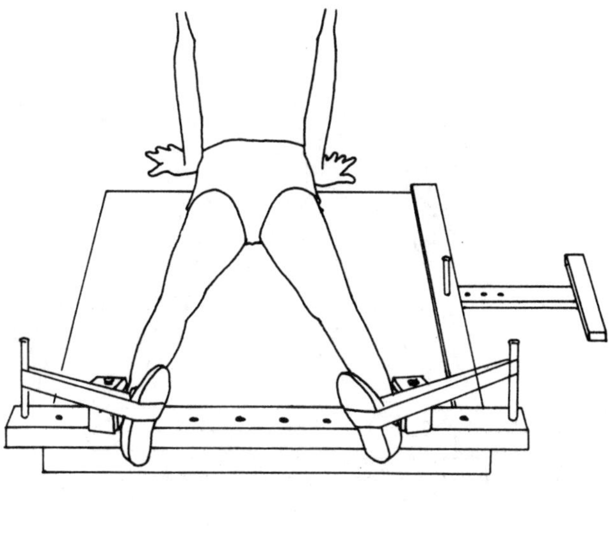

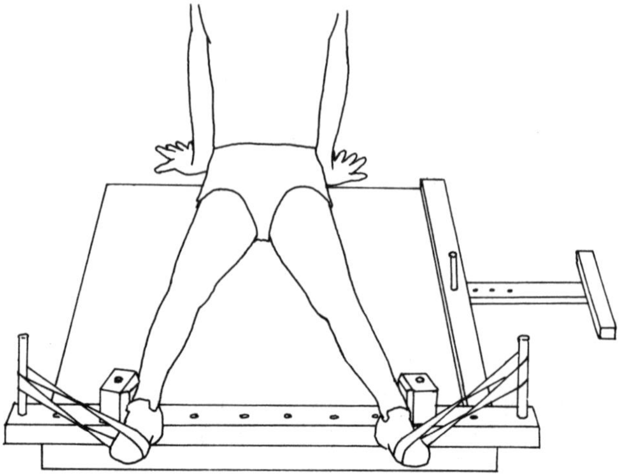

Supination in plantar flexion *Note that the toes are pointed downward in the beginning position, then are maximally turned in. This exercises a different group of muscles than plain supination does.*

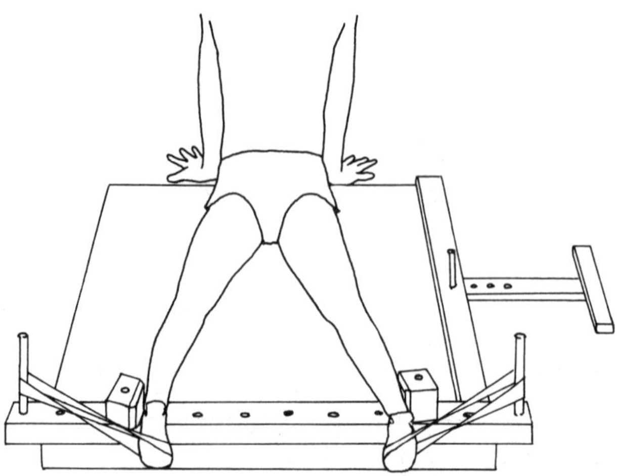

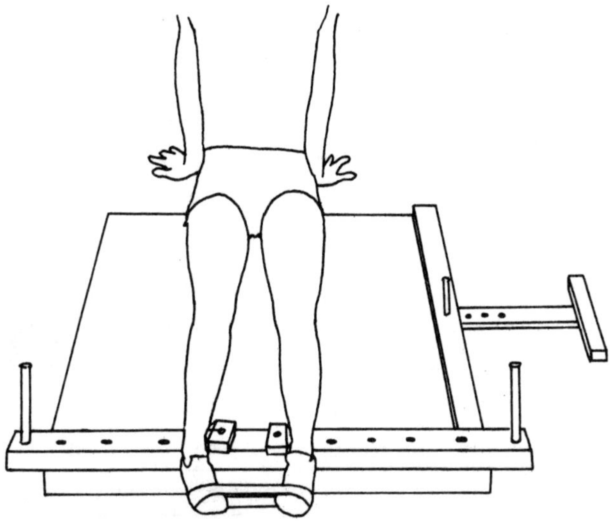

Pronation in plantar flexion *With the toes pointed down, turn the feet out. This exercises a different group of muscles than plain pronation does.*

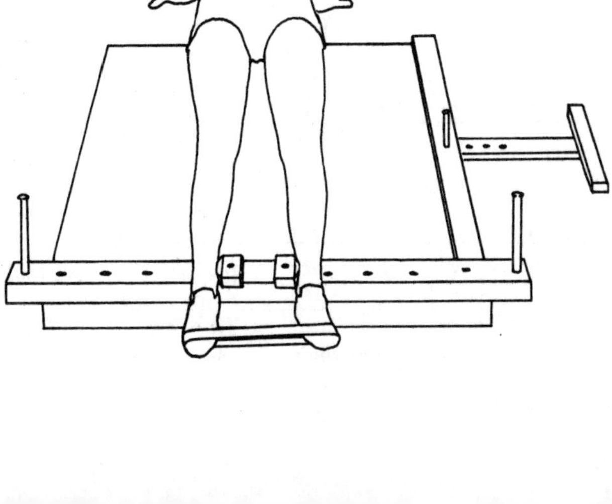

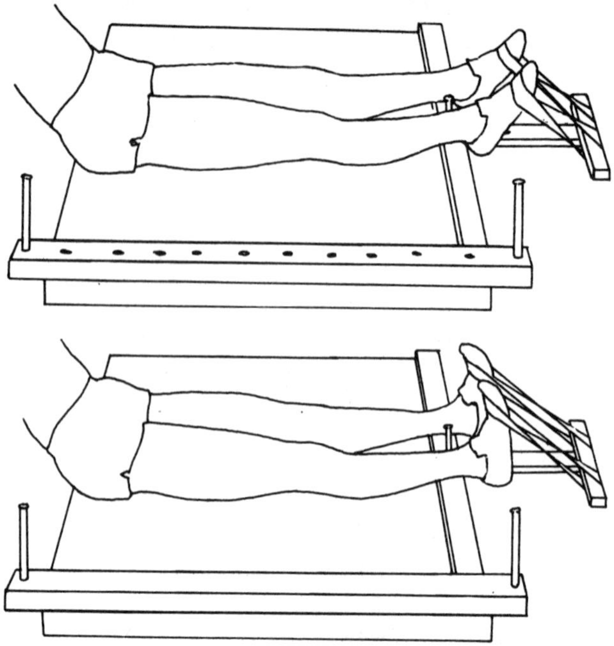

Dorsiflexion *The final position is an upward pointing of the toes.*

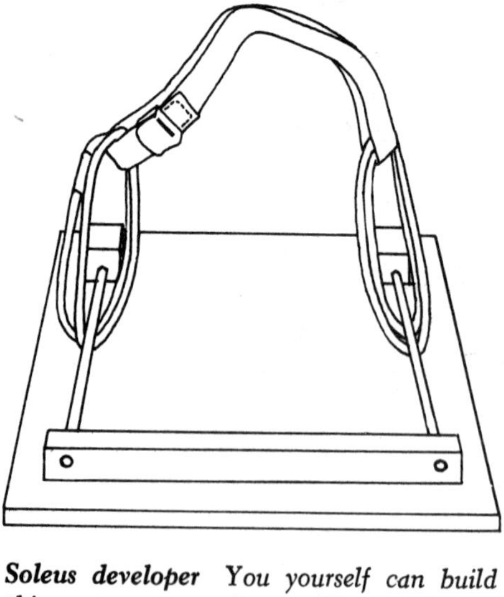

Soleus developer *You yourself can build this apparatus that will specifically strengthen the soleus muscle. It is extremely valuable for body builders or high-performance athletes who want to strengthen their calf muscles. It is the only way that we know of isolating the soleus for specific strengthening.*

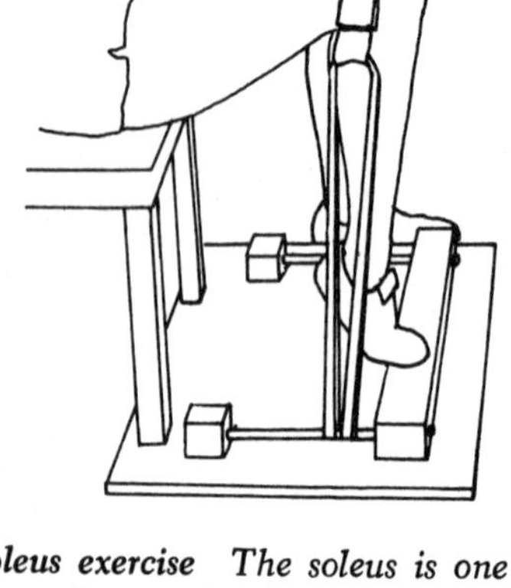

Soleus exercise *The soleus is one c the major muscles that pulls your foc down and moves the Achilles tendor This exercise will certainly improv your jumping and push-off ability.*

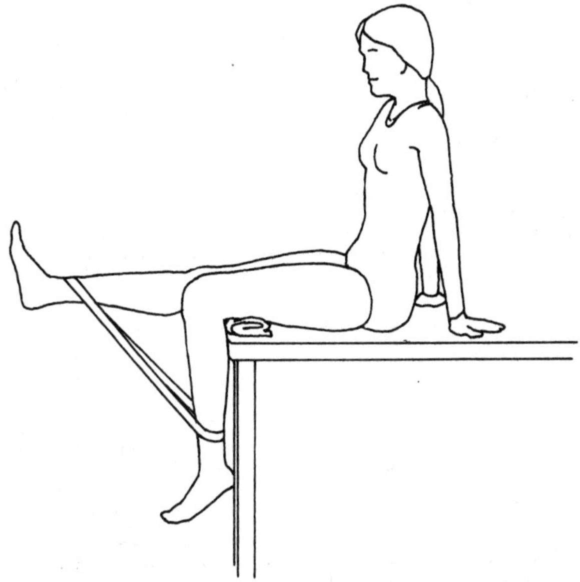

Knee extension *Start with your knees bent, then straighten one leg. Note the position of the bands and the rolled towel under the knee to aid in proper positioning.*

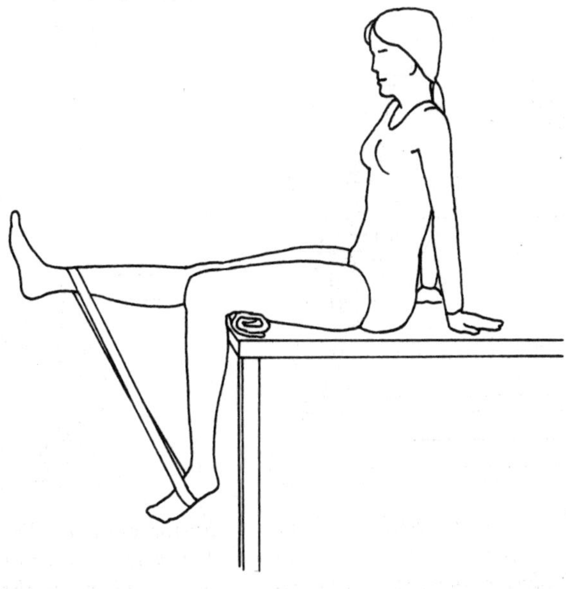

Knee extension *This differs from the previous exercise in the placement of the bands, but it is also very good for opposite knee flexion and calf development. Start with both knees bent, then straighten one leg. Note that the band is around the sole of one foot.*

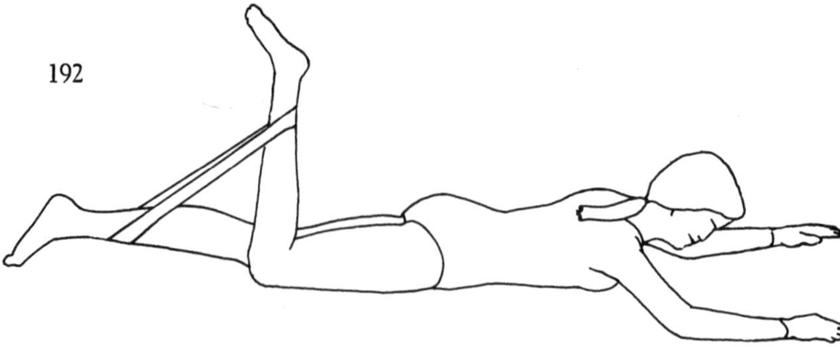

Hamstring strengthening *This is a knee flexion or hamstring-strengthening exercise. Start with both knees straight, then bend one up. You will need to exercise both legs.*

Internal rotation of the knee *Note that the knee is bent 90 degrees. Start with the foot pointed outwards, then turn the foot in against the tension of the band. This produces internal rotation of the knee, which is a very important exercise for any sports requiring cutting or for rehabilitation of the knee for maximum performance. This is also a very important exercise for eliminating breaststroker's knee.*

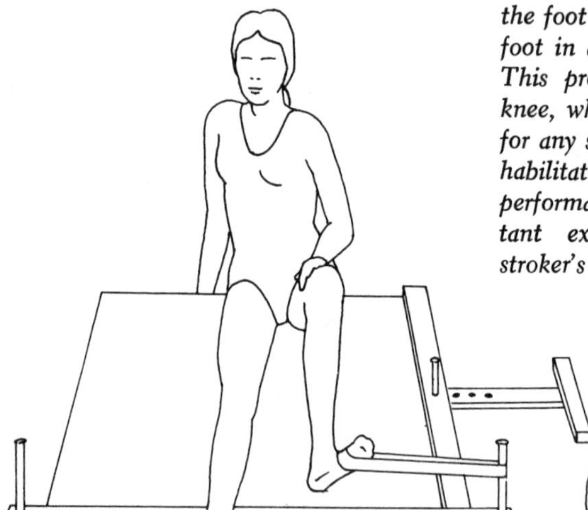

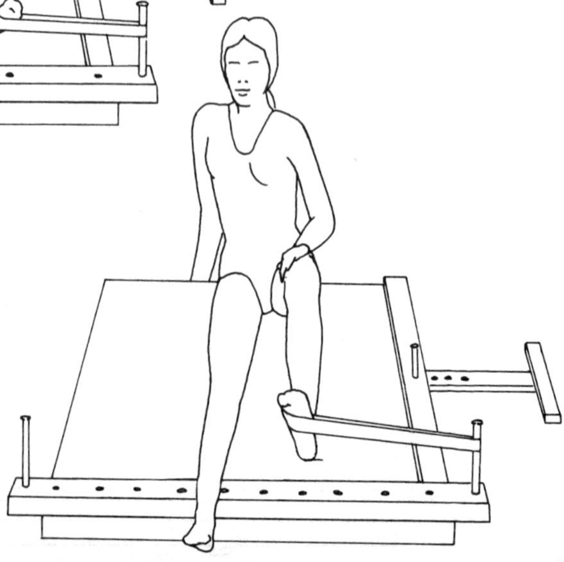

External rotation of the knee *This is the opposite of internal rotation, and like that exercise, it is extremely important. Turn the foot outward against the tension of the band.*

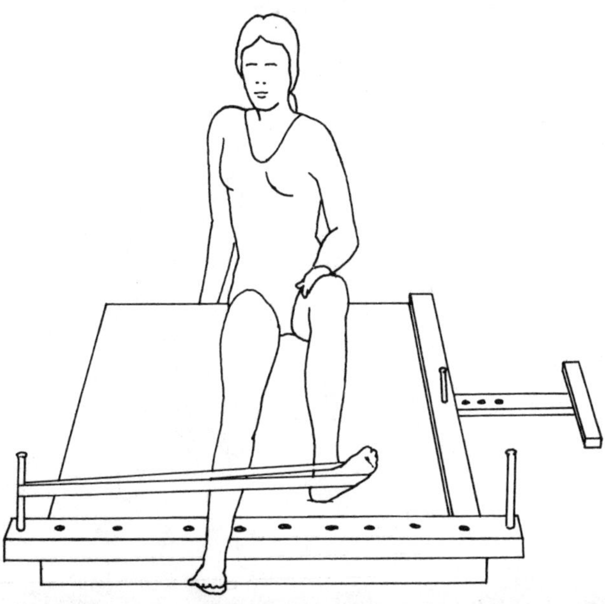

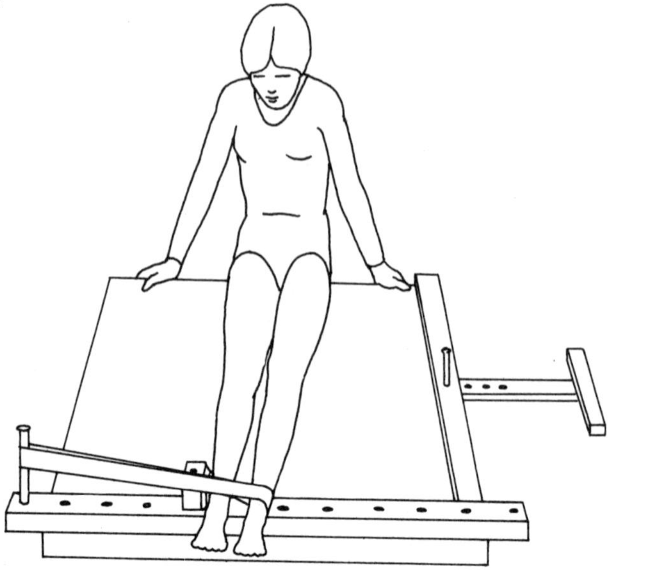

Hip abduction *Start with the feet together, then move one leg away from the post. Be sure to do both sides.*

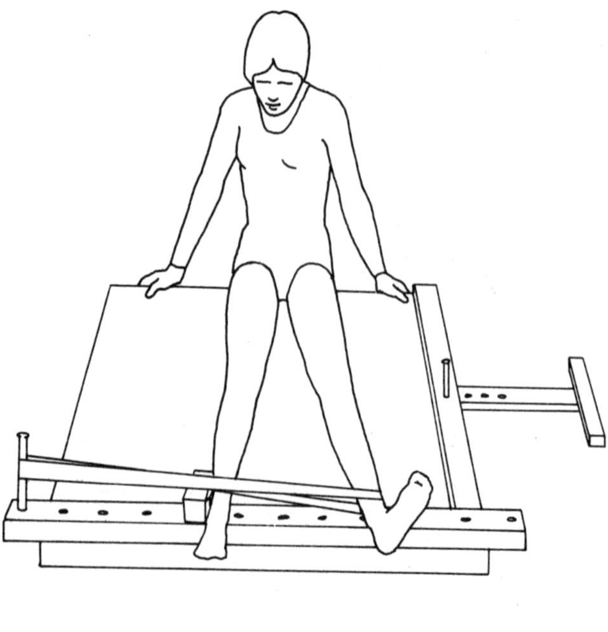

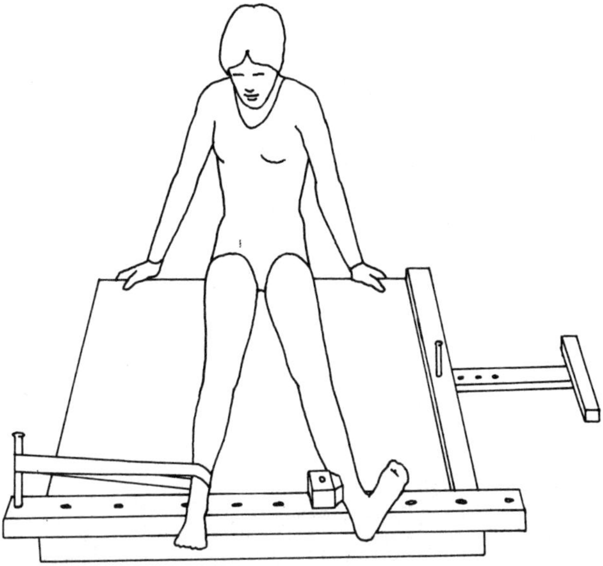

Hip adduction *Start with the feet apart, then move the leg in against the tension of the band. Be sure to do both sides.*

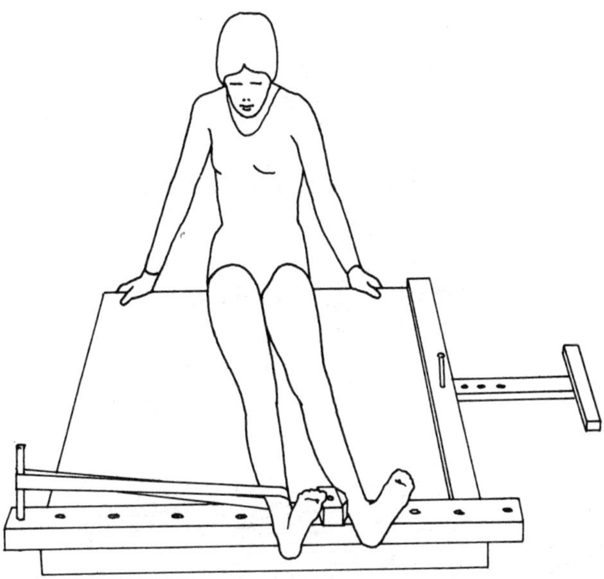

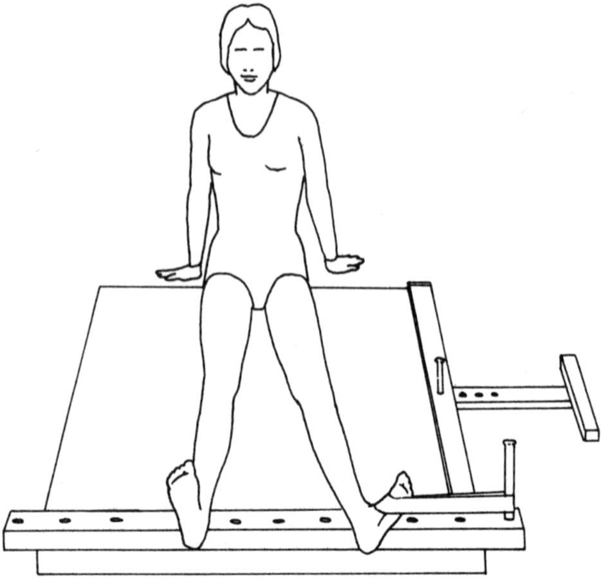

Internal rotation of the hip *This exercise helps strengthen the important internal rotators. Note that it is done with the knee locked.*

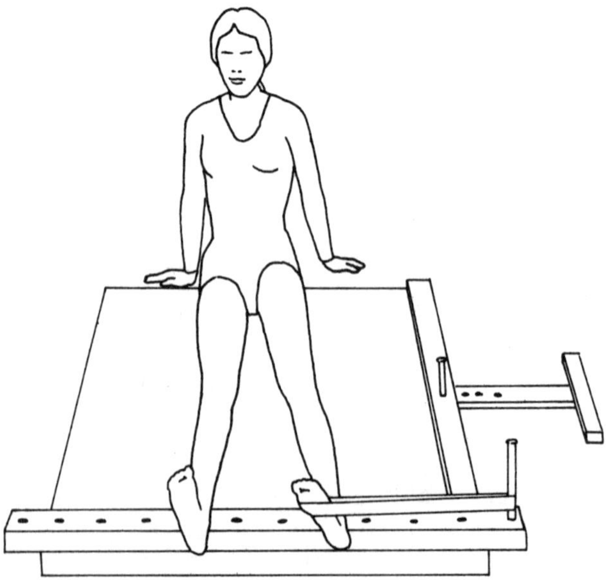

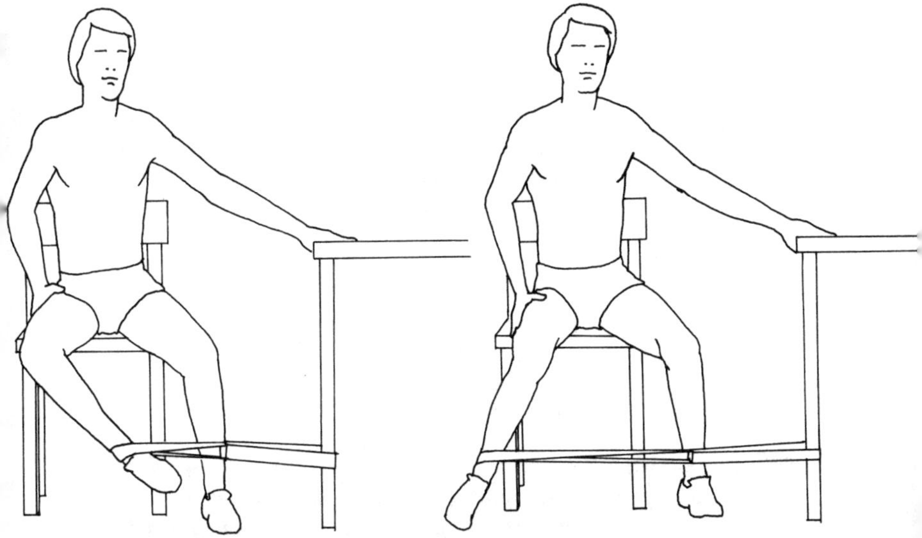

Internal rotation of the hip *Note that when the hip is internally rotated, the foot ends up outward.*

External rotation of the hip *Note that in the end position, the foot is inward. This rotates the hip outward.*

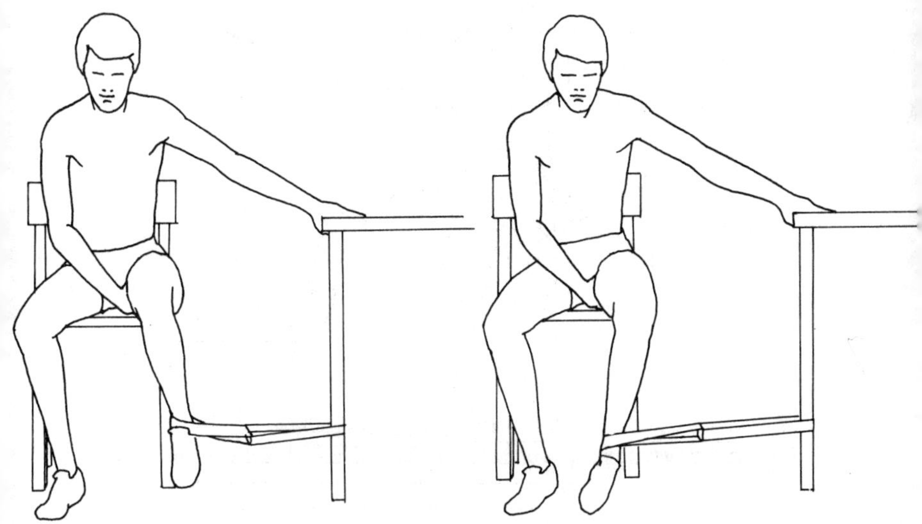

Scapular retraction *Begin with your arm extended. Keep elbow locked. Pull the band slowly toward you; then slowly let it return. This is a very important exercise in throwing sports because it helps train the shunt, or braking, function in the throwing maneuver and helps prevent many of the common arm and shoulder ailments in throwers and volleyball spikers.*

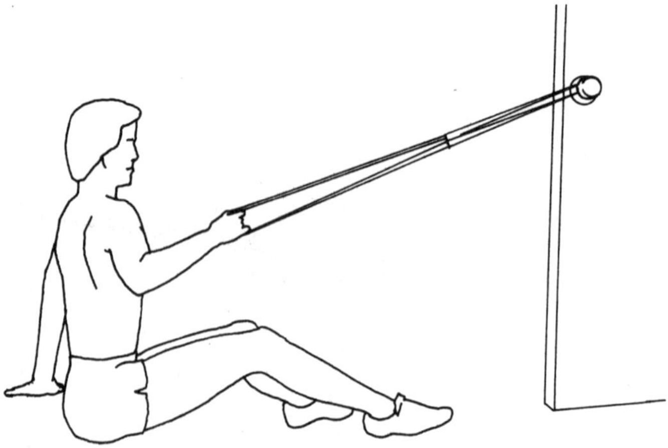

Shoulder extension *Begin with your arm extended, as above. Pull the band slowly toward you, bending the elbow with a rowing motion.*

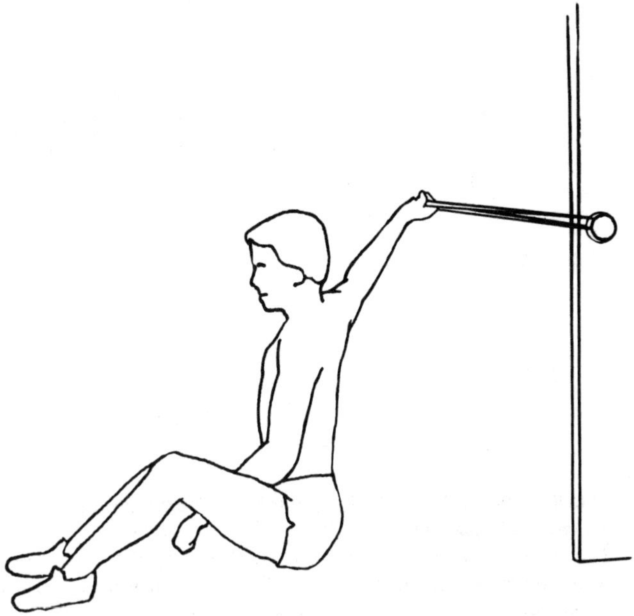

Internal rotation of the shoulder *Start with the arm back as shown, then rotate entire arm toward the middle.*

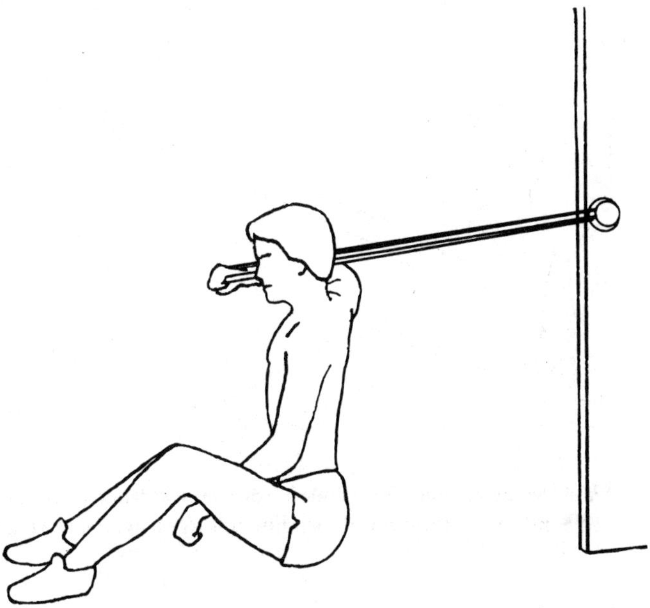

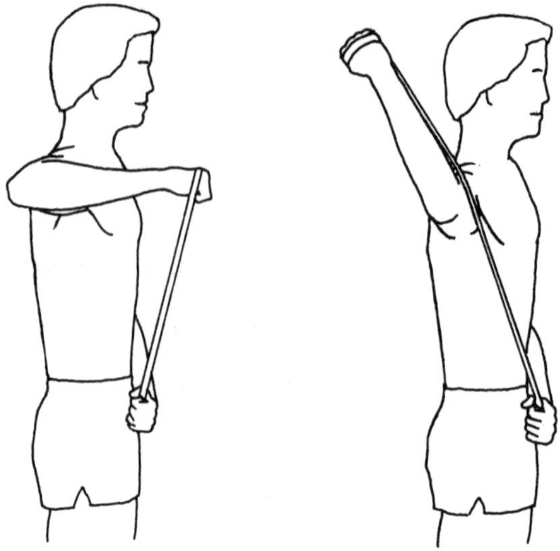

External rotation of the shoulder with arm abducted *Note the direction of the upper arm.*

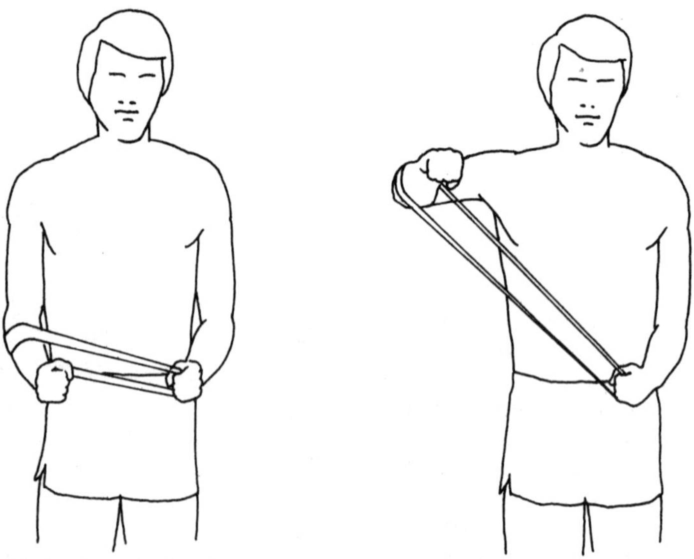

Abduction of the shoulder *Grasping the band in front of you in one hand and looping it around the other forearm, with elbows bent 90 degrees, move one arm straight out to the side and up, keeping the elbow bent. This is just one of many ways to exercise the shoulder; you are limited only by your imagination. It is particularly important to train the internal and external rotation of the shoulder.*

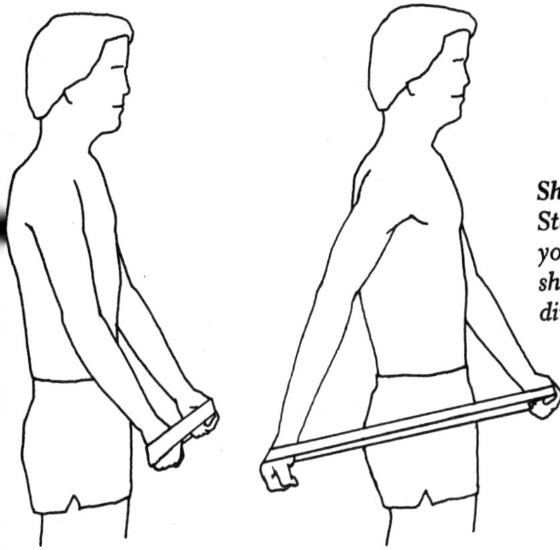

Shoulder hyperextension *Start with arm alongside your body, then end as shown, with arms pointed directly backwards.*

Triceps or elbow extension *Begin with both hands grasping the band in front of the chest, with elbows straight down at sides. Move one arm straight down, keeping elbow at side. Be sure to keep up resistance to pull of band when returning the arm to the starting position.*

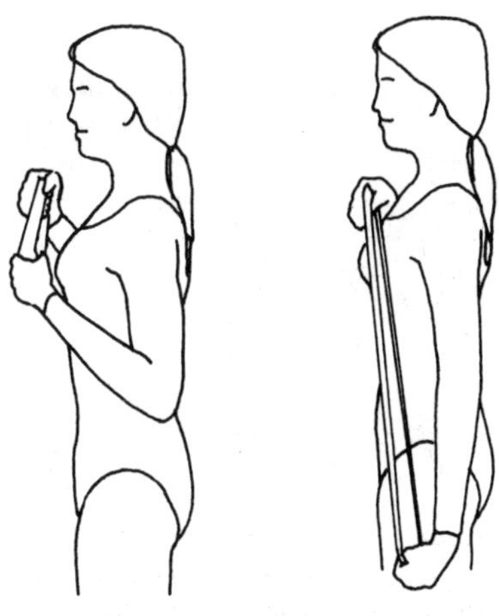

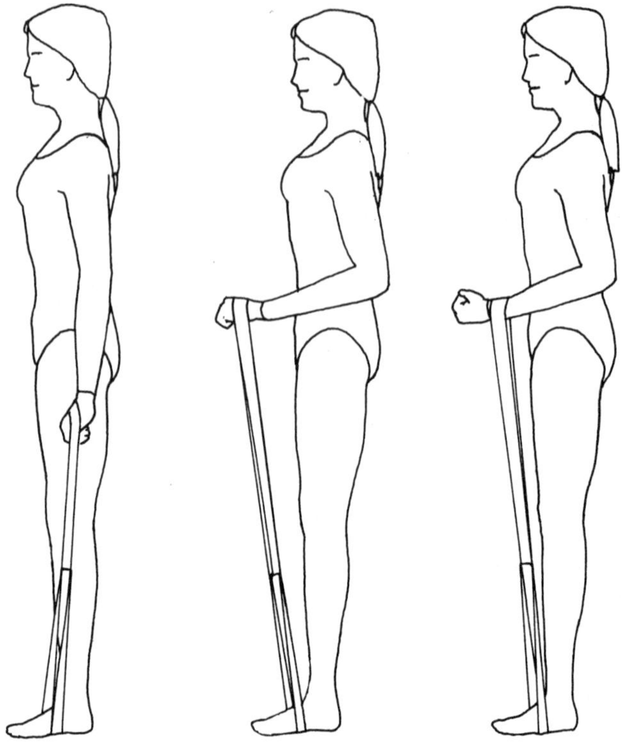

A B C

Biceps flexion *Figure A shows starting position. Note the difference of the hand position in figures B and C; each position exercises different muscles, so for maximum benefit do both palm-up and palm-down exercises.*

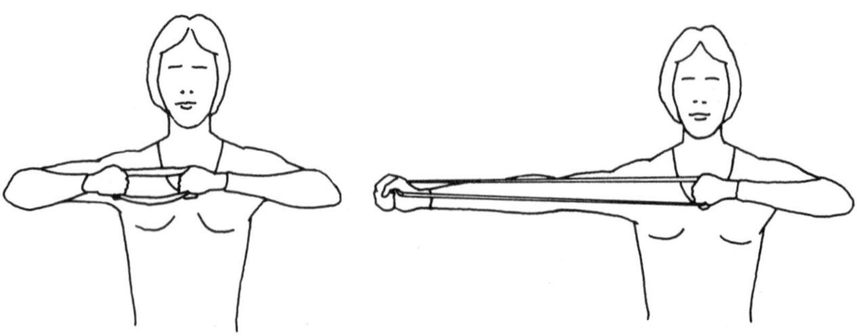

Triceps or elbow extension *This can also be a scapular exercise, if you pull backward with the shoulder blade muscles.*

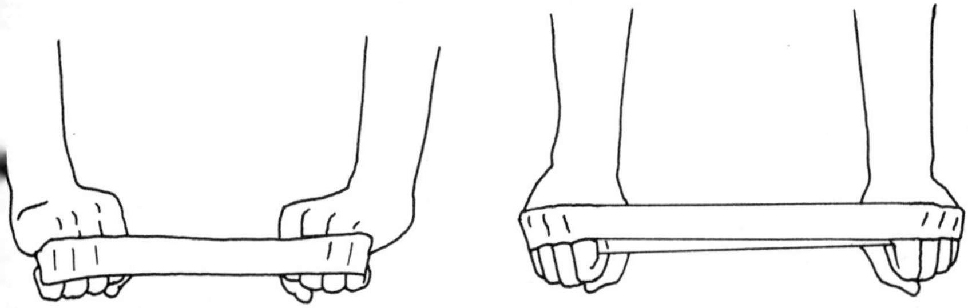

Ulnar flexion (adduction) *Bend the wrists to the side, toward the little fingers.*

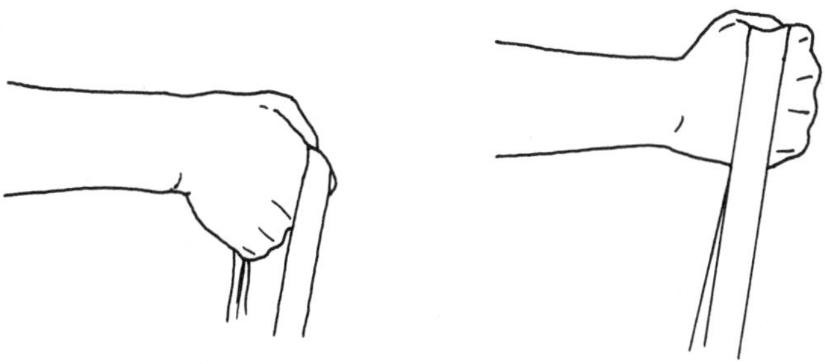

Radial flexion (abduction) of the wrist *Bend the wrists to the side toward the thumb.*

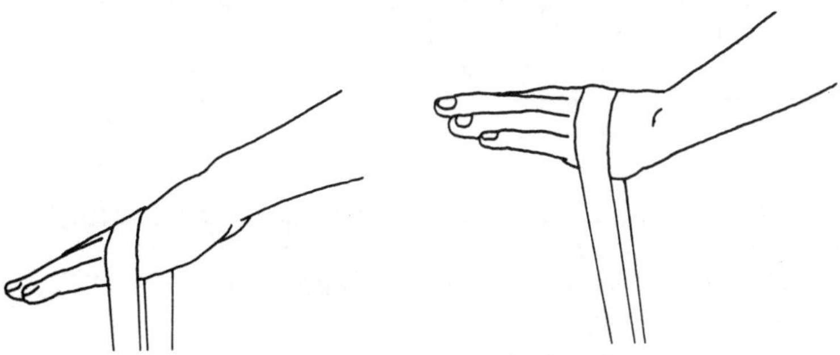

Dorsiflexion of the wrist *Bend the wrist backward.*

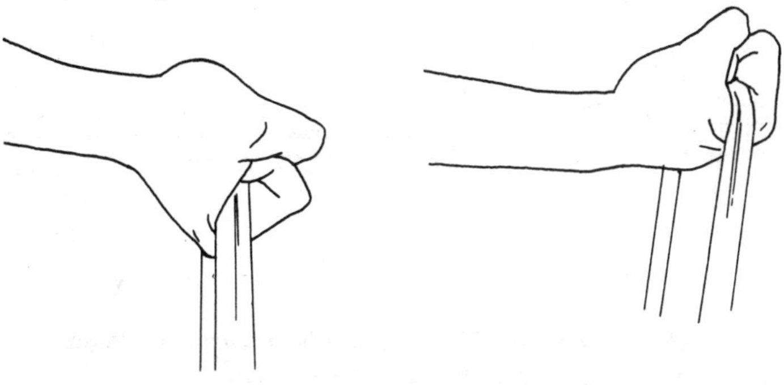

Flexion of the wrist *Bend the wrist in toward the palm.*

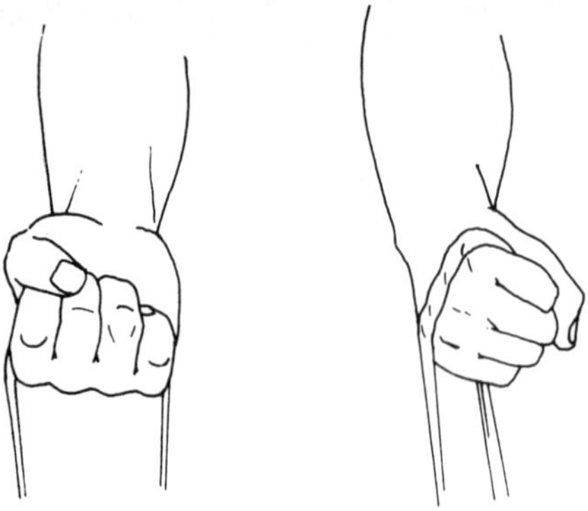

Rotation of the wrist *It is possible to rotate the wrist through an almost universal motion.*

Monster sidestep *This is an advanced use of the bands. The beginning position is standing up straight; then very quickly take as wide a step as possible and hold that position. Then bring the other foot slowly over to the foot that has just stepped. Make your first step a quick powerful motion, then the other step, coming back, a controlled step. This way you will walk sideways across the room; then begin stepping with the other leg and walk back.*

If this is too difficult with the band around the ankles, you can move the band up to the calves or even to the knees, which is the easiest position. As you advance, you should be able to lower the band down to ankle level and take very wide steps. The next stage is to do it while balancing on your toes. The most advanced stage is doing this in the linebacker squatting position.

This will exercise your hip muscles in a way they have probably never been exercised before.

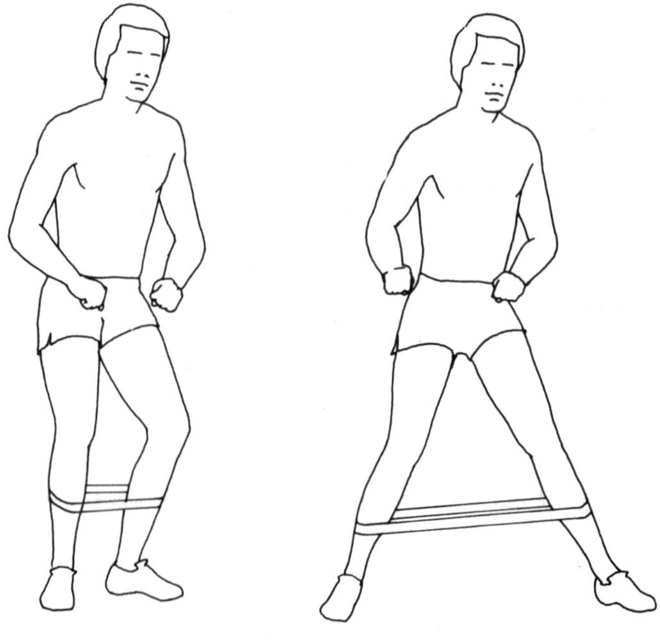

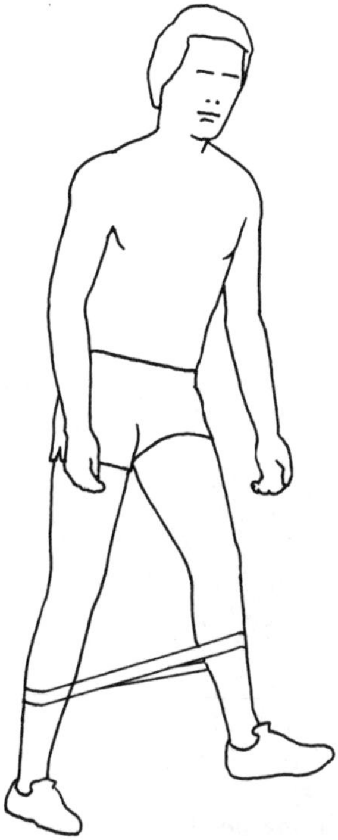

Monster forward step *After the monster side step, progress to this exercise. The band can be placed up to knee level or all the way down to ankle level. Kick out with your lead leg, then slowly bring the trailing leg up to meet it. After that, kick out with force again, as wide as possible, then let the trailing leg come in slowly with control. Do not let the band snap the trailing leg in. The idea is to exercise both legs. This is a very effective exercise for runners, hurdlers, soccer players, and all those whose sport requires kicking. The power band works very well for kickers, especially soccer players who want to do side kicks. With the band on a post, it is possible to mimic almost any kicking maneuver you want to train for.*

A

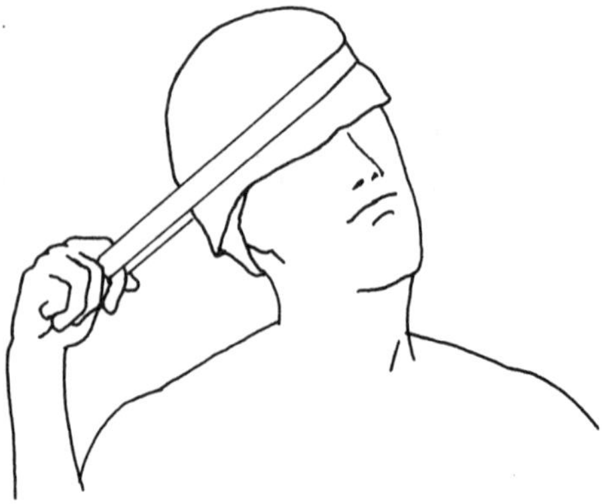

B

Neck exercises *Use a power band over a stocking cap to effectively help strengthen the neck muscles. The stocking cap is important to hold the band in place. When doing the neck extension exercise shown in figure A, it is important to have the cap over your eyes so you don't snap yourself in the eye if you accidentally let go of the band. Move from flexion to extension. Figure B shows lateral bending, C shows rotation of the neck.*

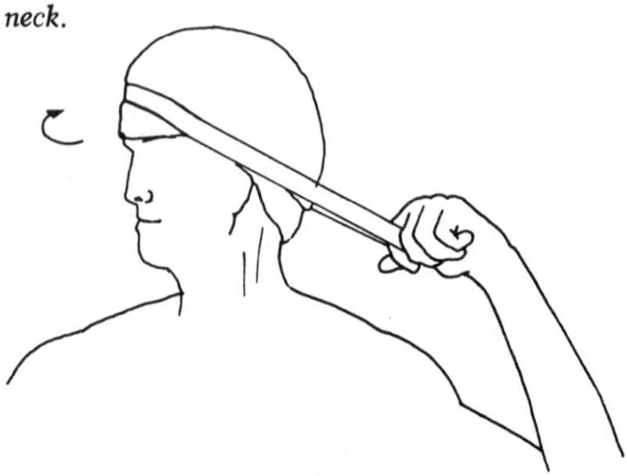

C

16

The Oscillating Beam

The oscillating beam, or O-beam, is a tremendous tool for developing balance, stabilizer strength, and movement patterns that can dramatically improve your performance in activities ranging from baseball to skiing, from bowling to football. Not only is the O-beam helpful for building you up and developing your motor skills, but it has another element that is hard to beat—it is fun.

We couple O-beam training with training on the kinesthetic primer board described in the next chapter to teach the principles of efficient motion. Bill Buckner won his first National League batting championship after he learned better balance on the O-beam and the K-board. Eric Soderholm was another greatly improved hitter and fielder following training. If you want further motivation, consider that the champion tennis players we have worked with do very well on the beam—they have the correct type of movements—but they also get even better. Whatever your sport, you will move better after training on the beam and the board.

The O-beam is a plank that can be made either professionally or in almost anyone's home carpentry shop. Sandwich a ¾-inch plank between two 2-by-4-inch pieces of board. Your final dimensions

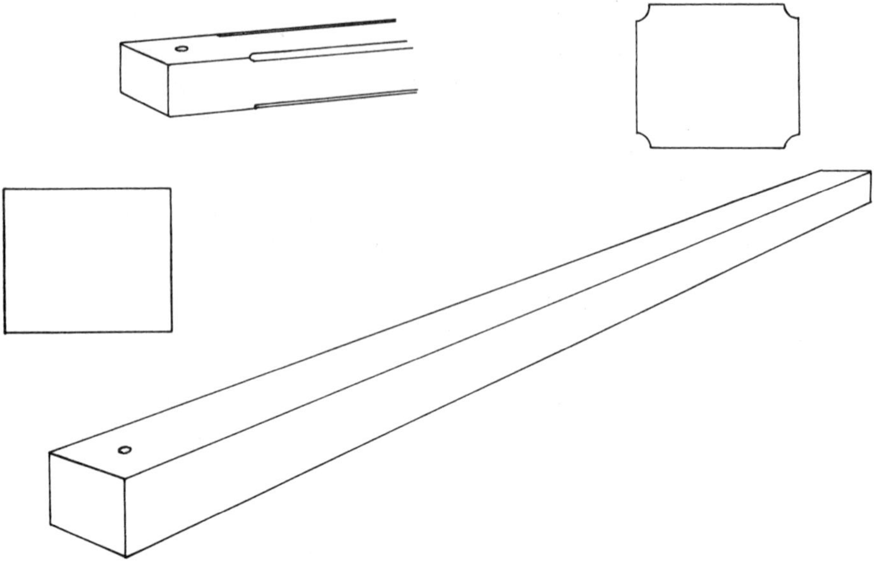

The oscillating beam

would be 3 by 3½ inches square and 12 to 14 feet long, beveled ½ inch on each corner. A spoke plane or a regular plane can be used to do the beveling. Beveling the corners takes away a little bit of the stability and makes your body do more. Having the beam different widths—with both a 3-inch and a 3.5-inch side—gives you the opportunity to increase the difficulty of the exercises as your performance increases.

If you don't have the room for that long a plank, you could use a 3- to 5-foot-long plank, but you then would obviously not be able to do all the stepping exercises.

The O-beam is used to practice a wide variety of postures and movement patterns. Training on the O-beam will help you develop stronger ankles and knees. It will also help you develop the stability to counterbalance excessive inward or outward rotation of the lower and upper leg. It will develop the muscles of your head and neck, spine and ribs, and spine and pelvis. Ultimately, working on the O-beam will give you a finely tuned sense of balance and enable you to perform any activity at higher levels.

The O-beam is, by its nature, an inexpensive and effective method of rehabilitation or preconditioning for the prevention of injuries in all sports that involve running, jumping, and squatting. Progressions range from static work—simply standing on it, on two feet or one foot—to dynamic work involving walking, hopping, and jumping Movement-mastery exercises range from stable standing, either erect or in a crouch, to accomplishing complex direction changes with eyes opened and, finally, closed.

Since the O-beam is 3 inches by 3½ inches, you can start out working on the broader surface, which does not oscillate (shake) as much as the narrower surface. After you have mastered the routines working on the broad side, you can turn the beam to its 3-inch side and hone your skills even finer. The important thing is to develop an awareness of structural integrity—proper alignment, stabilization, and strength; the feeling of motion and control; and careful wakefulness. In effect, the athlete must discover the limits imposed on his body by fear, weakness, or inexperience, and gradually transcend these limits and move to new levels. By progression we learn many previously unthinkable skills that build the mind and body toward high level of sports performance.

O-beams are currently being used in sports rehabilitation clinics and athletic training rooms by teams at all levels—grade school, high school, college, Olympic, and professional. The beam can be used at home, preferably on a rug area and in front of a mirror for posture feedback. While we always recommend supervision by a certified athletic trainer, corrective exercise therapist, physical education instructor, or physical therapist, we believe that an individual can work alone out of necessity—mindful that progression and a careful adherence to form are the keys to success.

The exercises are listed here in progression. Each progression should be mastered completely before advancing to the next level. The progressions should also be used as warm-ups for the more advanced movements and the training in more complex neuromuscular patterns. Another benefit of the progressions is that they help tone up unbalanced muscles that are too weak to do their antigravity stabilizer work.

The activities should be done in slow motion at first. Alternate movements frequently to keep up the interest, bearing in mind that the goal is a mastery of each movement. Always give yourself enough time to make adjustments within your body to the unstable nature of the beam.

Before working on the O-beam, you will need to know a few more facts about the body.

The feet oscillate and must be controlled. Rolling in (pronation) of the feet will cause the lower leg (tibia) to rotate in, and the upper leg (thigh) will also roll inward. The necessary counter-rotational force must be supplied or stability and balance will be lost.

The spinal vertebrae also oscillate. The spine has three continuous curves: a concave curve in the upper back (the cervical region), a convex curve in the middle back (the thoracic region), and a concave curve in the lower back (the lumbar region). For proper balance on the O-beam, these three curves must be made as straight as possible.

The concave curve of the upper spine should be extended in a straight line so that the ears are directly above the shoulders. This is accomplished by drawing the chin in and the head back until balance is achieved. The convex curve of the thoracic region of the spine is lessened by the "lengthening extension," in which the shoulder girdle is drawn backward and the scapulae are drawn together and down. Lessening the curve of the lower spine can be achieved by rolling the pelvis from a posterior tilt to an anterior fixed position—as if you are lifting the mons pubis upward from under and between the thighs. Note how this causes you to lose the potbellied look.

Erect posture is always emphasized for work on the O-beam. With the three regions of the spine in alignment, you will sense an "all together" feeling. When working on the beam, the three curves should be maintained in a static, rigid contraction. All sections of the core—head and neck, ribs and spine, and spine and pelvis—should be fixed and stable throughout all activities.

The spine has three basic functions, all of which will be emphasized by work on the O-beam:

1. Vertical action, which includes the erect static posture, forward bending, and backward bending. This vertical action demands a straightening of the spine or a reduction of the curves.
2. Side-to-side bending.
3. Rotation to the right or left.

Often an exercise will call for a combination of these movements.

The following techniques can help you master the beam exercises. Keep them in mind as you do your O-beam workouts.

- When standing still, the feet should remain in a straight line, with all the toes gripping the beam and sensing each subtle factor, from change in sense of balance to lightness of touch.
- The patella (kneecap) should always be in a straight line with the inside of the big toe and second toe.
- The rib cage should not be elevated; rather, it should be held down and together with abdominal contractile tension, about 30 percent more than you would normally use.
- The pelvis should remain fixed and stable unless specifically indicated otherwise.
- When moving with full vision, eyes should remain fixed and focused forward, not on the beam or the feet.

These points should be referred to before and during each lesson. As you become familiar with these techniques, you will find yourself using them automatically, with no conscious effort.

Movements forward on the beam should find the toes gripping the surface first, followed by the heel. In backward motions the toes should feel the board, then the heel should move down to the board. For lateral actions, the weight should be carried on the balls of the feet.

You may wish sometimes to move about the beam with your shoes off. Removing the shoes awakens the feet to the sensory feelings of performing the movement. The use of shoes on the O-beam is common because shoes are worn in most physical activities. Note that it is easy to slip on the beam when wearing only socks, and this can be dangerous. Be cautious and alert.

To minimize the routineness of these exercises, try variations on the basic activities. These could include:

- Different arm positions.
- Obstacles on or above the beam.
- Use of wands, hoops, beanbags, balls, ropes, etc.
- Closing eyes (this eliminates the righting eye reflex and places greater demand upon the other balancing systems).
- Balancing different objects on the beam and body parts.
- Use of partners.
- Mimetics.

These suggestions, coupled with your imagination, should result in a multitude of exciting, enjoyable activities.

O-BEAM BALANCE EXERCISES

The following routines will help improve your balance.

Pre-Basic

With eyes closed

1. Walk on line on floor.
2. Quarter squat on one leg on the floor.
3. Balance with both legs on the floor.
4. Balance on one leg on floor.

Basic

All activities from basic level are performed on beam.

1. Walk.
2. Quarter squat—on one leg, first in inclined position and then sitting position.
3. Toe raises—on two legs, in sideways position.
4. Walk, pivot, walk.
5. Walk on toes.
6. Swing step—move free leg alongside beam by depressing hip.
7. Walk backward.

Intermediate

1. Walk quickly.
2. Side shuffle.
3. Hop.
4. All fours.
5. Stork stand (hip flexed, on one leg).
6. Command touch—move hand to spot on body named by a partner.
7. Balance touch—touch an object on the floor with free leg while maintaining balance.
8. Toe raise—on one leg, in side position.
9. Lunge.

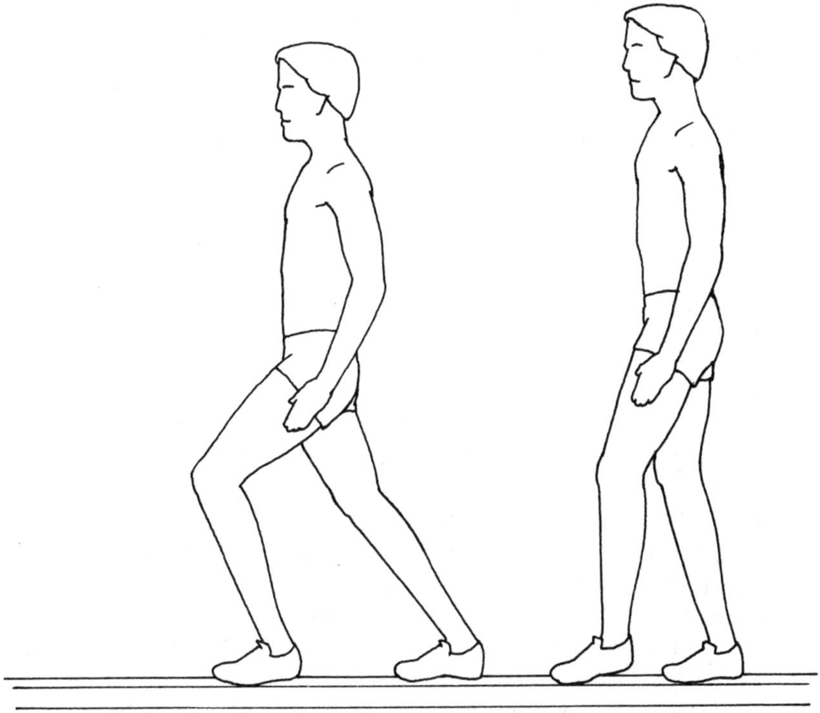

Using the O-beam *The illustrations show various positions of walking and stepping on the O-beam. Notice that for stability, the pelvis usually leads the motion. Also, toes should touch first; grab the beam with your toes; then bring your heel down.*

Lunge activities on the beam can be very helpful in creating movement patterns needed for higher performance. Work on the proper forms and feel of the lunge positions. The lunge activity should only be done at the appropriate level. Master the other elements of balance first.

The lunge position is illustrated in the drawing (below). The rear knee should be locked into the straight (extended) position. The feet should be pointed forward, with the knees kept in line with

Lunge *Note that the back knee is straight. Also observe the proper position of the hip, neck, and spine, centered over the pelvis.*

the inside of the foot. The ribs should be pulled down, the back extended, and the eyes should be focused straight ahead. Have your partner check for level hips and shoulders.

Once you are familiar with the lunge position, try pushing yourself upward using the forward-leg muscles only; then push yourself upward using the muscles of the extended rear leg only. Finally, push yourself upward using the muscles of both legs. Note the power that results from using two legs rather than one.

Advanced

1. Heel–toe walk.
2. Cross over (in front) moving sideways.
3. Cross over (behind) moving sideways.
4. Walk on all fours.
5. Walk quickly backward.

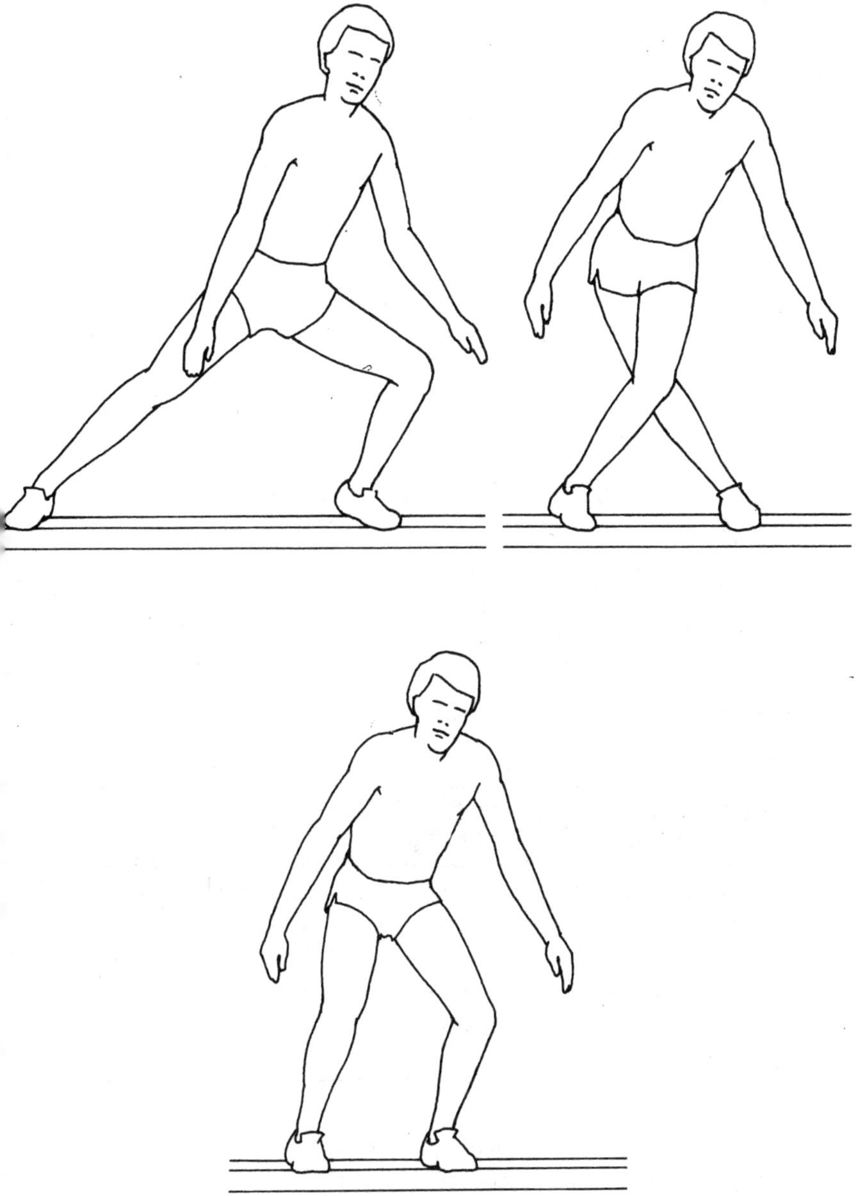

O-beam activities *The top left illustration shows the wide sidestep, or sideways lunge. The top right position is the crossover technique practiced on the O-beam. The bottom illustration is the proper semi-squat, or linebacking, position.*

6. Hop with quarter turn.
7. Hop sideways.
8. Lunge, jump up, return to lunge position.
9. Lunge, jump, switch lead leg.
10. Lateral squat—attempt to touch fingers of hands clasped behind back to beam.
11. Walk on all fours, then lift leg off beam. Secure balance and position.
12. Thread needle—step through clasped hands and return.

Skilled

1. Burst forward and stop.
2. Lunge, jump, half turn to lunge with same leg leading.
3. Lunge, jump, half turn to lunge with opposite leg leading.
4. Hop, half turn.
5. Jump up and land on beam.
6. Hop backwards.
7. Heel click, return.
8. Heel slap, return.
9. Squat thrusts.
10. Back lever—free leg extended, full squat, and return.

O-BEAM PERCEPTUAL MOTOR DEVELOPMENT EXERCISES

Motor perception exercises can benefit each and every athlete or rehabilitation patient. These exercises help develop:

- Equilibrium (balance).
- Kinesthesia (body-position sense).
- Bilateral coordination.
- Motor planning.
- Motor problem solving.
- Right and left discrimination.
- Ocular (eye) control.
- Tactile (touch) stimulation.
- Vestibular stimulation (balance control).
- Reflex inhibition.

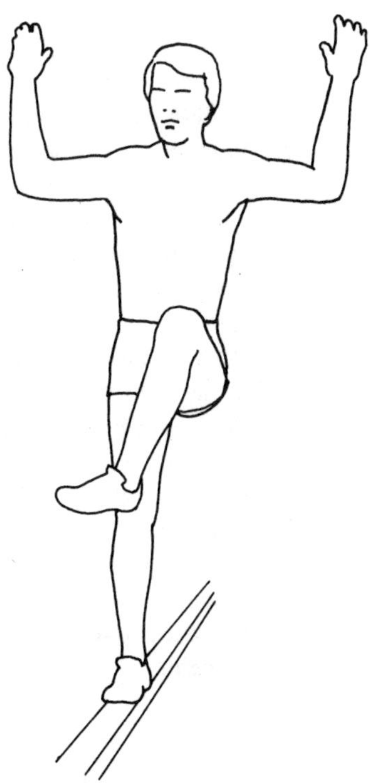

Advanced training maneuvers *These include hopping and standing on one foot.*

Get on the beam and have fun doing the following exercises. Master each before going on, but don't be afraid to repeat previously mastered exercises.

Static Postures

STANDING EXERCISES

1. Stand on beam, left foot in front of right. Hold position for 30 seconds.
2. Stand on beam, right foot in front of left. Hold position for 30 seconds.
3. Same as #1 except with eyes closed.
4. Same as #2 except with eyes closed.
5. Standing sideways with feet touching.
6. Standing sideways with feet spread apart to shoulder width.
7. Squat down and up while maintaining posture #6.

SIGHTLESS POSTURES AND MOTIONS

8. Repeat exercises #5 through #7 with eyes closed and record the number of seconds posture is maintained.

Dynamic Postures

1. Walk forward on beam, arms held at the side.
2. Walk backward on beam, arms held at the side.
3. Walk to end of beam, turn around, and walk back with arms held at the side.
4. Walk forward to middle of beam, do quarter turn, and walk remaining distance sideward to the left with weight on balls of feet.
5. Walk to middle of beam, quarter turn, and continue sideward to the right with weight on balls of feet.
6. Walk forward with left foot always in front of right.
7. Walk forward with right foot always in front of left.
8. Walk backward with left foot always in front of right.
9. Walk backward with right foot always in front of left.
10. Walk forward with hands on hips—feel hip movements as you proceed.
11. Walk backward with hands on hips—feel hip movements as you proceed.

Other options You are limited only by your imagination in training on the O-beam. For baseball training, learn to swing, then learn to hit nerf balls in the stable position.

12. Walk forward and pick up a shoe from middle of beam.
13. Walk forward to the center, kneel on one knee, rise, and continue to end of beam.
14. Walk forward with shoe balanced on top of head.
15. Walk backward with a 2.5-pound plate balanced on top of head.
16. Place shoe at center of beam; walk to center, place shoe on top of head, continue to end of beam.
17. Have a partner hold a wand twelve inches above center of beam; walk forward on beam and step over wand.
18. Walk backward and step over wand.
19. Have wand held at height of three feet; walk forward and pass under wand.
20. Walk backward and pass under wand.
21. Walk the beam backward with hands clasped behind body.
22. Walk the beam forward, arms held sideward, palms down, with 2.5-pound plate on back of each hand.
23. Walk the beam forward, arms held sideward, palms up, with a 2.5-pound plate on the back of each hand.
24. Walk the beam backward, arms held sideward, palms down, with a 2.5-pound plate on the back of each hand.
25. Walk the beam backward, arms held sideward, palms up, with a 2.5-pound plate on palm of each hand.

17

The Kinesthetic Primer Board for Movement Education

"Kinesthetic primer board" (K-board) is a fancy name for a teeter-board. While these balance-development boards have been used extensively in movement education and motor-perception-development classes, especially for primary-grade physical-education classes, K-boards have received little recognition for their value in sports rehabilitation.

That may change once people know that it was after Bill Buckner practiced batting using the K-board that he went out and led the league in batting. We've used the board extensively at our clinic for specific ankle, knee, pelvis, and back injuries. It is also a great performance-enhancer. It is our feeling that the state of the art of sports medicine will be greatly advanced by emphasizing the concepts and devices aiding perception development. And of these, the kinesthetic primer board is an all-star. The benefits are great, and you can make a K-board yourself.

You need two boards. The top board is 18 inches square by ¾ inch thick. The bottom board is 18 inches long, 2½ inches wide, and ¾ inch thick. Round the corners off the big board, then mount the smaller board exactly across the middle using screws and glue. To

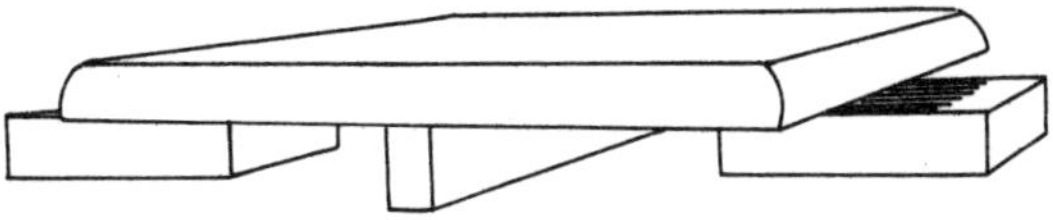

Kinesthetic primer board with cheater blocks *If you are recovering from an ankle injury, the primer board normally used may move too much, so putting blocks under either side will decrease the amount of force and exercise demanded of your ankles until you are recovered.*

aid traction you may wish to tread the surface with rubber matting like that used on stairs. You can round off the edges of the bottom board to make balancing more difficult.

If you wish to use a K-board for movement requiring a step, such as in batting, you can make a four-foot-long model. (A K-board this long only needs to be 15 inches wide.) For injuries where one side is more developed, we sometimes use two boards (one foot on each) to isolate the response of both the good and the bad leg. Furthermore, we sometimes use a higher board, with a bottom board that is ¾ inch thick by 3¼ inches wide. This makes balancing more difficult because there is farther to go to right the board. We round off the bottom edges of this higher K-board as well, so that balance is more difficult. In the clinic we usually convert our flat-bottomed boards into rounded-edged boards after much use, since the boards tend to wear down on the corners anyway. Using the flat-bottomed board on bare floor first, then later moving to carpet, will give you much the same effect as moving from a flat-bottomed board to a round-bottomed one.

USING THE BOARD

You can stand on the K-board two ways: with your feet perpendicular to the bottom board, so you can rock either frontward or backward (as to the right in the illustration), or with your feet parallel to the bottom board, so you can rock either to the left or to the right (as on the left in the illustration).

The same posture principles hold true on the K-board as on the O-beam. If you don't align all your body segments, you will end up flapping like a bird as your hands attempt to give you the balance that your core is not giving you.

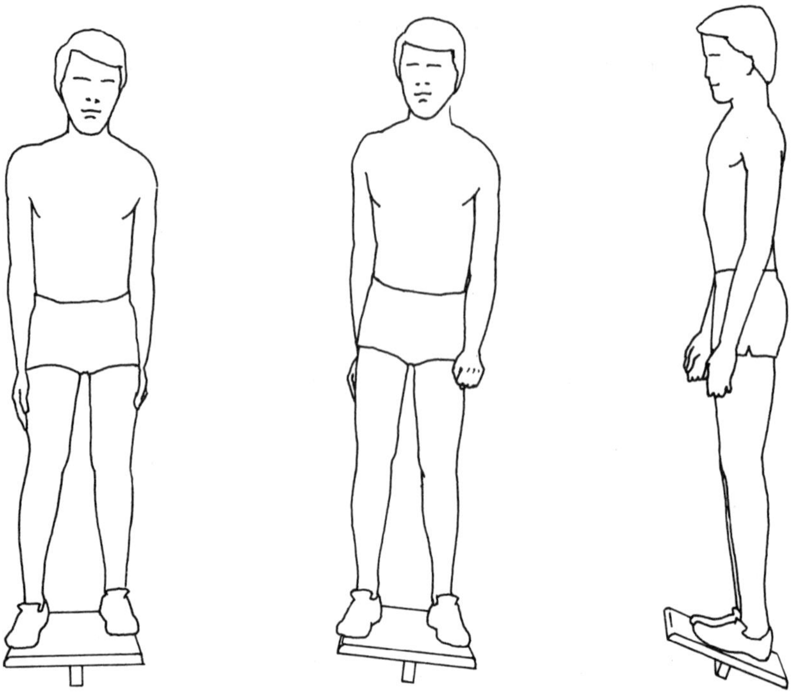

Use of the K-board *You need to train standing on the K-board both front to back and side to side. These two options exercise entirely different groups of muscles.*

Step on the K-board, balancing front to back. Attempt to sense or feel the surface flatness with your feet. This feeling or teaching of the feet is an important part of movement education. We recommend that you start barefooted in order to increase your feel for it. As you attempt to balance you will have much more success if you keep your chin in, press down with your ribs, rotate your pelvis forward, and tighten your butt. Once you are in good position you will discover that balance is provided best by rotating the pelvis. This explains an important factor in movement: The pelvis leads the motion. Many people and almost all children tend to lead with their heads; but in jumping, for instance, if you try leading with the pelvis instead of the head, you will notice an immediate difference in the height and ease of your leaps.

Control of the side-to-side motion is somewhat different. Again, you need good posture, with chin in, ribs down, butt tight, and feeling with the feet. But this time your control comes from a side-to-side shift of your waist, at approximately the level of your navel.

The following are basic movements. Learn to do each while holding steady, without rocking.

1. Erect standing, front to back.
2. Erect standing, side to side.
3. Squatting, front to back.
4. Squatting, side to side.
5. Single-leg standing, front to back.
6. Single-leg standing, side to side (foot is positioned exactly in the center).

After you learn to do each exercise with your eyes open, try it with your eyes closed. These exercises will further help you develop your sense of movement, which is like a sixth sense. In fact, the word *kinesthesia* means the sensation of bodily position, presence, or movement. The board allows you to train your motion senses so you can train your muscles. Kinesthetic awareness produces efficient effort, which means neither too much nor too little muscle force, but just the right amount.

After you have learned to do the above exercises, try jumping on the K-board. Set it up flat and then jump onto it. Once you can land with control, you are a "percher." That is when the board really becomes fun, as you learn to throw, juggle, hit, and stride, all the while maintaining perfect equilibrium. You'll be surprised at how efficient your body becomes at providing excellent balance for both everyday motions and for sports performance.

It is our observation that top athletes often have this ability to move efficiently, with balance and control. We are sure that your performance will improve as you get better on the O-beam and K-board.

While the physical demands of the board are unlike the effects of long-distance running, it is still amazing to see the exertion required to maintain equilibrium on the board. The lactic-acid levels rise quickly at first in the less used areas of the body. Athletes using the board will often report a burning sensation in the feet or ankles.

It has been our experience that use of the boards six days a week should be continued for about three weeks.

18

The Mini-Trampoline

One of the very valuable aids in training for specific stabilization strength and for synergy and a sense of your body is the mini-trampoline, or tram. The tram is an essential part of our rehabilitation program for ankle, knee, and hip injuries, but it is also valuable in performance enhancement and training for children and adults. Trams are now being vigorously marketed as alternatives to jogging and running on hard surfaces. Most of these trams do what they are advertised to do—that is, provide a soft resilient surface to jog or run in place on—and for this reason we agree they can be quite valuable in the rehabilitation of joint injuries, especially prior to full recovery and running on hard surfaces. Mini-trampolines come in many sizes and shapes, and they vary in cost and quality. If you cannot afford or do not have access to a tram, a bunch of overstuffed pillows or a bed that won't collapse will provide a workable substitute.

In 1976, the American Academy of Pediatrics recommended the abolition of large trampolines. Large trampolines were being used to try back flips, and because it was impossible to properly "spot" school children doing this, a statistically significant number of neck injuries were occurring on large trampolines. We agree with the recommendation of the American Academy of Pediatrics. However, you should not confuse large trampolines with mini-trampolines, since their use is quite different. You would have to be either an accomplished acrobat or very foolish to try to do flips on a mini-tram! We use it for training, running, and just for standing, not for attempting flips or any other hazardous activity.

In shopping for a tram, be sure to look for the following qualities:

- The tram bed itself should be approximately ten inches off the floor.
- The tram bed should have a foam-rubber padding and a covering of vinyl or a stronger material around the entire exterior frame and all of the springs, making it safe for both children and adults.
- The heart of any trampoline is its springs, which should be attached in a "V" pattern. This will give the surface tension and balance resilience that we are looking for rather than the tightrope effect that you find if the springs are attached straight like the spokes of a wheel. Buy a brand that has a reputation for good springs.

Properly constructed mini-trampolines are very safe and are valuable tools for rehabilitation as well as for performance training. They are also valuable in teaching both children and adults strength, balance, and coordination, all of which will improve skills and performance levels, regardless of the sport or exercise program.

In addition, trams are valuable aids for perceptual motor development training, especially in the training and rehabilitation of children. We are surprised that more physical educators have not utilized them in schools.

The program for training specific stabilization strength on the tram will not involve vigorous activity, but it can and will become quite strenuous even for a highly trained athlete who has been trained extensively in traditional conditioning programs. Remember, progress is not measured by the number of repetitions that you do, but by complete mastery and the ability to successfully perform the routine. The key to success is going to be mental training and concentration on your body. It will take a great deal of mind control to develop the body control we are aiming to teach you; this is a total training effort for all of your mind-body systems. In fact, because it demands so much of your mind, your body, and the fusion of these two components, the tram routine may have the same tranquilizing, meditative effect on you that it has on many of our athletes. Do not hurry, and do not get frustrated while doing the routines.

LESSON ONE: STANDING ON THE TRAM

Stand in the center of the tram with both feet apart, slightly wider than your shoulders. Spend approximately two minutes tuning in to your kinesthetic sense, and make the following assessments of various parts of your body:

- Are your feet shaky or solid?
- Do your knees rotate in or out?
- Are your legs rolling in or out?
- Is your pelvis tilted forward 45 degrees, backward 60 degrees, or somewhere in between?
- Is your spine straight?
- Are your shoulder blades back and pulled together?
- Is your chin locked, or are your head and neck out in the road-runner position?

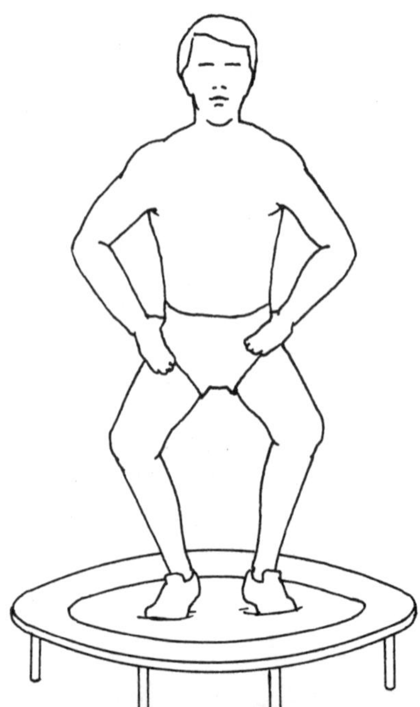

Stable position on tram *Knees are slightly bent for emphasis to show the outward rotation of the knees. This stable posture includes the head-up position.*

Now, close your eyes and reassess these seven areas. Don't be surprised if you find yourself wobbling at this point in the exercise. You have always been on smooth surfaces before this; the fluidlike unstable surface of the tram forces your body to continually correct itself and balance itself with the stabilizers and midcourse correctors that we have been talking about. You must remain stable not just in one plane, but in many planes—more than just the side-to-side plane of the O-beams and K-boards. We are now beginning to train you for maximum control of those movements and factors that prevent the rotations and counter-rotations in your feet, knees, and hips. In most people, the stabilizer and midcourse-corrector muscles are weak and have to be developed before performance is attempted. Reinjuries occur so frequently and rehabilitation fails for so many people because these stabilizing, correcting muscles have not been trained.

Your goal in this exercise is specific stabilization strength, which your body tone should accomplish. After assuming the basic standing position on the tram, focus first on your feet, which can roll inward (supination) or outward (pronation). Your toes should be pointed straight ahead and the weight of your body evenly distributed on your feet (on the big and little toes and the heels, if you have good arches.). The ability to keep your body from rolling, hold the arches from collapsing, and maintain a stable position is called eccentric supination strength. It is the foot's equivalent of grasping a bar with the hand.

When your feet are stable, move up to the knees, which should be pressed outward rather than caving inward in the X-kneed position which unfortunately we see so commonly.

Your pelvis should be tipped up maximally. You accomplish this by contracting or tightening up the gluteal muscles in your buttocks as much as possible.

Now to the core. Your spine should be erect and your shoulder blades back. Your chin should be tucked in, and your head and neck in the neck-lock position. Think tall!

Now, with your eyes closed, you should be feeling your body. What is it doing? Is it steady? Are any of the muscles burning? If you are getting that burn of fatigue (which is from lactic-acid buildup), it is a sign that those muscles are weak and definitely need training. You should be able to achieve this position and hold it for thirty seconds. If you cannot do this, then you should practice these exercises on the floor first, as you are not fit to be training on the tram. And if you are not fit to train on the tram, you certainly aren't fit to perform athletics.

LESSON TWO: SINGLE-LEG STANDING

After you can stand steadily on the tram for thirty seconds, you must advance to standing on one leg. This is done with one leg centered in the tram and the other bent back at the knee, so that you are standing like an ostrich. Work at eliminating the oscillations or wobbling. You must be able to do this equally with each leg. Your goal is to stand steadily on one leg—whether good or injured—for thirty seconds without wobbling. You should be able to do this with eyes open and with eyes closed.

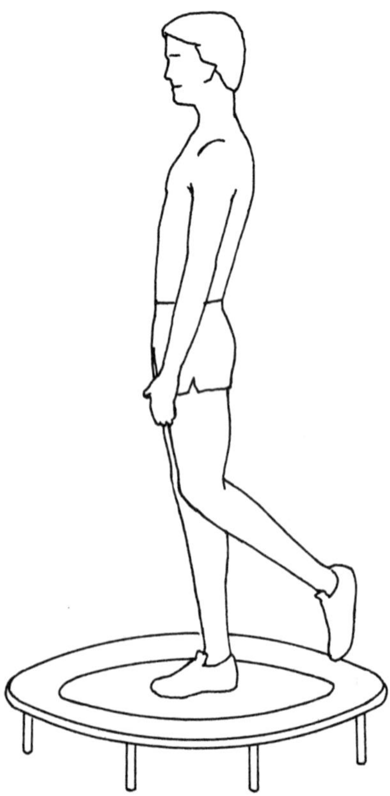

Single-leg standing

Full squat position *This is the true test of ability to run on an injury. If you can hold this position on a tram for 30 seconds and remain stable, then you are fit to run. Until you can do this, you do not have sufficient strength or stability to run without risking reinjury.*

LESSON THREE: SIT-SQUAT

The sit-squat is a true test of whether you are ready to run or not.

Assume the basic position in the center of the tram. Do your checks to be sure you are in the stable, proper body position. Then slowly begin a descent into a full squat position. Remember, this is not past 90 degrees of knee flexion. As your back moves down, the knee should follow a line made by the inside of the big toe. Don't forget to press your legs outward, and particularly concentrate on avoiding the X-knee, or valgus, position. You must keep your foot in the stable position and counter any wobbling of the foot by grabbing with your toes. Now repeat this with your eyes closed.

Once you can do the full squat, with your eyes open or closed, in the stable position, you are ready to do the one-legged squat. First try it with your good leg if you are rehabilitating an injured leg. Once you can do the squat in a stable, nonwobbly fashion with your good leg, you should be ready to do it on your injured leg. Until you can hold a one-legged squat at a full 90 degrees of knee flexion without wobbling for thirty seconds, we believe you should not be running. If you can do this one-legged full squat without any wobble, then rehabilitation has progressed satisfactorily and you are fit to begin running.

It is important while doing the one-legged squat that you maintain correct position. With the leg off the mat, you should have your toes pointed and knee straight. It is essential that your pelvis be tilted forward maximally and that your abdominal muscles be tightened throughout this entire exercise. You should lean backward slightly while going down slowly, concentrating on keeping your knee outward. It is important while doing this test to concentrate on maintaining stability and eliminating any wobbling.

LESSON FOUR: HEEL AND TOE RAISES

For the heel raise, assume the basic standing position and adjust your body tone to the maximum. Press your pelvis forward and maximally tighten the gluteus maximus muscles in your buttocks. Depress your ribs and lock your knees backward. You want to have a sense of rigidity throughout your body. Slowly raise your heels off the tram and hold at a maximum height for about five seconds, then slowly

Heel raise

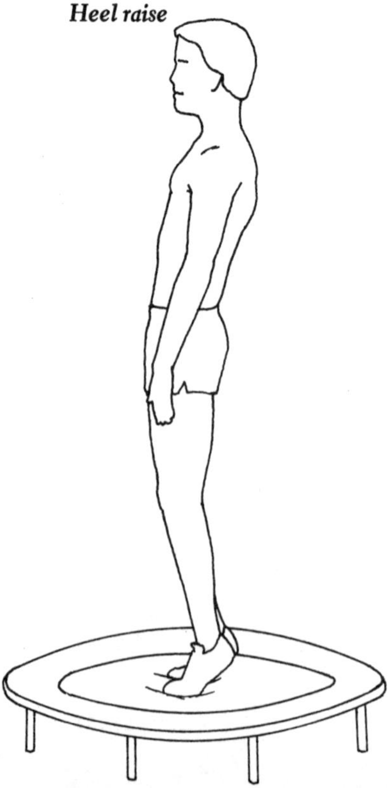

Toe raise

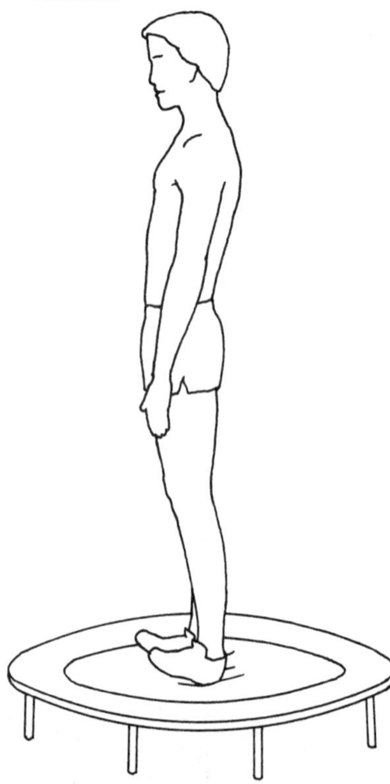

return. Then raise your toes in the same fashion. Continue to concentrate on damping out any rocking from side to side, wobbling, or oscillation in the feet. It is important that the feet be in a straight plane so that you get maximum support from the balls of your feet or the heels. These are essential in maintaining a steady position. These exercises will work the slow-twitch muscle fibers in your feet and your pelvis, as well as the short external rotators of the hip. Once you do them with eyes open and then eyes closed, do them one leg at a time, eyes open and eyes closed.

All of the exercises in Lessons One through Four are superb additions to knee and ankle rehabilitation strengthening programs.

LESSON FIVE: HIP EXERCISES

All hip exercises are done one leg at a time, alternating legs, and with eyes open and then closed: These exercises should first be done in a slow-motion pattern, then you can do them faster. We must warn you that only superb athletes can do these exercises in fast motion with their eyes closed.

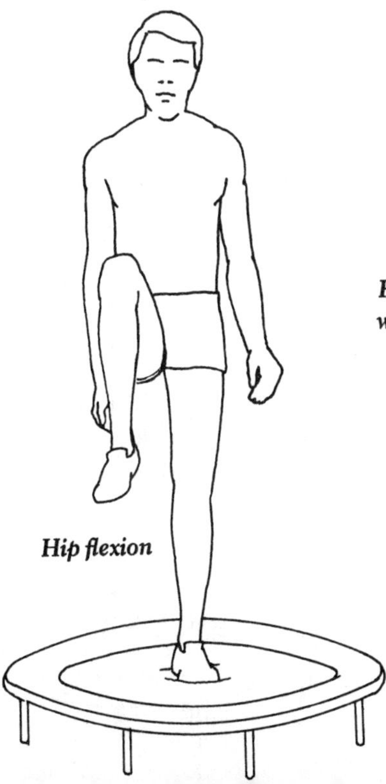

Hip flexion

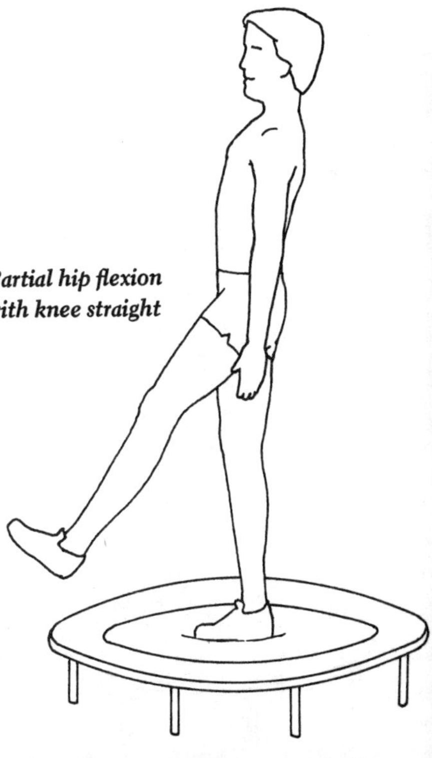

Partial hip flexion with knee straight

Hip Flexion

Assume the basic standing position on one leg, with the foot held firm, knee locked, pelvis locked and tipped upward, spine aligned, vertically, and chin locked. Bend the knee of the free leg to a 90-degree angle by raising the foot off the floor and pointing the toes. Now raise the knee even higher, to 125 degrees, and slowly move it back and forth in this straight plane while maintaining maximum tone on the other leg. As always on the mini-tram, you must work to eliminate any shakiness and unsteadiness.

Hip Hyperextension

Assume the basic standing position, then move your thigh backwards 15 degrees; hold, then move it forward. Maintain steadiness. Then do the opposite leg.

Hip hyperextension

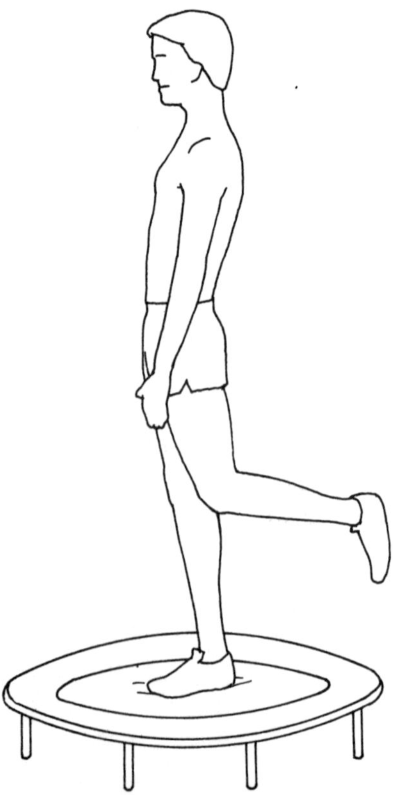

Variation of hip hyperextension

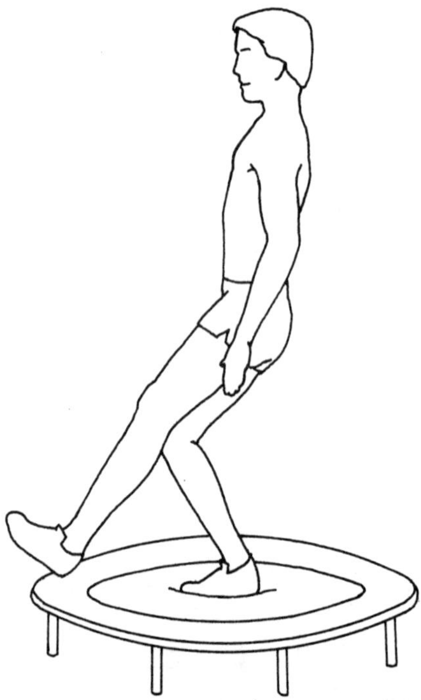

Hip Abduction

Assume the basic position. Bend your knee, move it forward approximately 45 degrees, then lift your leg upward and to the side 45 degrees, and return. Of course, maintain the stable, steady position, eliminating rocking. Then do the opposite leg.

Hip Rotation

For both internal and external rotation, assume the basic standing position, then bend one knee to 90 degrees. Move the foot of that leg outward; this will cause inward rotation of the hip. Move the foot all the way inward, and this will cause external rotation of the hip. Then work the other leg in the same way.

Hip abduction

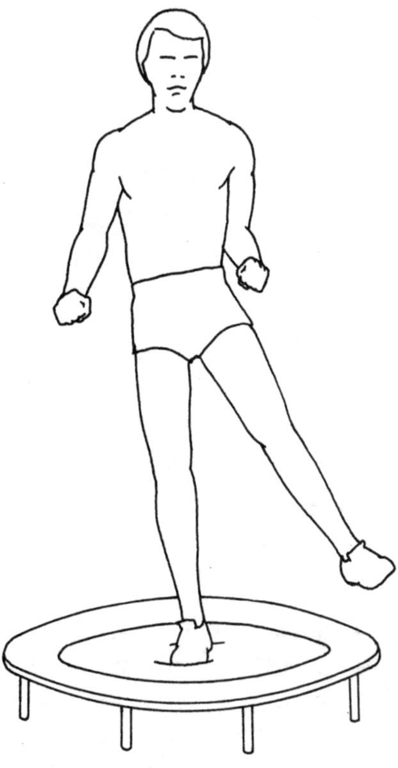

Hip rotation *Note that turning the lower leg inward rotates the hip out, and vice versa.*

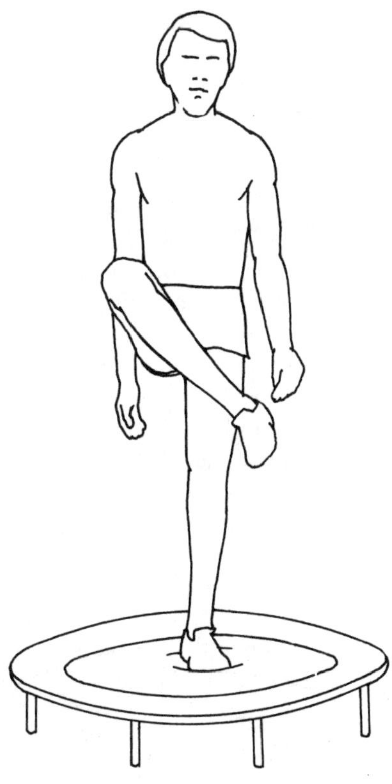

Hip Hiker

Assume the basic standing position. With one foot off the ground, hike the hip up on one side, leaning over onto the other side. After you are stable, do the opposite side.

For an advanced version of this exercise, start in the one-leg standing position with the hip bent 90 degrees and the leg straight out in front of you. Gradually move the leg out to the side in the hip abduction movement and then, while starting to move forward, move your leg out behind you so that you will almost form a T. This is the most advanced form of the exercise.

It should be obvious to you by now that there are many variations of specific stabilization exercises that can be done. But all of these are the same exercises that we do in the D'ROM routines. They are simply more advanced and effective strengthening exercises if done on the tram. So once you are at an advanced level, the tram is an effective strengthening modality that is wide open for your creativity.

Upper-extremity strengthening and stability can be developed using the tram as well. Here is one very valuable exercise that develops and strengthens your entire shoulder girdle as well as the muscles in the arms and those that cross the elbows and the wrists. It is very important to do this exercise properly.

Make a tight fist with each hand and assume the position you would assume if you were going to do a push-up, except that your fist will be on the trampoline bed instead of the floor, and the weight of your body should be carried primarily on the knuckles of the index and middle fingers. Extend your legs out as far from your arms as possible. It is very important to keep your abdominal muscles tight and pulling and to keep your spine straight or even slightly arched. Do not sag and develop a swayback.

You will notice that your arms shake and wobble just as your feet and legs did at the beginning of the exercises for the lower body. Once you have achieved stability in the basic position, you should learn to protract and retract your shoulder blades. When you can do this, you can move on to advanced levels by raising your feet off the floor and propping them on a chair or bench. We do not recommend that you attempt this exercise with your eyes closed. Once you have the ability to do a full squat on each leg on the mini-tram, you are ready to progress to jump training. Assume the full squat position,

Hip hiker

High-performance training *This is the proper stable landing position for jump training, an essential part of high-performance training.*

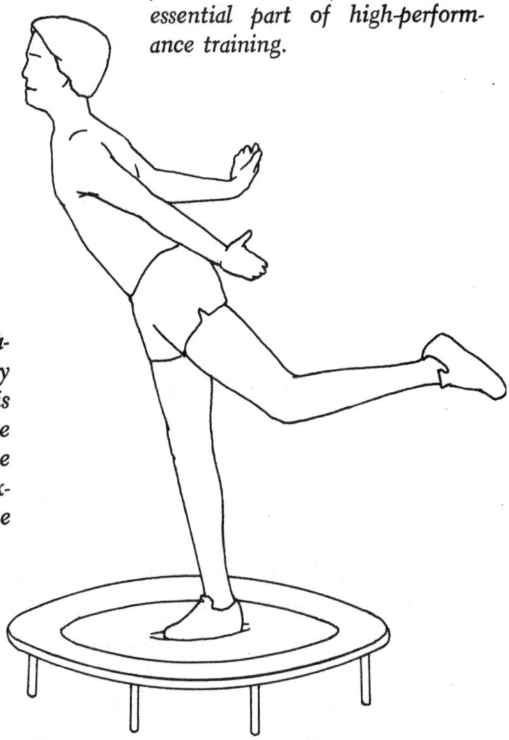

Other high-performance maneuvers *This is one of many advanced maneuvers. Another is the partial squat with the knee flexed and hip extended on one leg, and the hip flexed, knee extended, and toes pointed on the other.*

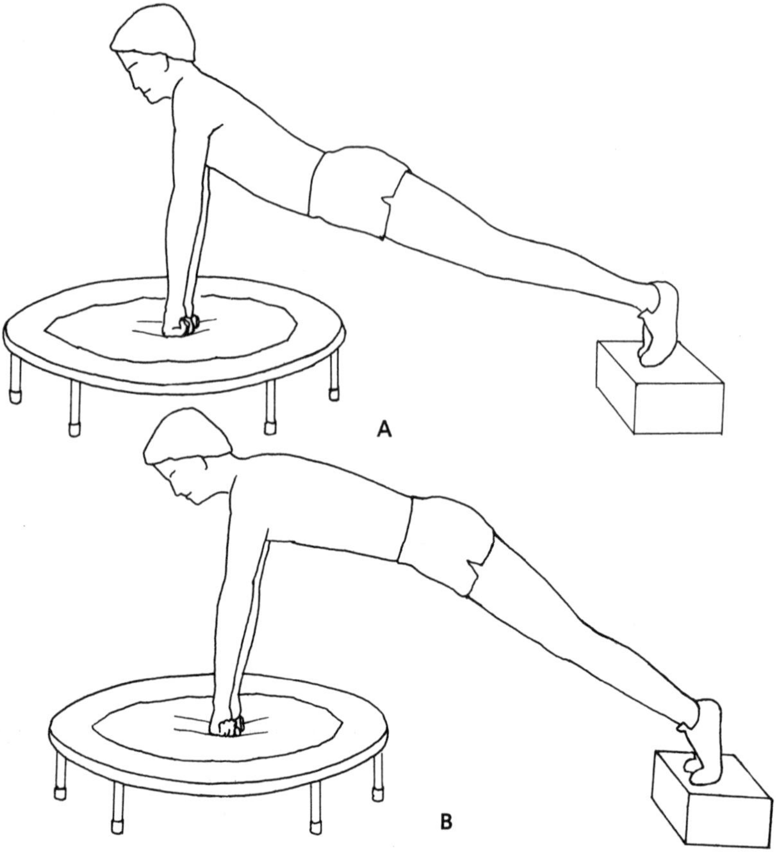

Upper extremity stability *Figure A shows the improper swayback position. Position B is obviously more stable.*

jump up, then come back down, holding yourself stable without wobbling.

It is very important to be able to jump up from a full squat position and land without wobble. This is a very safe, soft way to begin jump training, which is discussed in the next chapter. It will force you into good technique and proper landing form, and familiarize you with all the muscles it takes to perform jump training.

After you have completed this chapter's series of training exercises, we are sure you will be able to appreciate your body's functions better, as well as its weak points. Also, you will have learned a great deal about how to stabilize your body, and obtained an excellent level of fitness and improved performance.

19

The Soft Down Jump Box

The soft down jump box (SDJB) is actually two five-sided wooden boxes, structured so that the larger box slips over the smaller box. The top box can be adjusted by increments to five different height levels. The lowest level is when both boxes sit firmly upon the floor; height increases are achieved by passing two dowels through holes drilled through the inside box, then placing the larger box over the smaller one. The inside box remains on the floor while the top box is supported by the dowels. The holes nearest the bottom of the smaller box are narrowly spaced, while the next set up are wider, the third set of holes is again narrow, while the fourth and highest set is wider. It is important to note that the narrow-spaced holes give less support and thereby create a more wobbly landing surface.

If you wish to make your own boxes, here are the dimensions. Use six-ply plywood, and make it strong. The larger box should measure 30 inches long and 23 inches wide, and be 30 inches high. The smaller box fits inside and should measure 27 inches long and 19 inches wide, and be 20 inches high.

Drill 1½-inch holes in the narrow sides of the smaller box in the following sequence:

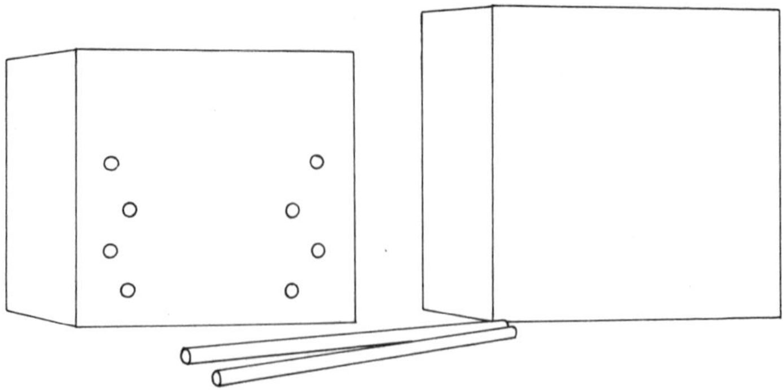

The soft down jump box *The jump box is actually one large box mounted over a smaller box with a pair of dowels. Mats are used on the ground around the jump box; it is best to jump from a soft surface and, especially, to land on a soft surface.*

- 3¼″ from the top; 2½″ from each side
- 7½″ from the top; 4¼″ from each side
- 11½″ from the top; 2½″ from each side
- 15½″ from the top; 4½″ from each side

You will use two poles, each 3 feet long and 1½ inches in diameter. They are put through the holes, then the larger box is set on top of them.

The SDJB is a movement-learning device. The learning objectives are:

1. Soft landing—both onto box from floor and onto floor from box.
2. Perching—jumping from equilibrium to a posture of equilibrium.
3. Raising the center of gravity.
4. Landing in sequence—defusing or dispersing downward force by muscular effort rather than bone; to hit the floor by toe–knee–hip action while maintaining proper fixed and stable core alignment.
5. Full body extension.
6. Leg counter-torsion—keeping knees in line.
7. Learning not to stop short, but rather moving to a full squat.
8. Learning not to relax on the way down, but rather to have strong, concentrated resistance to the floor.

Once you have fully mastered the O-Beam and K-board you are ready for the boxes. Our goal is for you to learn to be stable and land in a soft, controlled fashion. *Do not overtrain on boxes.* Follow these important guidelines:

- Only train on alternate days; your body will need a day in between to recover from the training.
- Always jump down onto a mat, not onto concrete, tile, or even a wooden gym floor.
- Fifteen minutes per session is enough.

If you violate these rules you will probably get tendinitis and really set yourself back.

A SOFT DOWN JUMP BOX TRAINING ROUTINE

1. Assume the stable position with the big toe lined up with the patella and your knees slightly turned out. Have your back in the stable position. Now move your body into a full squat (not beyond 90 degrees).
2. From this squat position, jump toward the top of the box.
3. Land atop the box. It will be unsteady. Once you are stable and steady, assume the stable position on the box.
4. Jump up into the air and fully extend, as shown in Figure 4 in the illustration. Be sure your toes are pointed down. Note that in this position it is the pelvis that leads your jump, not your head. Never lead with your head.
5. Land toes first, gently taking the landing force from toes to ball of foot to heel to legs, bending your knees. With practice you will learn to land softly and on both feet at the same time. (Most people favor one side.) It is essential to do this exercise properly. Form is important!

After completing this sequence, assume the stable position again. Then jump up and turn around to face the box, and repeat the jump sequence.

This training is very important because once you learn to land on both feet at the same time in a soft, stable fashion, you will greatly minimize the most common cause of tendinitis and knee ligament injuries in jumpers. Not only will you decrease your injury rate significantly, but because of proper motor development, a beautiful by-product of this training technique is a dramatic increase in your vertical leaping ability. Of course, this is what all jumpers are looking for.

Remember, there are no shortcuts. Form is important. Don't break the rules and don't overtrain.

1

2

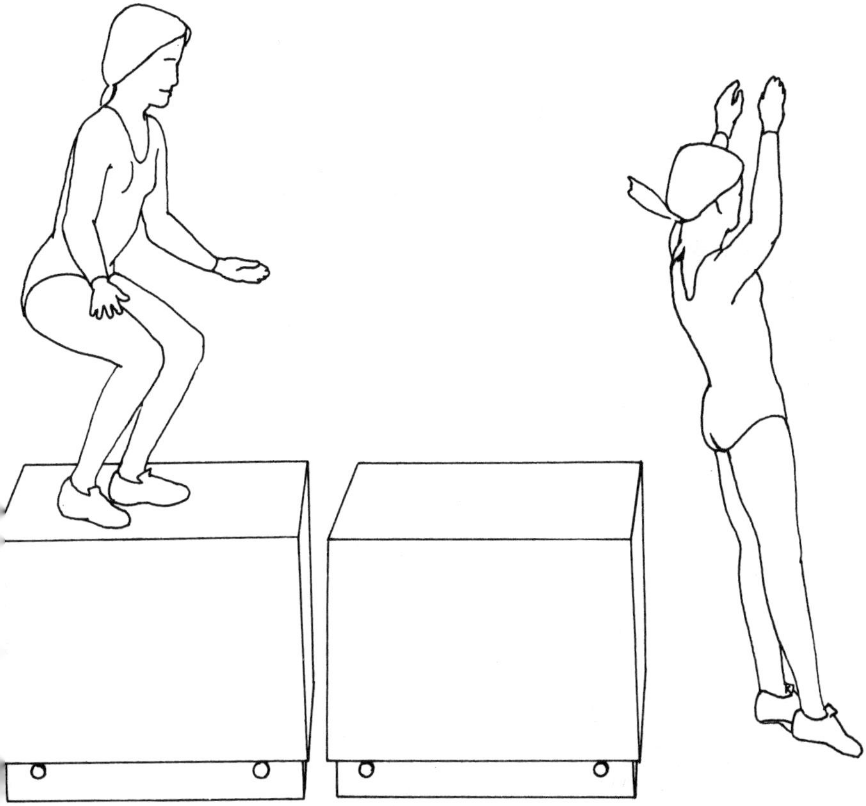

4

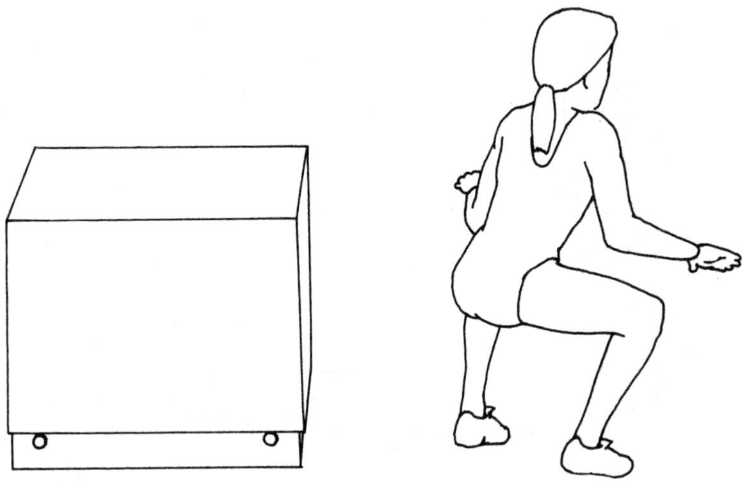

5

20

Balls

This section will permit you to use your creative genius. If you perform in a sport where a ball is used or if you are working with children, you should enjoy this.

The balls we recommend are the Nerf (soft foam) type, either round or football-shaped. Various sizes of balls can be used for different activities, and for children and adults. After you have completed the O-beam and the K-board routines and are stable on these devices, it is time for balls. Playing with Nerf balls is part of the advanced course in stability and balance training, but it is also applicable to any catching and throwing experience.

The key factor is that *critical millisecond*: the time you lose when you move your head to see something.

If there is one phrase that is true, that has been used so much that it is one of our oldest clichés, but that is not often trained, it is "Keep your eye on the ball." How often have you heard an elite athlete say he is performing well because he is seeing the ball better? "It was as big as a grapefruit!" the hero of the ball game will exclaim as he describes the pitch he hit over the fence. A millisecond is a very short period of time—one-thousandth of a second—and often it is not recognized as being lost. But every time you move your head, you lose that amount of time.

We believe that this critical millisecond is the difference between a foul ball and a home run, or between a goal and a near miss. The reason is that by staying stable you minimize the corrections your brain has to make. Willie Horton used to ask, "Why do I hit so well every time I have a stiff neck?" We believe that because he was following the ball with his eyes instead of turning his head, he didn't have to make those adjustments and thus saw the ball better and moved his core better while hitting. Then, when his neck got better, he started turning his head and losing that critical millisecond. If you have ever heard your golf instructor, your batting coach, or your tennis pro tell you to keep your eye on the ball, they are all saying the same thing—keep your eye on the ball and *don't move your head.*

We've already discussed the importance of the stable position and how you can achieve it. The next phase is to assume the stable position with your eyes on the ball, then learn how to follow the ball, catch it, or hit it without moving your head. No matter how skilled or unskilled you might be, you can improve to some extent with this training. We go back to our prime example of the Chicago Cubs' Bill Buckner, who spent hours in off-season drills, hitting and catching Nerf balls while standing and balancing on one or both legs upon K-boards and O-beams. Not only did he win the batting crown, but he also had his best fielding year to date. These exercises, we feel, were the racer's edge.

The most important elements in catching and hitting balls are head control and eye tracking.

As the head goes, so goes the body. Head control is the central factor in balance development. If you don't believe it, get on the K-board and move your head. Your balance will change. But not only does your balance change, you also lose the critical millisecond. Get your head in position, then keep it still.

Tracking is the ability to have your eyes follow a ball while not moving your head. It includes both lateral and up-and-down tracking.

A BALL TRAINING ROUTINE

1. While standing in equilibrium upon an O-beam or K-board, follow thrown balls with your eyes only. Then follow the balls while lunging to your left and right.

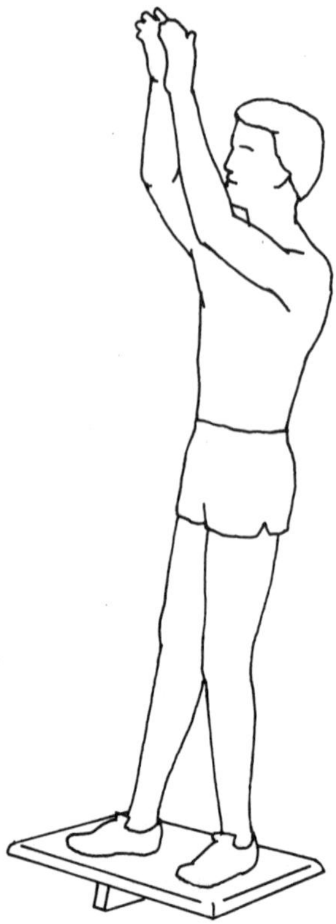

A

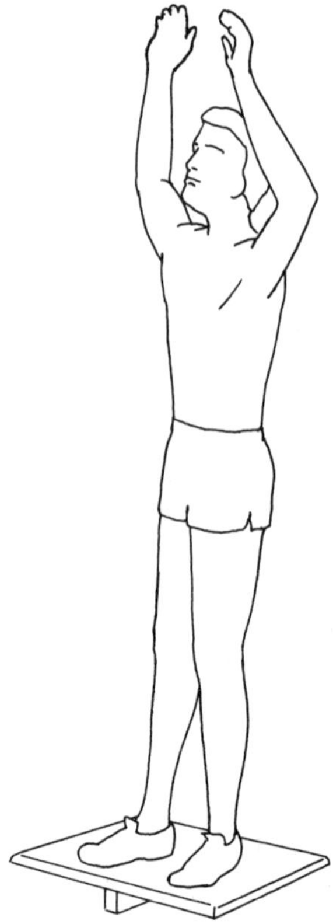

B

Catching balls *Figure A shows proper body position for catching. Improper head motion, shown in figure B, will throw you off. Movement of the head rather than using the eyes for tracking is the biggest failing of baseball players and other ball players. Track the ball with your eyes and keep your head stable; don't lose that critical millisecond.*

2. Catch balls, using the same process as when you just tracked them. Learn to stay in balance. Then catch while moving to your right and to your left. Also catch balls crossing your field of vision from the left and from the right.
3. Strike the ball, with either your hand or a bat. This will put greater demands upon your balance but will keep you in good form. If you are a baseball player, use the larger board for appropriate striding.

Proper batting position *Practice batting on one or two K-boards. Note the proper head position, and remember to track the ball with your eyes, not by moving your head.*

We believe that the repetition of these tracking and catching maneuvers, requiring such concentrated practice, will aid you greatly. Furthermore, in an age of traveling or absent fathers and working mothers, the hour or so per week that a parent spends with a child in their garage, backyard, or living room—throwing, hitting, and catching not big, heavy balls but Nerf balls—will have good results. When the child finally gets to the heavier and harder balls, he or she will be more confident and more efficient—and probably happier, too.

21

The Dynamic Axial Resistance Device

The Dynamic Axial Resistance Device, or "DARD" for short, was developed by Robert Gajda to solve a specific problem in training high-performance athletes and body builders. It is an apparatus that is designed to work the muscles in the front part of the shin called the anterior tibial group of muscles. The DARD was originally designed to aid in dorsiflexion of the foot, or toe-ups. It turned out, however, that the DARD had many other uses. It is a very efficient and effective way to strengthen against pronation and supination of the foot. It is probably the most valuable weight-resistance exercise device in preventing shin splints and in strengthening the muscles of the shin in runners.

The DARD is also an extremely inexpensive but effective way to train knee extension. The advantage of it for knee extension is that it does not require a great deal of weight for a maximum amount of resistance training, and it achieves all the training benefits we look for in a device; that is, it demands dynamic stabilization, it works the midcourse correctors, and it permits a full range of motion. In addition, as the word "axial" indicates, you can train rotation with the device.

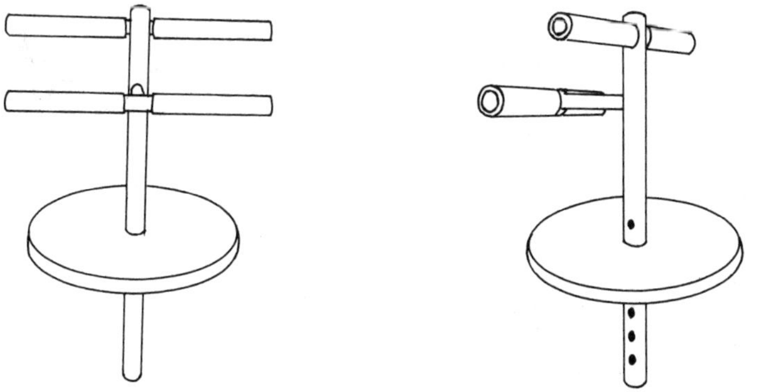

The DARD *Note the key spacing of the cross-pipe in the DARD. This is significant if you are going to use it properly.*

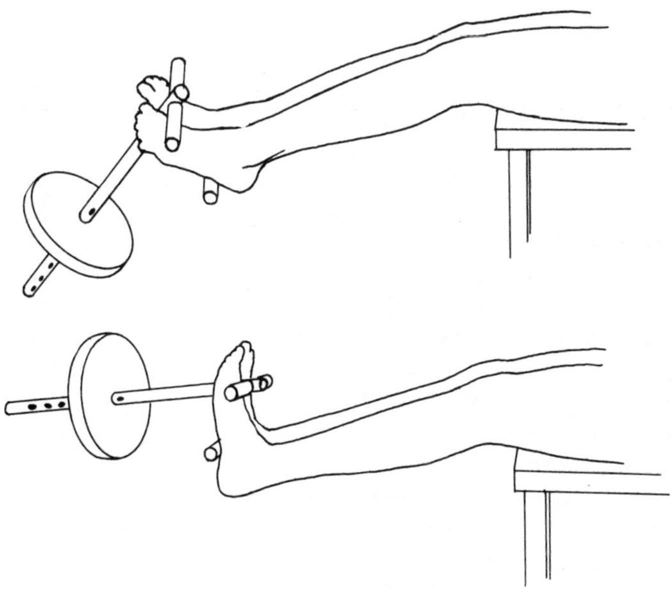

Dorsiflexion *This is the best exercise we know for preventing shin splints.*

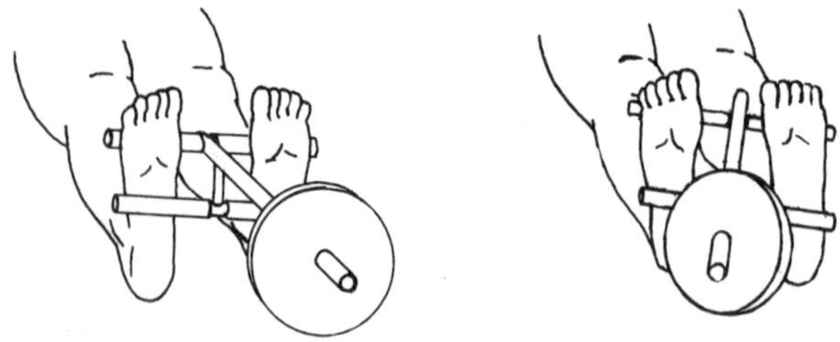

Inversion and eversion of the heels

Body builders who discovered these devices lying around the Institute began using them for wrist-training exercises. The DARD is a superb way to strengthen the forearm muscles through wrist dorsiflexion, volar flexion, and side-to-side bending and rotation at the wrist (called radial and ulnar deviation).

Last but not least, the DARD is terrific for the traditional arm-curl exercise. It gets the maximum amount of resistance with the minimum amount of weight.

The beauty of the DARD is that it is extremely portable and very inexpensive to make if you have access to a few segments of threaded pipe, "T" connectors and bicycle handlebar tubing. (When the benefits of this device become better known, it will be commercially available for a minimal price as well.)

The holes on the end of the device are used for gradually increasing the amount of resistance with only one plate. The DARD works just like any other lever: The closer the weight plate is to your foot or hand, the less the resistance. As you move the plate out, you dramatically increase the amount of resistance that you are exercising against. So one weight plate goes a long way with a DARD to give you a tremendous variety of resistances. If you prefer not to use the free weight, you can easily hook the end of this up to an isokinetic pulley or a power band.

We didn't know what to call this exercise device, so we came up with dynamic axial resistance device and decided to use the acronym DARD. It is *dynamic* because it is related to the dynamic activities of walking, running, and jumping, and because it is not meant to sit on a closet shelf but rather to be kept in motion. It is *axial* because it can be used for training rotation around an axis. It allows for a great range of *resistance* and it is unmistakably a *device.*

22

Knee Rehabilitation Program

All knee injuries can be rehabilitated. After successful treatment, almost all athletes can return to their sports. Their level of performance will vary with the success of the rehabilitation, the quality of the rehabilitation program, and the severity of the injury.

Our experience has proved that most athletes can even return to an elite level of performance with proper rehabilitation. Professionals who have successfully used our system include Tom Hicks, linebacker for the Chicago Bears; Gary Fencik, All-Pro safety for the Chicago Bears; Arno Steffenhaggen, all-star midfielder for the Chicago Sting Soccer Club; and Eric Soderholm of the New York Yankees. We believe ours is the best program for rehabilitating any knee injury and also for protecting the other knee from becoming injured.

The problem with most rehabilitation programs for knees is that they are designed as though there were only two important muscles about the knee, the quadriceps in front and the hamstring muscles in back, and as though the knee only bends.

Our program acknowledges the fact that there are thirteen muscles that cross the knee joint—in front, in back, on each side, and curving around the knee—and that the balanced functioning of all of these muscles is important for the proper functioning of the knee. So we emphasize training all of these muscles. We also know and stress the fact that the knee is not simply a hinged joint that bends. The knee is a complex joint that can also glide and rotate as it bends. This combination of bending, gliding, and rotation is the normal, stable way in which the knee moves. The most common cause of disability after treatment of a knee injury is what is called a rotatory (or rotation) instability. However, most programs fail to train for rotation. We emphasize rotation training in knee rehabilitation.

It is the properly balanced functioning of all the muscles, combined with the proper movement on the complex track of the knee, that leads to a stable, functioning knee. Our emphasis is on training stability in the knee in all planes of motion.

This unique knee-rehabilitation program will work for many people who thought they were washed up. You can use it successfully because we will show you how to train all the muscles across your knee. We will show you how to retrain your knee so that it tracks properly within its groove, and thereby functions normally. And, most important, we will show you how to train for stability in *all* positions.

In order to accomplish all this, we must emphasize training of the hip and ankle as well as the knee. This is both because many of the muscles that cross the knee also cross the hip and ankle, and because the hip and ankle muscles become appallingly weak after any knee injury. Since your good knee is going to be bearing the brunt of all the work for a while, we also emphasize that you must keep it strong by following the same training routine for it that you follow for the injured knee.

The knee rehabilitation program does not require expensive machines. We will use equipment described in this book in the chapters on power bands, boards, the O-beam, the DARD, and the mini-trampoline. Most of this equipment can be hand-made. The equipment that can't be made is relatively inexpensive to purchase.

The most commonly asked question after any knee injury or surgery is, "Doc, when can I return to running?." Here is a simple test that answers the question, and you can perform it right now. In bare feet or stocking feet, can you stand on your injured leg? Do you rock back and forth or wobble? If you do, you are definitely not fit to run or perform any athletics. If you are stable and secure standing on the injured leg, try doing a quarter squat and then a half squat on it. If you are too weak to do the squat, then clearly you are too weak to run. If you wobble, then that is a sure sign that you have not strengthened all of the muscles about your knee. These muscles are important midcourse correcters that balance and stabilize. The secondary stabilizers keep the knee in its proper track while moving. Kinesiologists call this constant correction and stabilization "essential synergy." Our goal is to take the wobble out so you will be secure and can eventually return to running.

Unfortunately, most athletes and many trainers look on running as a form of rehabilitation, when actually it is a maximum-performance activity that should be seen as a goal of rehabilitation rather than a form of it. Do not under any circumstances resume running until you can do a stable one-legged half squat. The reasons for this are several. First, you have not developed all the muscles in your leg for the proper tracking mechanism if you cannot do a one-legged half squat. Second, while running you will spend half your time on one leg or the other. If the leg is too weak to do a simple squat in a stationary position, the forces are going to be at least four times as great in running and you are likely to reinjure your knee. Third, don't forget that there are very few athletic events where you run in a straight line. The ability to change directions while running is going to put incredible rotational forces upon the knee, and if you do not have the strength to hold your knee on track for a straight-ahead maneuver, think of the damage you can do by trying to pivot on it without having properly rehabilitated it. That is why we must train all of the knee's rotating and stabilizing muscles.

If you can pass the half-squat test, then you can begin to run on a soft surface. We prefer a mini-trampoline because it decreases the shock of running.

After severe ligament injuries in the knee, ideally you should not run for one year, because it takes that long for the ligaments to regain their full strength. With intensive complete rehabilitation, however, we have seen many successful results in running after only six months. Do not forget that running is a goal and not a means of rehabilitation. The ideal time to return to running is when you can hold a thirty-second one-legged squat, ideally on an O-beam or a mini-tram.

The stable position for the knee is slightly rolled out with your kneecap pointed approximately over the second toe. Your foot should be flat on the ground and you must avoid the X-kneed rolled-in position. There should be a slight arch to your back and your shoulder blades should be squeezed together. This is your ideal stable position, and it will decrease the stresses across the knee joint.

We begin knee rehabilitation by gently exercising the hip muscle, because a stable hip is important and some of the muscles across the hip joint also move the knee joint. So this is an indirect and gentle way to help strengthen the knee. The same is true of some muscles that move the ankle. Ankle exercises are another effective, indirect, and important way to strengthen and begin rehabilitation of the knee.

The quadriceps muscle is a group of four muscles that cross in front through the kneecap and attach to the tibia. They are emphasized in all rehabilitation programs, and unfortunately have been overemphasized so much that the other muscles have been neglected. The hamstring muscles are the group of muscles in the back of the knee and are now being recognized by many rehabilitation programs, but unfortunately they are usually exercised as a group. The biceps femoris is the outermost hamstring muscle; the semitendinosus is the innermost, and the semimembranosus is the hamstring in the middle. Other muscles that curve around the knee are the sartorius and the gracilis (see drawing on page 21). From their location it is obvious

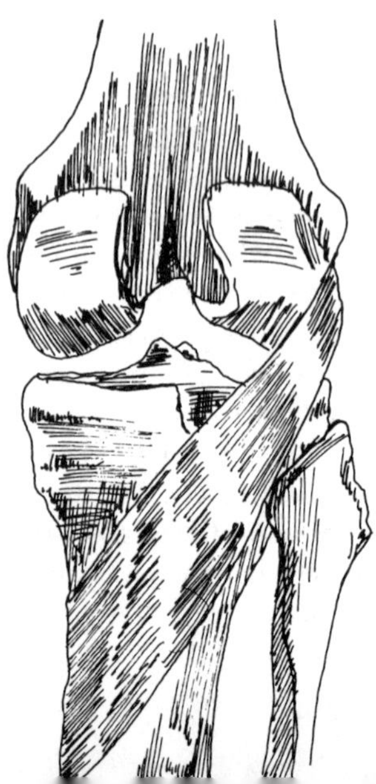

The popliteus muscle *One of the strong muscles involved in proper knee rotation and tracking is the popliteus muscle. Unfortunately, most training programs neglect the training of this very important muscle.*

that these muscles can control or can rotate the knee and also help bend it. The balanced use of all of these is helpful in restoring essential synergy to the knee function. The popliteus has been an ignored muscle for a long time. It is a primary rotator of the knee. We emphasize strengthening the popliteus because we believe it is important and essential to normal knee functioning. The gastrocnemius is the large muscle that helps move the Achillies tendon, but it also helps to flex the knee against the thigh. The gastrocnemius can also prevent motion. These muscles are the "shakiness removers," or what kinesiologists call neutralizers, but they are important to essential synergy. They are the midcourse correctors that keep us in line while walking, and, even more important, while running, cutting, and jumping. It is essential to strengthen these specific muscles after an injury since there may be some decrease in ligamentous stability.

The problem of using only machines for strength training as a means of knee rehabilitation is that machines will not train these muscles individually so that they can regain their normal stabilizing and rotational functions. There is no rotation training on any of the commonly available exercise machines for the knee. So this essential function cannot be trained on expensive exercise machines but can be with inexpensive methods that we will outline.

After any knee injury, most athletes are concerned about the loss of motion that occurs and always want to get back to stretching the knee to get full motion back. A full range of motion is important, but it is even more important not to rush after any injury and not to do any harmful stretching. Increasing motion and elasticity of all the tissues about a joint is a natural phase of healing that occurs with proper muscle training and use. It is important not to strain or cause pain in the rehabilitative phase and not to rush it.

As soon as you are in a cast, you should start your rehabilitation program. We do not wait until the cast comes off but begin exercises in a cast. Before you do any of this, however, get the permission of your treating physician or surgeon to be sure that the injury can be exercised. Do not do these exercises without your doctor's permission.

As a general rule, controlled exercises will enhance healing and speed up recovery. But timing is important, and you must have the cooperation of your physician for this treatment to be successful.

Here is our knee rehabilitation routine, in two parts: one series of exercises to be performed immediately after an operation, and another for after removal of the cast. These exercises will be familiar from earlier chapters. They are presented here in a program specifically designed, in sequence, frequency, and number of reps, to rehabilitate an injured knee.

AFTER THE OPERATION

This routine can be started immediately after surgery, while the cast is still on, with your surgeon's permission. It should be done three times per week, with one to three sets of ten to fifteen reps in a slow, steady, sustained fashion. *Do not swing the cast.* You must move it in a controlled fashion. The following exercises should be helpful after most knee operations, but we must emphasize that you should get permission from your physician before doing them.

The Knee

KNEE LOCK

This is a static exercise based on contracting, then relaxing.

1. Assume a sitting position with one or both legs straight out.
2. Point your toes straight up.
3. Keep your knees down. (Obviously, a cast on one leg will do this for you.)

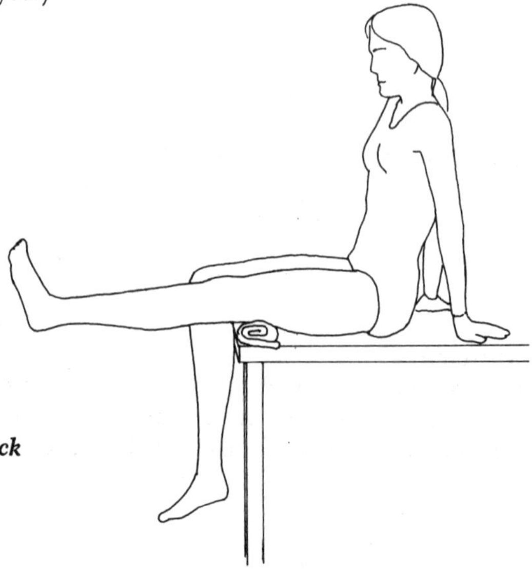

Knee lock

4. Contract the muscles of your upper leg, specifically the quads. Making this muscle hard is sometimes called the "quad set." If you were describing the activity of a muscle in terms of a light switch, as either being on or off, you would say that the quads were on.

The Hip

A. HIP FLEXION

This means a bending at the hip, or forward leg raise.

1. Lie on the floor on your back. Maintain a flat lower back throughout the movement. This is important because you are then in a stable position and will avoid injuring your back.
2. Lift your leg straight up. Stop when you can't keep your leg straight anymore, or at 90 degrees. Hold the position. Then slowly lower the leg back down.
3. Repeat using the other leg. Remember that you want to develop strength in both the good and the injured leg.

Hip flexion

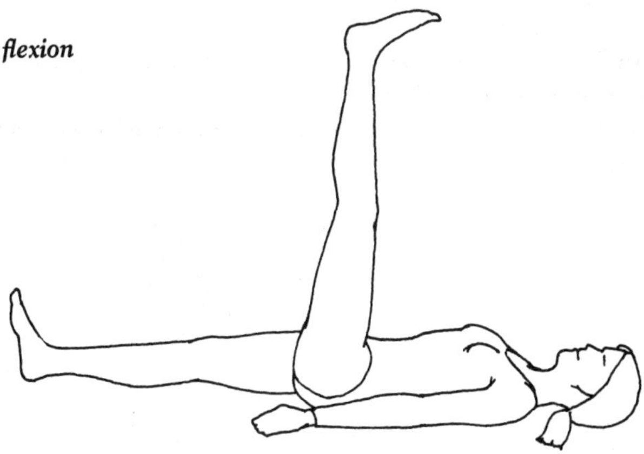

B. HIP ADDUCTION

Adduction means coming toward the midline of the body. The opposite is abduction, which means going away from the midline of the body. Because of the great similarity of the names for these

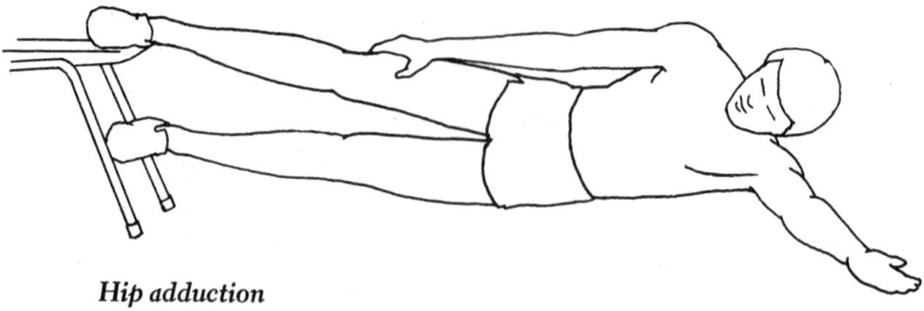

Hip adduction

opposite movements, physicians and therapists tend to pronounce the first two letters of the words as "a-*d*-duction" and "a-*b*-duction."

1. Lie on the floor on your side with your legs straight.
2. Have a chair by your feet and put your top leg on the chair. Flex both quads.
3. Raise the other leg up almost to chair height, keeping the leg straight and your body on its side. Hold! Then slowly lower the leg.
4. Reverse and repeat the procedure for the other leg.

C. HIP HYPEREXTENSION

Hip hyperextension means to bend backward at the hip beyond the midline of the body. It is the opposite of hip flexion (forward bending).

1. Lie face down on the floor. Put your hands under your hips. Flex your quads.
2. Lift one leg up so that the thigh clears the floor. Keep your leg straight; stop when your hand feels your hip beginning to lift. Hold. Then slowly lower the leg.
3. Repeat with the other leg, being sure always to lift in a slow, steady, sustained fashion.

Hip hyperextension

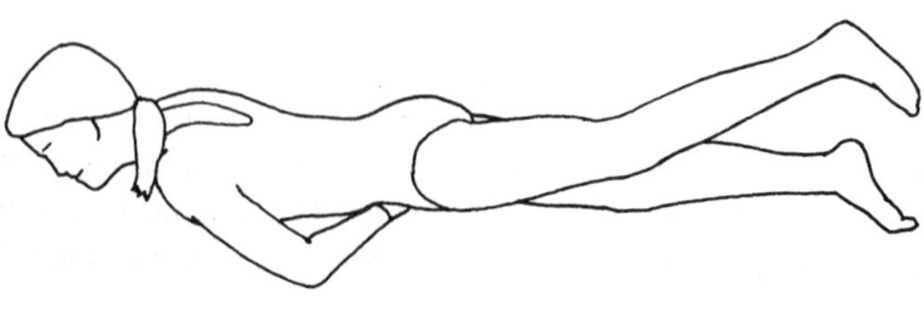

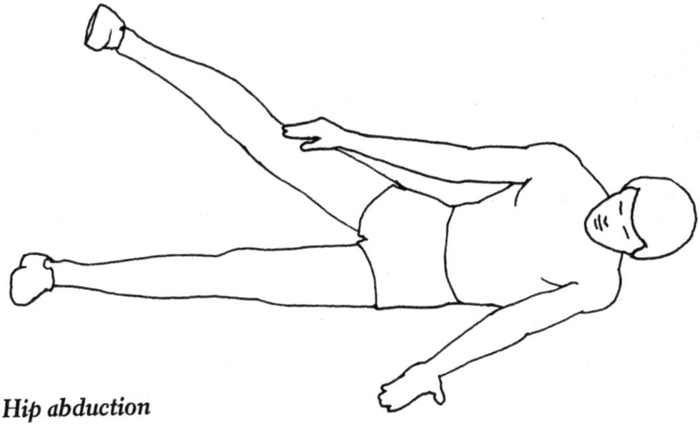

Hip abduction

D. HIP ABDUCTION

Abduction means moving away from the middle of your body.

1. Lie on your side with your legs straight.
2. Flex your quads, then lift the upper leg, being careful not to twist your body. Hold, then slowly lower the leg.
3. Repeat with the other leg.

There are several other exercises that may be done under certain conditions, but they are not allowed if the leg should not be weight-bearing. We will include them in the next section and suggest that everyone wait until the cast comes off.

AFTER THE CAST COMES OFF

During the initial post-cast physical therapy, which will last from three to four weeks, we do not want you to stretch or force full extension and full flexion of the knee. We know that there is a great desire to exercise fully to get back into shape quickly, but our experience is that you will get back quicker if you follow the natural patterns of healing and don't force it.

At first you will be working only 15 degrees of extension and flexion. Obviously, individuals vary, and some may proceed to a movement arc of 30 degrees during the second week if tenderness and pain do not exist. The primary considerations during the initial cycle are *building up the muscle,* which has atrophied or gotten smaller and distorted due to nonuse—therapists use the term "readjusting" to mean this restoring of the muscle groups—and *working other support systems* such as the foot, ankle, and countertibial torsion muscles like the tibialis anterior and posterior and the peroneals. A range of fifteen to thirty degrees of extension and flexion during the initial period allows you to walk. If, however, the tenderness and pain are extreme with this movement arc, you may just have to work on muscle-setting exercises like the quad sets. Remember, in many rehabilitation programs, people are in too much hurry to do flexion. Progress takes time!

As with the exercises you did before the cast was off, remember to do them in a slow, steady, sustained fashion. Don't use swinging movements, but instead focus on the feel of contraction and never stretch.

You must now exercise four muscle groups: the hip, the knee, the ankle and lower leg, and the core.

The Hip

Do three sets of ten to twenty reps of these exercises, three to six days per week. At first do fewer days, then increase as you get stronger. Trade off frequency with number of reps. If you can only do three days a week, be sure it is alternate days.

The first four hip exercises are the same as were used for in-cast exercises. Be sure to note the increased reps and frequency.

A. HIP FLEXION (See p. 255)

B. HIP ADDUCTION (See p. 255)

C. HIP HYPEREXTENSION (See p. 256)

D. HIP ABDUCTION (See p. 257)

E. HIP INTERNAL ROTATION (See p. 259)

F. HIP EXTERNAL ROTATION (See p. 259)

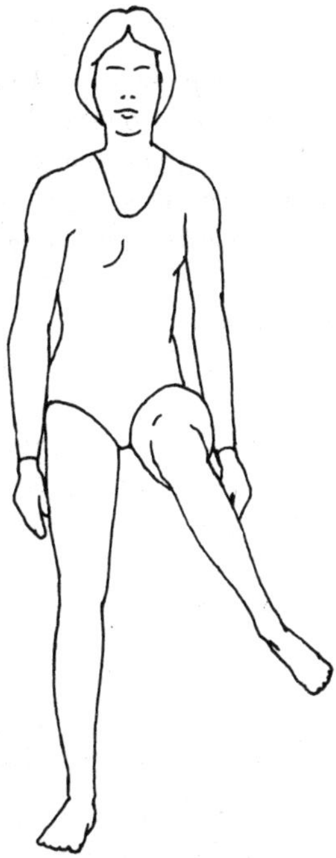

Hip internal rotation

Hip external rotation

The Knee

The sets and reps remain the same as for the hip exercises. However, you will not be doing extension or flexion of more than 30 degrees for the first three to four weeks.

A. KNEE LOCK (See p. 254)

B. KNEE EXTENSION

This extends the range of motion and helps pull the kneecap where it belongs.

1. Sit on a chair or bench, and put a folded towel under the upper thigh near the knee.
2. Contract the muscles of your upper leg, specifically the quads. This will extend your leg as much as possible, as much as your muscles can extend.

3. Perform what are called "terminal extensions." Move your leg up and down over those last 15 degrees. As you repeat this over some days, you will note that the amount of extension you can do will increase, demonstrating a practical application of the range-of-motion theory. Your muscles will increase your ROM up to the point that is mechanically allowable by your joint construction—without dangerous stretching exercises that could weaken or destroy part of your joint.

The Ankle and Lower Leg

Knee problems are often caused by or aggravated by weak ankles. The following exercises are designed to strengthen the ankle and provide a good, stable foundation for your knees. Again, do three sets with fifteen or twenty reps—or until the muscles "burn," whichever comes first. The burning sensation, caused by lactic acid building up, indicates that the muscles are nearing a fatigue point. Start with three days a week, on alternate days. For many of these exercises you will need the DARD or the power bands.

A. HEEL RAISE

This exercises the muscles of the calf.

1. Stand on the bottom step of the stairs, holding on to the railing for balance.
2. Place the ball of your foot on the edge of the stairs and then allow the weight of your body to lower the heel.
3. Raise the foot as high as possible, then lower gently back into the starting position.

B. TOE-UP (DORSIFLEXION)

You will need the DARD for this. It will exercise the muscles on the front of the shin.

1. Sit on a bench with your legs hanging over the end.
2. Place a light weight on the DARD and then place it so one bar is under the arch of the feet and the other bar is on the top of the arch. Point your toes downward.
3. Point your toes upward, then release slowly back to the original position of the toes pointed down. Note the pull on the muscles of the lower leg.

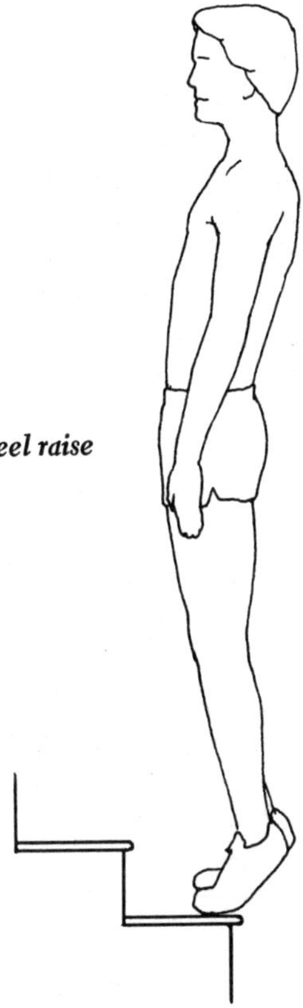

Heel raise

Dorsiflexion *The final position is an upward pointing of the toes.*

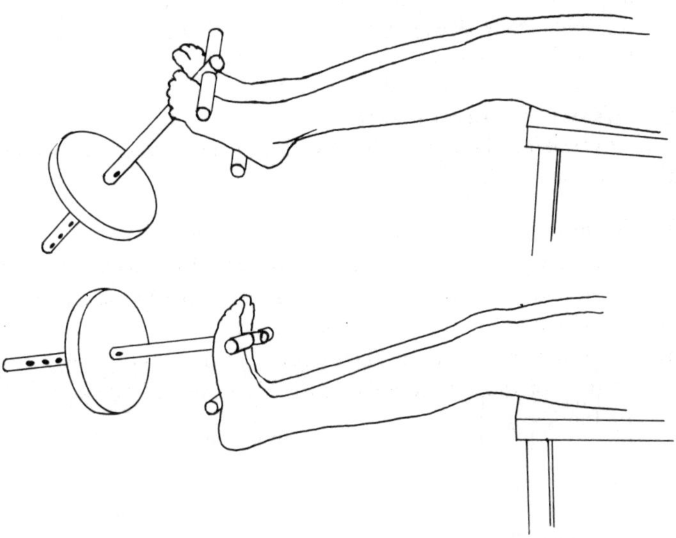

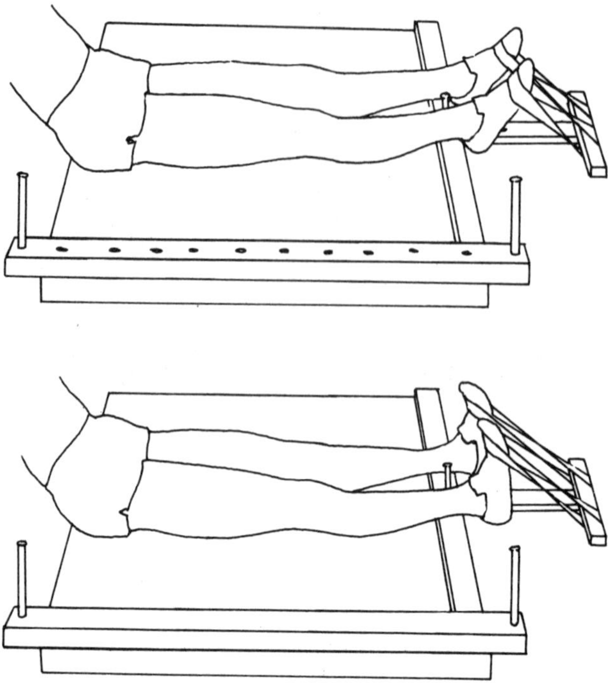

Straight pathway dorsiflexion

C. STRAIGHT PATHWAY DORSIFLEXION

Remember, dorsiflexion means "toes to nose."

1. Place a power band around a table leg, hook, or a chair with someone sitting on it. Lie on the floor and place the power band over the top of the forefoot.
2. Move or pull toes backwards toward your body.
3. Increase tension by pulling body further away from the leg or the hook.

D. HEEL INVERSION

In this exercise, the foot is held in static supination. By rolling the foot bottom inward, you exercise the muscles on the inner side of the calf.

1. Place band around a table leg, a hook, or a chair with someone sitting on it. Lie on the floor and place the band over the top of the forefoot. Keep the toes pointed out straight.

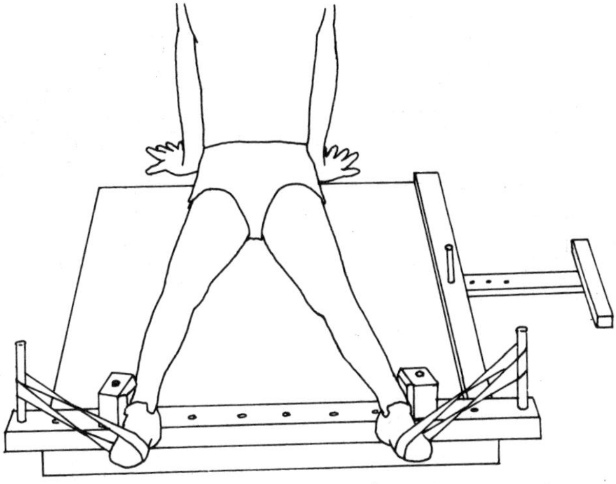

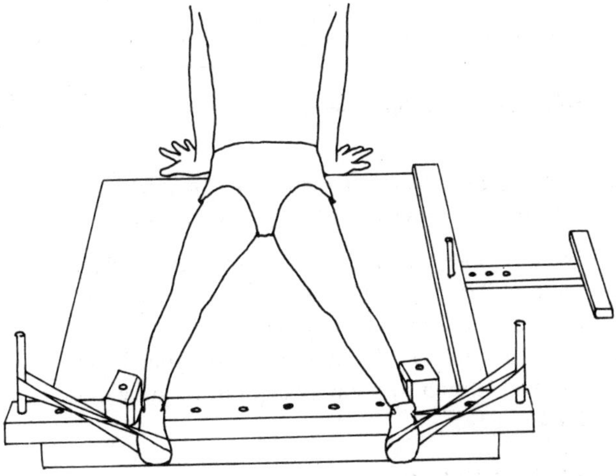

Heel inversion

2. Move or pull toes inward. You will feel this exercising the muscles on the innerside of your calf.
3. Increase tension by pulling body farther away from table leg, hook, or chair.

E. HEEL EVERSION

This is the same exercise as above, except the foot is held in static pronation. Since pronation is a rolling out of the heel, you are exercising the outer muscles at the ankle, the peroneal muscles. You can feel these muscles turn on and off if you put your hand on the lower, outer part of the leg.

Heel eversion

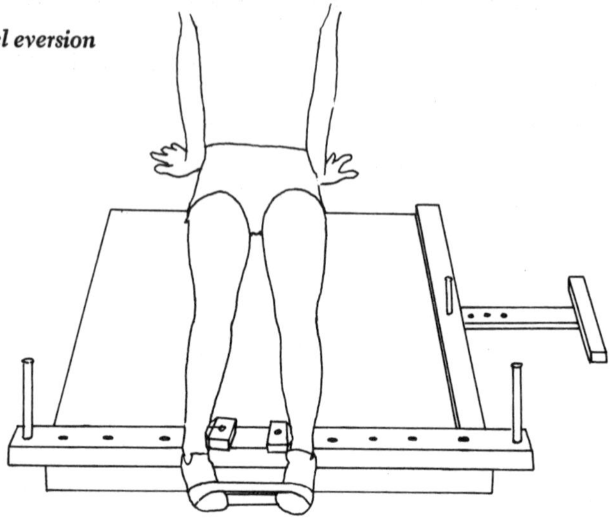

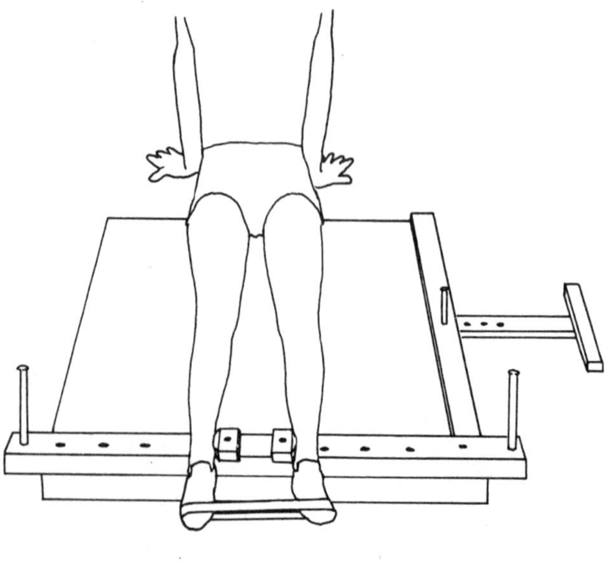

F. HEEL SUPINATION

While the three exercises above are pulling exercises, the next two will be pushing exercises. "Supination" means rolling inward.

1. Sit with your foot elevated off the ground.
2. Loop the power band under the front part of the foot, and make an angle of 45 degrees upward away from the midline of the body.
3. Keep your foot pointed upward and maintain that dorsiflexion (toes pointed upward) at all exercise positions.
4. Rotate the foot from outward to inward.

Heel supination

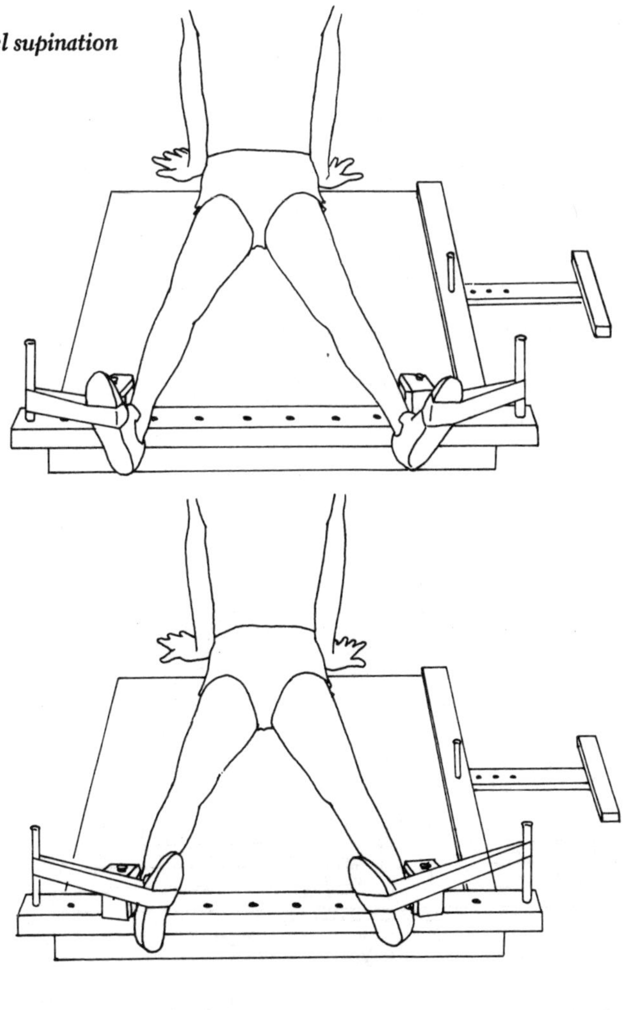

G. HEEL PRONATION

1. Sit with your legs fully extended (straightened).
2. Place power bands around both feet.
3. Turn inside edge of the feet outward, then hold and finally allow your feet to return to the original position slowly. Remember, the benefit derived from the exercise comes with the concentration and the proper performance of the exercise.

Heel pronation

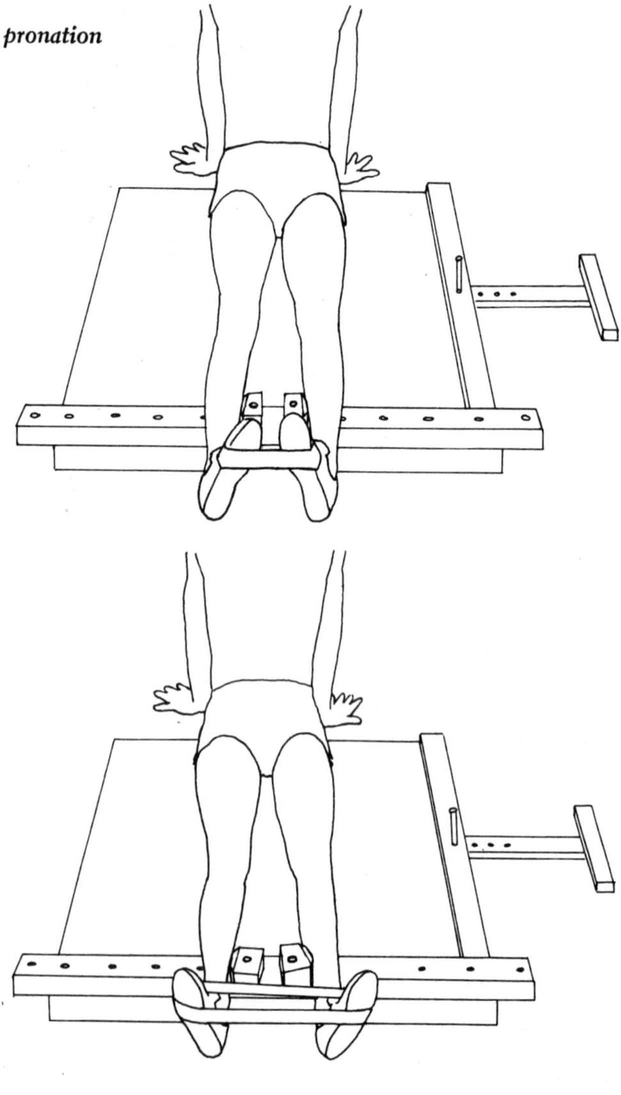

H. IN AND OUT ROTATION

1. Sit on the floor with your legs fully extended.
2. Place bands around one or both feet.
3. Dorsiflex the feet (dorsiflexion means point toes toward nose). Now turn the inside edge of the foot outward, then hold, and finally allow your foot to return to the original position, but slowly in resistance.

In and out rotation

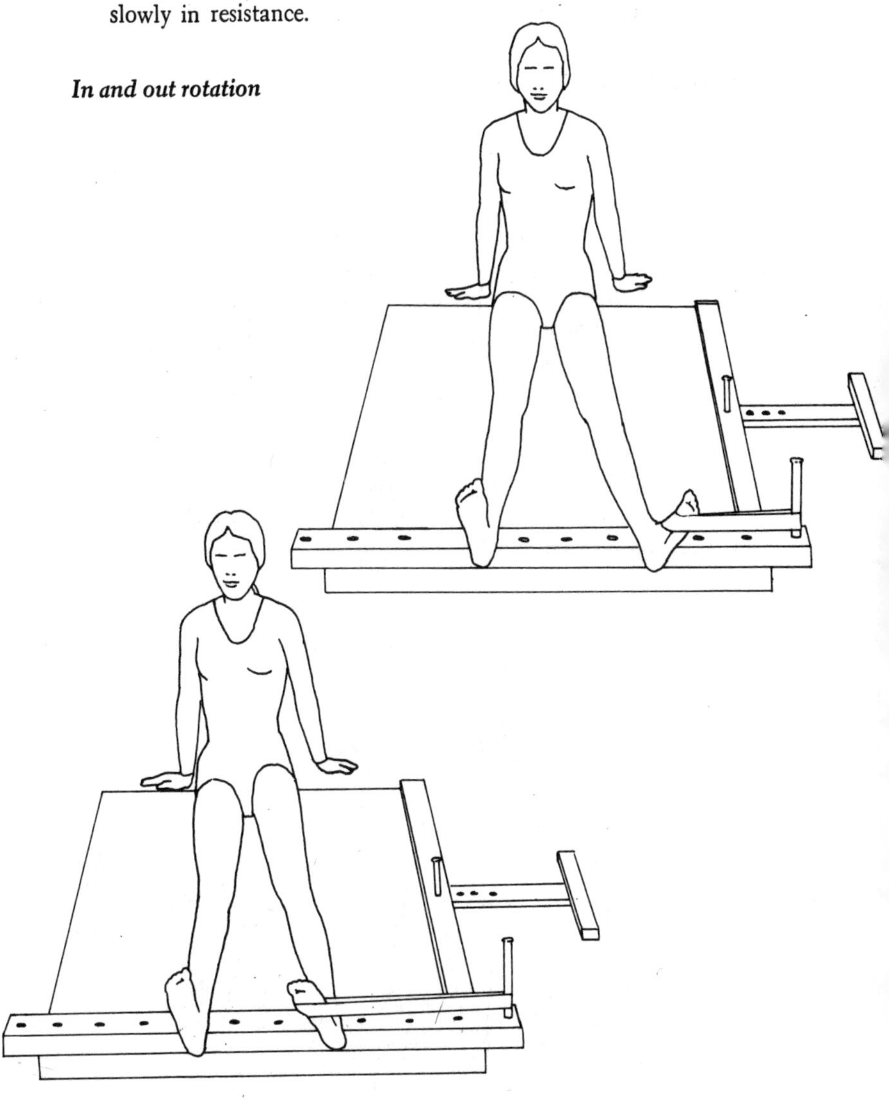

Core Build Up

In Chapter 2 we described in great detail what the core is and why the exercises for the core are important. We strongly recommend that you read the chapter if you have not, and specifically recommend that you do the following core exercises:

- Torso curl.
- Torso hyperextension.
- Side bend.
- Rotational exercise—do three sets, with ten to fifteen reps, or until your muscles burn.

By the time you get this far in your rehabilitation program you should start to feel stronger. After three to four weeks you should note a definite increase in range of motion and greater strength in the injured knee, and will be ready to proceed with your aim toward maximum performance in rehabilitation. The exercise routines for this maximum performance and rehabilitation, which we know you want to achieve, are listed in order in the chapters on dynamic range of motion, bands, beams, boards, and boxes.

We never promised you it would be easy—just that it would be effective. If you want to maximize your rehabilitation and maximize your athletic performance abilities, then you must go through this routine *step by step* and *not take any short cuts.*

Conclusion

In the beginning we promised you help for the healthy, hope for the injured, and aid to those wanting maximum performance. We said that if you followed this comprehensive training system you could live up to your physical potential and even improve your performance.

What we have given you is a low-cost holistic system that involves a unique way of thinking. You will have discovered that there is no single or magical pathway to rehabilitation and increased performance. Instead, we have given you a number of tools with which to improve the material of your body so you can be steps ahead of your competition.

Our goal throughout has been to help you train smart. For example, we've urged you not to waste time and perhaps your body by doing stretching exercises. Instead, we've recommended that you start your warmups with a routine that puts every one of your joints through the complete range of motion. We've shown you how to think about the differences between strength, endurance, and power, and to train specifically for each of the three. If you understand these differences you'll realize that it's a waste of time to debate the relative values of free weights and various types of exercise machines, because they all leave much undone.

Training smart also requires alternation of training styles—sometimes training hard, sometimes easy. It means training properly with lighter weights and resistance rather than improperly with the heaviest weights and resistance you can manage. It means mastering the oscillating beam, the kinesthetic primer board, the power band routine, and the jump box, and building up vulnerable parts of your body, such as your neck. And training smart means concentrating on the core and on eye and head control.

Furthermore, once you have learned the basis of performance enhancement you will be able to use power bands in a creative fashion to train specifically for activities like hitting, kicking, and jumping. We have given you a solid basis for improving most athletic functions but there is plenty of room for using these training devices creatively to train for each individual sport.

We wish you well, we wish you great success, and most important, we wish you tremendous satisfaction.

Index

MOVING FORCE SYSTEMS, INC.

DANGEROUS DOZEN

Exercise One

Yoga Plow – This exercise can pinch off one of the essential arteries in the neck, causing a possible stroke. It is also devastating to the lower back muscles and ligaments

Exercise Two

Shoulder Stand – This exercise places great strain on the spine and arteries of the neck. The stretch and stress on the blood vessels can cause a stroke or cut off circulation to the brain and spinal cord.

Exercise Five

Hurdlers Stretch – This exercise stretches the muscles and ligaments in the groin region farther than they were normally intended to go. This can lead to chronic pull or at least make you more vulnerable to groin pull.

Exercise Six

Ballet Stretch – Ballet exercises place inordinate abnormal demands on the hips, ankles and feet. Ballet stretches excessively stretch the back of the knee, low-back ligaments, muscles, joints, discs and especially the sciatic nerve.

Exercise Nine

Stiff Leg Raise – This exercise puts great strain on the lower back because you must keep your spine flat to the ground as you lift your legs. This movement risks injury to the ligaments, muscles, or even discs in the lower back.

Exercise Ten

Cross-legged Toe Touch – This exercise puts enormous strain on all the structures in the lower back and stresses the ligaments far beyond their normal limits. It can cause severe and permanent lower back injury.

Exercise Three

Shoulder Stand Variation – This exercise causes severe stress and strain on the delicate vertegrae of the neck, puts incredible pressure on discs and ligaments, and takes away the natural protection of each interlocking verte- brae, so pressures on bone and connective tissue are tremendous.

Exercise Four

Sitting on your Haunches/Knees – This exercise causes many injuries by putting extreme pressure on the lateral meniscus (lateral cartilage) in the knee, and can cause a tear of this cartilage which results in permanent disability and requires surgery.

Exercise Seven

Sit and Reach – This exercise stretches the posterior longitudinal ligament beyond its normal anatomical bounds and puts a great deal of stress on the sciatic nerve. Stretching either or both of these structures is a common cause of back pain and sciatica.

Exercise Eight

Toe Touch – This exercise is one of the most common causes of back pain in runners because it puts under stress one of the main supporting ligaments in the spine, the posterial longitudinal. It is also possible to injure a disc by putting your spine in this dangerous position.

Exercise Eleven

Wide Stance Alternate Toe Touch – This exercise also stretches the muscles and ligaments in the lower back and groin far beyond their normal anatomical limits. The muscles of the back and groin cannot give and support you when you are toe touching; you are actually stretching and hanging by your ligaments.

Exercise Twelve

Lotus Position – This exercise combines several dangerous stretches. It places incredible pressure on the knee/ankle and pelvic joints by placing them in an unnatural position. It also places pressure on the ligaments and muscles of the lower back.

"FLEXIBILITY" RE-EXAMINED

The Myth

"Increasing flexibility prevents injury"

It is our purpose to dispel the above myth and all misconceptions it has created!

THE BONES ONLY GO SO FAR!

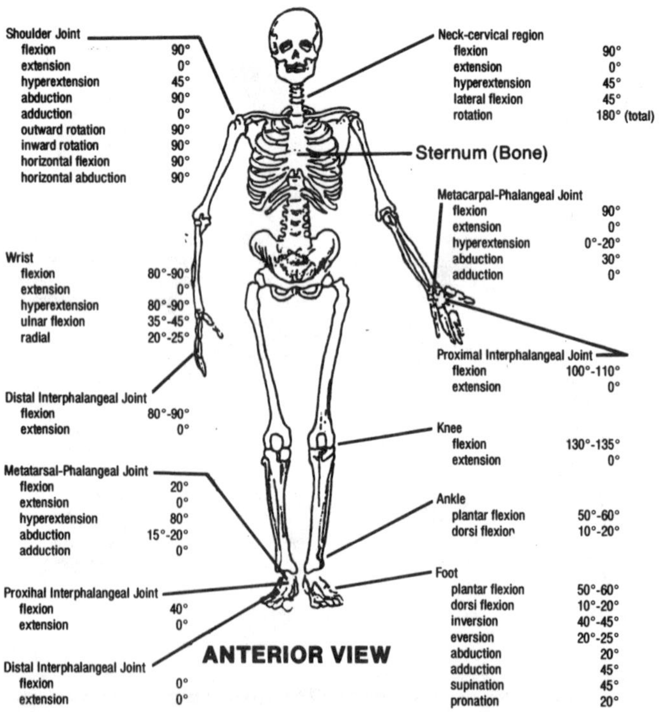

"FLEXIBILITY" WHAT DOES IT MEAN?

Robert Gajda M.S.

Flexibility is a cliche. Today it is used to describe easy going personalities, limber bodies, fishing poles, business schedules, bank accounts, etc. Dr. Bender of Southern Illinois University suggested physical educators shy away from the term "flexibility" due to its lack of specificity. Therefore, at Health Plus Network, we use joint RANGE OF MOTION when referring to degree of body movement. Every joint is designed to move within normal limits. Anatomical structures limiting joint ROM include:

bone ligament muscles tendon fasciae

The following chart defining joint ROM limits was researched and documented by professor R.E. Shelton at the University of Illinois.

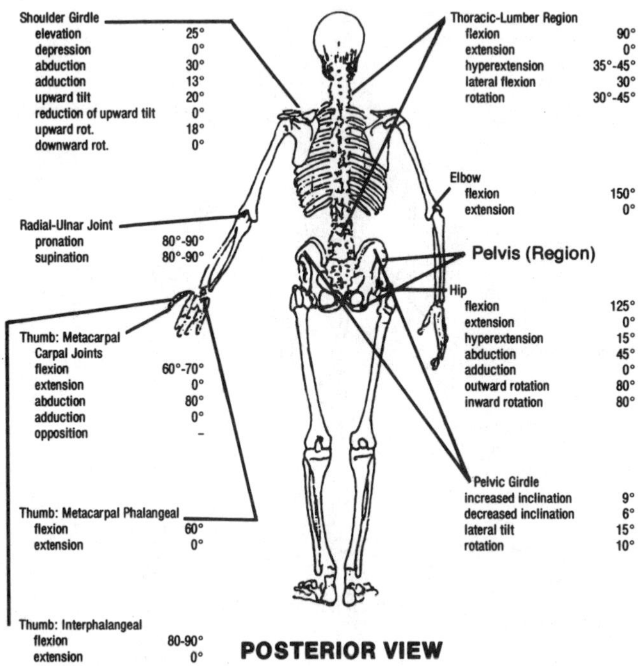

POSTERIOR VIEW

MOVING FORCE SYSTEMS, INC.

ORDER FORM

			Retail Price	Shipping
☐	Core Bench	(CB100)	$ 300.00	$ 30.00
☐	CMF	(CF100)	$ 1,600.00	$ call
☐	Dard	(DD100)	$ 40.00	$ 7.00
☐	K-Primer Board	(KP200)	$ 40.00	$ 8.00
☐	Deluxe KPB	(KP210)	$ 55.00	$ 8.00
☐	Lex Board	(LX300)	$ 300.00	$ 15.00
☐	Tennis Handle	(TH200)	$ 15.00	$ 3.50
☐	G-2 Max	(GG400)	$ 1,500.00	$ call
☐	Balance Stand	(BS100)	$ 125.00	$ 20.00

Total Merchandise $ ________

Sales Tax $ ________

Shipping $ ________

TOTAL ENCLOSED $ ________

Enclosed Is: ☐ Check ☐ Money Order Charge To: ☐ MasterCard ☐ Visa

Account Number ☐☐☐☐☐☐☐☐☐☐☐☐☐☐☐☐ Expires ________

NAME ________

SIGNATURE ________

SHIP TO NAME ________

ADDRESS ________

CITY ________ STATE ________ ZIP ________

PHONE (________) ________

MAIL TO: Moving Force Systems, Inc., 660 Ravine Road, East Dundee, IL 60118

1-800-884-4878

MOVING FORCE SYSTEMS, INC.

ORDER FORM

	Item	Code	Retail Price	Shipping
☐	Core Bench	(CB100)	$ 300.00	$ 30.00
☐	CMF	(CF100)	$ 1,600.00	$ call
☐	Dard	(DD100)	$ 40.00	$ 7.00
☐	K-Primer Board	(KP200)	$ 40.00	$ 8.00
☐	Deluxe KPB	(KP210)	$ 55.00	$ 8.00
☐	Lex Board	(LX300)	$ 300.00	$ 15.00
☐	Tennis Handle	(TH200)	$ 15.00	$ 3.50
☐	G-2 Max	(GG400)	$ 1,500.00	$ call
☐	Balance Stand	(BS100)	$ 125.00	$ 20.00

Total Merchandise $ ________

Sales Tax $ ________

Shipping $ ________

TOTAL ENCLOSED $ ________

Enclosed Is: ☐ Check ☐ Money Order Charge To: ☐ MasterCard ☐ Visa

Account Number ☐☐☐☐☐☐☐☐☐☐☐☐☐☐☐☐ Expires ________

NAME ________

SIGNATURE ________

SHIP TO NAME ________

ADDRESS ________

CITY ________ STATE ________ ZIP ________

PHONE (______) ________

MAIL TO: Moving Force Systems, Inc., 660 Ravine Road, East Dundee, IL 60118

1-800-884-4878